QUEUE

Reading Comprehension Long Passages

6

by Jonathan D. Kantrowitz

Edited by Patricia F. Braccio

Class Pack ISBN: 978-0-7827-1217-9 • Student Book ISBN: 978-0-7827-1216-2
Item Code QWK1524 • Copyright © 2005 Queue, Inc.

Queue, Inc. • 80 Hathaway Drive • Stratford, CT • 06615
(800) 232-2224 • Fax (800) 775-2729 • www.qworkbooks.com

Table of Contents

TO THE STUDENTS

In this workbook, you will be asked to answer many different kinds of multiple-choice questions.

As you read and answer the questions, please remember:

- Read each question very carefully and choose the **best** answer.

- Indicate the correct multiple-choice answers directly in this workbook. Circle or underline the correct answer.

from "THE WOMAN WHO TRIED TO BE GOOD"

by Edna Ferber

On the day that Blanche Devine moved in there was wild agitation among the white, ruffled, bedroom curtains of the neighborhood. Later on certain odors, as of burning dinners, pervaded the atmosphere. Blanche Devine, flushed and excited, her hair slightly askew, her diamond eardrops flashing, directed the moving, wrapped in her great fur coat; but on the third morning we gasped when she appeared out-of-doors, carrying a little household ladder, a pail of steaming water, and sundry voluminous white cloths. She reared the little ladder against the side of the house, mounted it cautiously, and began to wash windows with housewifely thoroughness. Her stout figure was swathed in a gray sweater and on her head was a battered felt hat—the sort of window-washing costume that has been worn by women from time immemorial. We noticed that she used plenty of hot water and clean rags, and that she rubbed the glass until it sparkled, leaning perilously sideways on the ladder to detect elusive streaks. Our keenest housekeeping eye could find no fault with the way Blanche Devine washed windows.

By May, Blanche Devine had left off her diamond eardrops—perhaps it was their absence that gave her face a new expression. When she went downtown we noticed that her hats were more like the hats the other women in our town wore; but she still affected extravagant footgear, as is right and proper for a stout woman who has cause to be vain of her feet. We noticed that her trips downtown were rare that spring and summer. She used to come home laden with little bundles; and before supper she would change her street clothes for a neat, washable housedress, as is our thrifty custom. Through her bright windows we could see her moving briskly about from kitchen to sitting room; and from the smells that floated out from her kitchen door, she seemed to be preparing for her solitary supper the same homely viands that were frying or stewing or baking in our kitchens. Sometimes you could detect the delectable scent of browning, hot tea biscuit. It takes a determined woman to make tea biscuit for no one but herself.

Blanche Devine joined the church. On the first Sunday morning she came to the service there was a little flurry among the ushers at the vestibule door. They seated her well in the rear. The second Sunday morning a dreadful thing happened. The woman next to whom they seated her turned, regarded her stonily for a moment, then rose agitatedly and moved to a pew across the aisle.

Blanche Devine's face went a dull red beneath her white powder. She never came again—though we saw the minister visit her once or twice. She always accompanied him to the door pleasantly, holding it well open until he was down the little flight of steps and on the sidewalk. The minister's wife did not call.

She rose early, like the rest of us; and as summer came on we used to see her moving about in her little garden patch in the dewy, golden morning. She wore absurd pale-blue negligees that made her stout figure loom immense against the greenery of garden and apple tree. The neighborhood women viewed these negligees with Puritan disapproval as they smoothed down their own prim, starched gingham skirts. They said it was disgusting—and perhaps it was; but the habit of years is not easily overcome. Blanche Devine—snipping her sweet peas, peering anxiously at the Virginia creeper that clung with such fragile fingers to the trellis, watering the flower baskets that hung from her porch—was blissfully unconscious of the disapproving eyes. I wish one of us had just stopped to call good morning to her over the fence, and to say in our neighborly, small-town way: "My, ain't this a scorcher! So early too! It'll be fierce by noon!" But we did not.

I think perhaps the evenings must have been the loneliest for her. The summer evenings in our little town are filled with intimate, human, neighborly sounds. After the heat of the day it is pleasant to relax in the cool comfort of the front porch, with the life of the town eddying about us. We sew and read out there until it grows dusk. We call across lots to our next-door neighbor. The men water the lawns and the flower boxes and get together in little, quiet groups to discuss the new street paving. I have even known Mrs. Hines to bring her cherries out there when she had canning to do, and pit them there on the front porch partially shielded by her porch vine, but not so effectually that she was deprived of the sights and sounds about her. The kettle in her lap and the dishpan full of great ripe cherries on the porch floor by her chair, she would pit and chat and peer out through the vines, the red juice staining her plump bare arms.

I have wondered since what Blanche Devine thought of us those lonesome evenings—those evenings filled with friendly sights and sounds. It must have been difficult for her, who had dwelt behind closed shutters so long, to seat herself on the new front porch for all the world to stare at; but she did sit there—resolutely—watching us in silence.

She seized hungrily upon the stray crumbs of conversation that fell to her. The milkman and the iceman and the butcher boy used to hold daily conversation with her. They—sociable gentlemen—would stand on her door-step, one grimy hand resting against the white of her doorpost, exchanging the time of day with Blanche in the doorway—a tea towel in one hand, perhaps, and a plate in the other. Her little house was a miracle of

2

cleanliness. It was no uncommon sight to see her down on her knees on the kitchen floor, wielding her brush and rag like the rest of us. In canning and preserving time there floated out from her kitchen the pungent scent of pickled crab apples; the mouth-watering smell that meant sweet pickles; or the cloying, divinely sticky odor that meant raspberry jam. Snooky, from her side of the fence, often used to peer through the pickets, gazing in the direction of the enticing smells next door.

Early one September morning there floated out from Blanche Devine's kitchen that fragrant, sweet scent of fresh-baked cookies—cookies with butter in them, and spice, and with nuts on top. Just by the smell of them your mind's eye pictured them coming from the oven-crisp brown circlets, crumbly, delectable. Snooky, in her scarlet sweater and cap, sniffed them from afar and straightway deserted her sand pile to take her stand at the fence. She peered through the restraining bars, standing on tiptoe. Blanche Devine, glancing up from her board and rolling pin, saw the eager golden head. And Snooky, with guile in her heart, raised one fat, dimpled hand above the fence and waved it friendlily. Blanche Devine waved back. Thus encouraged, Snooky's two hands wigwagged frantically above the pickets. Blanche Devine hesitated a moment, her floury hand on her hip. Then she went to the pantry shelf and took out a clean white saucer. She selected from the brown jar on the table three of the brownest, crumbliest, most perfect cookies, with a walnut meat perched atop of each, placed them temptingly on the saucer and, descending the steps, came swiftly across the grass to the triumphant Snooky. Blanche Devine held out the saucer, her lips smiling, her eyes tender. Snooky reached up with one plump white arm.

"Snooky!" shrilled a high voice. "Snooky!" A voice of horror and of wrath. "Come here to me this minute! And don't you dare to touch those!" Snooky hesitated rebelliously, one pink finger in her pouting mouth.

"Snooky! Do you hear me?"

And the Very Young Wife began to descend the steps of her back porch. Snooky, regretful eyes on the toothsome dainties, turned away aggrieved. The Very Young Wife, her lips set, her eyes flashing, advanced and seized the shrieking Snooky by one arm and dragged her away toward home and safety.

Blanche Devine stood there at the fence, holding the saucer in her hand. The saucer tipped slowly, and the three cookies slipped off and fell to the grass. Blanche Devine stood staring at them a moment. Then she turned quickly, went into the house, and shut the door.

As winter came on she used to sit up before her grate fire long, long after we were asleep in our beds. When she neglected to pull down the shades we could see the flames of her cosy fire dancing gnomelike on the wall. There came a night of sleet and snow, and wind and rattling hail—one of those blustering, wild nights that are followed by morning-paper reports of trains stalled in drifts, mail delayed, telephone and telegraph wires down. It must have been midnight or past when there came a hammering at Blanche Devine's door—a persistent, clamorous rapping. Blanche Devine, sitting before her dying fire half asleep, started and cringed when she heard it, then jumped to her feet, her hand at her breast—her eyes darting this way and that, as though seeking escape.

She had heard a rapping like that before. It had meant bluecoats swarming up the stairway, and frightened cries and pleadings, and wild confusion. So she started forward now, quivering. And then she remembered, being wholly awake now—she remembered, and threw up her head and smiled a little bitterly and walked toward the door. The hammering continued, louder than ever. Blanche Devine flicked on the porch light and opened the door. The half-clad figure of the Very Young Wife next door staggered into the room. She seized Blanche Devine's arm with both her frenzied hands and shook her, the wind and snow beating in upon both of them.

"The baby!" she screamed in a high, hysterical voice. "The baby! The baby—!"

Blanche Devine shut the door and shook the Young Wife smartly by the shoulders.

"Stop screaming," she said quietly. "Is she sick?"

The Young Wife told her, her teeth chattering:

"Come quick! She's dying! Will's out of town. I tried to get the doctor. The telephone wouldn't—I saw your light! For God's sake—"

Blanche Devine grasped the Young Wife's arm, opened the door, and together they sped across the little space that separated the two houses. Blanche Devine was a big woman, but she took the stairs like a girl and found the right bedroom by some miraculous woman instinct. A dreadful choking, rattling sound was coming from Snooky's bed.

"Croup," said Blanche Devine, and began her fight.

It was a good fight. She marshaled her inadequate forces, made up of the half-fainting Young Wife and the terrified and awkward hired girl.

4

"Get the hot water on—lots of it!" Blanche Devine pinned up her sleeves. "Hot cloths! Tear up a sheet—or anything! Got an oilstove? I want a tea-kettle boiling in the room. She's got to have the steam. If that don't do it we'll raise an umbrella over her and throw a sheet over, and hold the kettle under till the steam gets to her that way. Got any ipecac?"

The Young Wife obeyed orders, white-faced and shaking. Once Blanche Devine glanced up at her sharply.

"Don't you dare faint!" she commanded.

And the fight went on. Gradually the breathing that had been so frightful became softer, easier. Blanche Devine did not relax. It was not until the little figure breathed gently in sleep that Blanche Devine sat back, satisfied. Then she tucked a cover at the side of the bed, took a last satisfied look at the face on the pillow, and turned to look at the wan, disheveled Young Wife.

"She's all right now. We can get the doctor when morning comes—though I don't know's you'll need him."

The Young Wife came round to Blanche Devine's side of the bed and stood looking up at her.

"My baby died," said Blanche Devine simply. The Young Wife gave a little inarticulate cry, put her two hands on Blanche Devine's broad shoulders, and laid her tired head on her breast.

"I guess I'd better be going," said Blanche Devine.

The Young Wife raised her head. Her eyes were round with fright.

"Going! Oh, please stay! I'm so afraid. Suppose she should take sick again! That awful—breathing—"

"I'll stay if you want me to."

"Oh, please! I'll make up your bed and you can rest—"

"I'm not sleepy. I'm not much of a hand to sleep anyway. I'll sit up here in the hall, where there's a light. You get to bed. I'll watch and see that everything's all right. Have you got something I can read out here—something kind of lively—with a love story in it?"

So the night went by. Snooky slept in her white bed. The Very Young Wife half dozed in her bed, so near the little one. In the hall, her stout figure looming grotesque in wall shadows, sat Blanche Devine, pretending to read. Now and then she rose and tiptoed into the bedroom with miraculous quiet, and stooped over the little bed and listened and looked—and tiptoed away again, satisfied.

The Young Husband came home from his business trip next day with tales of snowdrifts and stalled engines. Blanche Devine breathed a sigh of relief when she saw him from her kitchen window. She watched the house now with a sort of proprietary eye. She wondered about Snooky; but she knew better than to ask. So she waited. The Young Wife next door had told her husband all about that awful night—had told him with tears and sobs. The Very Young Husband had been very, very angry with her—angry, he said, and astonished! Snooky could not have been so sick! Look at her now! As well as ever. And to have called such a woman! Well, he did not want to be harsh; but she must understand that she must never speak to the woman again. Never!

So the next day the Very Young Wife happened to go by with the Young Husband. Blanche Devine spied them from her sitting-room window, and she made the excuse of looking in her mailbox in order to go to the door. She stood in the doorway and the Very Young Wife went by on the arm of her husband. She went by—rather white-faced—without a look or a word or a sign!

And then this happened! There came into Blanche Devine's face a look that made slits of her eyes, and drew her mouth down into an ugly, narrow line, and that made the muscles of her jaw tense and hard. It was the ugliest look you can imagine. Then she smiled—if having one's lips curl away from one's teeth can be called smiling.

Two days later there was great news of the white cottage on the corner. The curtains were down; the furniture was packed; the rugs were rolled. The wagons came and backed up to the house and took those things that had made a home for Blanche Devine. And when we heard that she had bought back her interest in the House with the Closed Shutters, near the freight depot, we sniffed.

"I knew she wouldn't last!" we said.

"They never do!" said we.

1. How did Blanche Devine's new neighbors react when she first moved in?
   a. surprised
   b. happy
   c. welcoming
   d. upset

2. When Blanche went outside to wash her windows, the neighbors were
   a. surprised.
   b. happy.
   c. welcoming.
   d. upset.

3. By May, the only thing at all out of the ordinary for Blanche was her
   a. diamond earrings.
   b. food.
   c. footgear.
   d. house dress.

4. What is the **best** way to describe how the neighbors acted in the spring?
   a. friendly
   b. nosy
   c. uninterested
   d. unusual

5. When Blanche joined the church, she was embarrassed by
   a. where the ushers seated her.
   b. the flurry among the ushers.
   c. the minister.
   d. the woman sitting next to her.

6. How did the minister treat Blanche?
   a. He ignored her.
   b. He was kind to her.
   c. He followed his wife's lead.
   d. He called on Blanche with his wife.

7. According to the neighbors, what was Blanche's biggest mistake?

    a. wearing a gingham skirt while gardening
    b. wearing a negligee
    c. snipping sweet peas
    d. saying good morning over the fence

8. In the evenings, townspeople tended to

    a. sit alone indoors.
    b. sit alone on their front porches.
    c. chat and socialize.
    d. do chores by themselves.

9. By the summer, Blanche was able to chat with all of the following **except**

    a. the Very Young Wife.
    b. the milkman.
    c. the iceman.
    d. the butcher boy.

10. Which of the following would you be **least** likely to find in Blanche's kitchen?

    a. pickled crab apples
    b. sweet pickles
    c. raspberry jam
    d. dirt

11. Snooky waved and seemed to be friendly because

    a. her mother told her to.
    b. she wanted some cookies.
    c. she had a good heart.
    d. she liked Blanche Devine.

12. When Blanche heard the knocks on the door, at first she thought it was

    a. Snooky.
    b. the minister.
    c. the Very Young Wife.
    d. the police.

    8

13. The Very Young Wife had come to Blanche's door, but **not** because

    a. the baby was sick.
    b. telephone lines were down.
    c. her husband was out of town.
    d. she knew Blanche was a friend.

14. Blanche was **not** able to _____ right away.

    a. reach the doctor
    b. rush to the neighbor's house
    c. rush up the stairs
    d. find the baby's room

15. Blanche did **not** want the Very Young Wife to faint because she

    a. was worried about the Wife's health.
    b. needed the Wife to call the doctor.
    c. thought it would set a bad example for the servant.
    d. already had one person to take care of.

16. When do you think Blanche's baby died?

    a. the night
    b. the night before
    c. the summer
    d. a long time ago

17. Blanche pretended to read because she

    a. did not know how to read.
    b. was too concerned about the baby.
    c. was too concerned about the Very Young Wife.
    d. was too concerned about the Very Young Wife's Husband.

18. Why do you think everyone reacted the way they did to Blanche Devine?

_____

_____

_____

_____

_____

_____

_____

_____

19. Why was Blanche Devine so upset?

_____

_____

_____

_____

_____

_____

_____

_____

20. Why do you think the Husband behaved the way he did?

_____

_____

_____

_____

_____

_____

_____

_____

21. Why do you think the Wife behaved the way she did?

_____

_____

_____

_____

_____

_____

_____

_____

from "ONE OF OURS"
by Willa Cather (1873–1947)

Claude Wheeler opened his eyes before the sun was up and vigorously shook his younger brother, who lay in the other half of the same bed.

"Ralph, Ralph, get awake! Come down and help me wash the car."

"What for?"

"Why, aren't we going to the circus today?"

"Car's all right. Let me alone." The boy turned over and pulled the sheet up to his face, to shut out the light which was beginning to come through the curtainless windows.

Claude rose and dressed,—a simple operation which took very little time. He crept down two flights of stairs, feeling his way in the dusk, his red hair standing up in peaks, like a cock's comb. He went through the kitchen into the adjoining washroom, which held two porcelain stands with running water. Everybody had washed before going to bed, apparently, and the bowls were ringed with a dark sediment which the hard, alkaline water had not dissolved. Shutting the door on this disorder, he turned back to the kitchen, took Mahailey's tin basin, doused his face and head in cold water, and began to plaster down his wet hair.

Old Mahailey herself came in from the yard, with her apron full of corn-cobs to start a fire in the kitchen stove. She smiled at him in the foolish fond way she often had with him when they were alone.

"What air you gittin' up for a-ready, boy? You goin' to the circus before breakfast? Don't you make no noise, else you'll have 'em all down here before I git my fire a-goin'."

"All right, Mahailey." Claude caught up his cap and ran out of doors, down the hillside toward the barn. The sun popped up over the edge of the prairie like a broad, smiling face; the light poured across the close-cropped August pastures and the hilly, timbered windings of Lovely Creek,—a clear little stream with a sand bottom, that curled and twisted playfully about through the south section of the big Wheeler ranch. It was a fine day to go to the circus at Frankfort, a fine day to do anything; the sort of day that must, somehow, turn out well.

12

Claude backed the little Ford car out of its shed, ran it up to the horse-tank, and began to throw water on the mud-crusted wheels and windshield. While he was at work the two hired men, Dan and Jerry, came shambling down the hill to feed the stock. Jerry was grumbling and swearing about something, but Claude wrung out his wet rags and, beyond a nod, paid no attention to them. Somehow his father always managed to have the roughest and dirtiest hired men in the country working for him. Claude had a grievance against Jerry just now, because of his treatment of one of the horses.

Molly was a faithful old mare, the mother of many colts; Claude and his younger brother had learned to ride on her. This man Jerry, taking her out to work one morning, let her step on a board with a nail sticking up in it. He pulled the nail out of her foot, said nothing to anybody, and drove her to the cultivator all day. Now she had been standing in her stall for weeks, patiently suffering, her body wretchedly thin, and her leg swollen until it looked like an elephant's. She would have to stand there, the veterinary said, until her hoof came off and she grew a new one, and she would always be stiff. Jerry had not been discharged, and he exhibited the poor animal as if she were a credit to him.

Mahailey came out on the hilltop and rang the breakfast bell. After the hired men went up to the house, Claude slipped into the barn to see that Molly had got her share of oats. She was eating quietly, her head hanging, and her scaly, dead-looking foot lifted just a little from the ground. When he stroked her neck and talked to her she stopped grinding and gazed at him mournfully. She knew him, and wrinkled her nose and drew her upper lip back from her worn teeth, to show that she liked being petted. She let him touch her foot and examine her leg.

When Claude reached the kitchen, his mother was sitting at one end of the breakfast table, pouring weak coffee, his brother and Dan and Jerry were in their chairs, and Mahailey was baking griddle cakes at the stove. A moment later Mr. Wheeler came down the enclosed stairway and walked the length of the table to his own place. He was a very large man, taller and broader than any of his neighbors. He seldom wore a coat in summer, and his rumpled shirt bulged out carelessly over the belt of his trousers. His florid face was clean shaven, likely to be a trifle tobacco-stained about the mouth, and it was conspicuous both for good-nature and coarse humour, and for an imperturbable physical composure. Nobody in the county had ever seen Nat Wheeler flustered about anything, and nobody had ever heard him speak with complete seriousness. He kept up his easy-going, jocular affability even with his own family.

As soon as he was seated, Mr. Wheeler reached for the two-pint sugar bowl and began to pour sugar into his coffee. Ralph asked him if he were going to the circus. Mr. Wheeler winked.

"I shouldn't wonder if I happened in town sometime before the elephants get away." He spoke very deliberately, with a State-of-Maine drawl, and his voice was smooth and agreeable. "You boys better start in early, though. You can take the wagon and the mules, and load in the cowhides. The butcher has agreed to take them."

Claude put down his knife. "Can't we have the car? I've washed it on purpose."

"And what about Dan and Jerry? They want to see the circus just as much as you do, and I want the hides should go in; they're bringing a good price now. I don't mind about your washing the car; mud preserves the paint, they say, but it'll be all right this time, Claude."

The hired men haw-hawed and Ralph giggled. Claude's freckled face got very red. The pancake grew stiff and heavy in his mouth and was hard to swallow. His father knew he hated to drive the mules to town, and knew how he hated to go anywhere with Dan and Jerry. As for the hides, they were the skins of four steers that had perished in the blizzard last winter through the wanton carelessness of these same hired men, and the price they would bring would not half pay for the time his father had spent in stripping and curing them. They had lain in a shed loft all summer, and the wagon had been to town a dozen times. But today, when he wanted to go to Frankfort clean and care-free, he must take these stinking hides and two coarse-mouthed men, and drive a pair of mules that always brayed and balked and behaved ridiculously in a crowd. Probably his father had looked out of the window and seen him washing the car, and had put this up on him while he dressed. It was like his father's idea of a joke.

Mrs. Wheeler looked at Claude sympathetically, feeling that he was disappointed. Perhaps she, too, suspected a joke. She had learned that humour might wear almost any guise.

When Claude started for the barn after breakfast, she came running down the path, calling to him faintly,—hurrying always made her short of breath. Overtaking him, she looked up with solicitude, shading her eyes with her delicately formed hand. "If you want I should do up your linen coat, Claude, I can iron it while you're hitching," she said wistfully.

14

Claude stood kicking at a bunch of mottled feathers that had once been a young chicken. His shoulders were drawn high, his mother saw, and his figure suggested energy and determined self-control.

"You needn't mind, mother." He spoke rapidly, muttering his words. "I'd better wear my old clothes if I have to take the hides. They're greasy, and in the sun they'll smell worse than fertilizer."

"The men can handle the hides, I should think. Wouldn't you feel better in town to be dressed?" She was still blinking up at him.

"Don't bother about it. Put me out a clean colored shirt, if you want to. That's all right."

He turned toward the barn, and his mother went slowly back the path up to the house. She was so plucky and so stooped, his dear mother! He guessed if she could stand having these men about, could cook and wash for them, he could drive them to town!

1. What time did Claude get up?
    a. midnight
    b. before dawn
    c. morning
    d. noon

2. Why did Claude wash his face in the tin basin?
    a. The washroom sinks were dirty.
    b. They had no running water.
    c. They had no hot water.
    d. Old Mahailey told him to.

3. Old Mahailey was probably
    a. Claude's mother.
    b. Claude's sister.
    c. Claude's grandmother.
    d. a family servant.

4. The Wheelers lived

    a. in the mountains.
    b. on the prairie.
    c. in a city.
    d. in a town.

5. What time of year was it?

    a. spring
    b. summer
    c. fall
    d. winter

6. Claude's first task of that day was to

    a. feed the stock.
    b. wake his brother.
    c. start a corn-cob fire.
    d. wash his car.

7. Which of the following would **best** describe Claude's father?

    a. small
    b. easily upset
    c. good-natured
    d. serious

8. Claude's father wanted Claude and Ralph to

    a. take cowhides into town on the wagon.
    b. take cowhides into town in the car.
    c. take Dan and Jerry in the car.
    d. leave the cowhides home.

9. Claude's father said he was **not** upset that Claude had washed the car because

    a. he believed that mud preserves the paint.
    b. he was joking.
    c. Claude wanted to drive the car.
    d. Claude took better care of the car than the horses.

16

10. Why do you think Claude's father made Claude take the wagon, hides, and hired men?

_____

_____

_____

_____

_____

_____

_____

_____

_____

_____

_____

_____

_____

_____

_____

_____

_____

17

PREPARING FOR THE NIGHT BATTLE OF DECEMBER 23rd

After getting control of Lake Borgne, the next British problem—finding a way to New Orleans—was solved by Captain R. Spencer of the Royal Navy and Lieutenant John Peddie of the Quartermaster Department. Disguised as fishermen, these officers reached the Mississippi. They found that small boats could go through the bayous most of the way to the great river. They had penetrated by way of Bayou Bienvenue. They had found no sign of American preparation. The British spies had seemingly found the only unguarded bayou. Their commanders decided to advance along this route.

Before reaching the mouth of Bayou Bienvenue, however, the British had to cross the shallow Lake Borgne. The troops on the heavy ships had to load into vessels that drew less water. They then went to Pea Island, near the mouth of Pearl River, for regrouping. From Pea Island the invaders went in open boats to the mouth of the bayou. Even the lighter boats sometimes grounded. Many seamen were at the oar for the greater part of four or five days. During these journeys, the British had no fires or warm food and they were exposed to drenching rains. Once, after a heavy rain, the skies cleared. The night became bitter cold. Ice formed before morning. Many of the West Indian Blacks, unused to such a climate, died of exposure.

Pushing on despite these hardships, the invaders captured the small American detachment at the mouth of Bayou Bienvenue about midnight on December 22nd, before other Americans could be warned of the attack. Joseph Ducros, a native of Louisiana, was among the captives. When questioned by Admiral Cochrane and Major General John Keane, he told the British officers that there were twelve to fifteen thousand American soldiers in New Orleans. He also said there were five thousand more farther down the river. Cochrane and Keane were impressed, though not convinced. They continued to move forward cautiously.

The British advanced along the bayous. Some were in boats. Some marched along the banks. They finally reached firm ground at the edge of the Villeré plantation. Late on the morning of the 23rd, they rushed the plantation house. They surprised and captured a militia detachment. The British had scored a tremendous tactical advantage. They had reached, almost unopposed, a spot within nine miles of their goal.

However, their presence was soon made known. Major René Philippe Gabriel Villeré had escaped. Other Americans had also seen the invaders. That morning, Jackson had received a message from Colonel Pierre Denis de La

Ronde saying that the British fleet was in a position that suggested landing. Augustin Rousseau galloped to headquarters on Royal Street with astounding news. He had barely delivered his message when others, including young Villeré, arrived muddy and nearly out of breath.

According to an often repeated story, Jackson was still not well. He was lying on a sofa in his headquarters about 1:00 in the afternoon when the news came that the enemy was in force only nine miles below New Orleans. He jumped up from the sofa, and, "with an eye of fire and an emphatic blow on the table" cried, "By the eternal, they shall not sleep on our soil."

Then, quickly becoming calm, Jackson called his aides, and said, "Gentlemen, the British are below. We must fight them tonight."

Jackson's decision to attack at once was as important as any ever made by a commander. The British could have entered New Orleans easily at this time. There were no important forces or defensive works between them and the city.

Jackson's move was more than the impulse of a man who at last could attack an enemy hated since boyhood. The British troops were tired. His were fresh. He had the advantage of darkness and surprise. He hoped also that action would improve morale, especially of the civilian population.

When Jackson learned that the British had landed, Carroll's and Coffee's men were four or five miles above the city. Major J.B. Plauche's Battalion was at Fort St. John on Lake Pontchartrain. Daquin's Battalion of San Domingo Men of Color and the Louisiana Militia under Claiborne were on Gentilly Road. Regulars were scattered about the city. The naval commander, Commodore Patterson, was also some distance away.

Orders to assemble brought quick action. The first troops arrived in the narrow streets of the Old French Quarter by midafternoon. Plauche's Battalion ran to the city (a feat which is commemorated yearly by a race from the old Spanish fort to Jackson Square). The Tennesseans under Carroll and Coffee arrived less than two hours after orders were issued.

Carroll and his men were ordered to join Governor Claiborne in case the landing at Villeré's was a feint. The others started about sunset on their way along the road toward the enemy. Colonel Thomas Hinds's Dragoons, recent arrivals from Mississippi Territory, and Coffee's Brigade of mounted infantry formed the advance. They were followed by the Orleans Rifle Company under Captain Thomas Beale, Jugeat's Choctaws, Daquin's Battalion, two pieces of artillery commanded by Lieutenant Samuel Spotts, the 7th Regular United

States Infantry under Major Henry D. Peire, a detachment of United States Marines under Lieutenant F.B. Bellvue, the 44th Regular United States Infantry under Major Isaac L. Baker, and Plauche's Battalion. Altogether, some two thousand men marched with Jackson along the Mississippi River in the winter twilight.

Meanwhile the schooner *Carolina* went to take position opposite the British encampment. Captain John D. Henly commanded. Commodore Patterson was on board.

About 4:00 p.m. a reconnoitering party on land had clashed with a British outpost. This party returned without a good estimate of the enemy's numbers. They had picked up copies of a proclamation to the Creoles. It said that if they remained quiet, their property and slaves would be respected. It was signed by Vice Admiral Cochrane and General Keane.

At nightfall, Jackson's forces reached the spot where the De La Ronde Oaks stand today. (These trees, probably planted about 1820 are often miscalled "Pakenham Oaks" or "Versailles Oaks.")

There the little army divided. General Coffee commanded one division. It consisted of part of his brigade of Tennessee mounted infantry, the Orleans Rifle Company, and the Mississippi Dragoons. The other division was under command of Jackson himself. It consisted of the artillery on the road along the levee. Then, on a line almost perpendicular to the river, were the Marines, the 7th and 44th Infantry, the battalions of Plauche and Daquin, and the Choctaws. By then it was dark, except for the light of a dim moon.

Coffee was guided by Colonel de La Ronde. He was a plantation owner familiar with the terrain. Coffee was to circle to the left and attack from that side. Every man was to keep quiet until the *Carolina*'s opening volley. It was to be the signal for the battle to begin.

While all this was happening, the British had been enjoying food and wine from the plantations. They were getting their first rest in several days. Campfires showed plainly the position of those between Villeré's house and the levee. Outposts and sentinels had been posted, including a detachment not far from Jackson's army. Only part of the British land forces were there when the fighting began. They totaled about 1,680 men. Others were on the way.

1. To get to Bayou Bienvenue, the British had to work their way across

   a. Pea Island.
   b. the Pearl River.
   c. Lake Borgne.
   d. the Mississippi River.

2. The light British boats traveled to the mouth of the bayou by means of

   a. river currents.
   b. men rowing.
   c. wind in their sails.
   d. steam power.

3. _____ was **not** part of the British forces.

   a. Captain Spencer
   b. John Peddie
   c. John Keane
   d. Joseph Ducros

4. The British captured American forces at

   a. the mouth of Bayou Bienvenue and the Villeré Plantation.
   b. the mouth of Bayou Bienvenue and Pea Island.
   c. the mouth of Bayou Bienvenue and the mouth of the Pearl River.
   d. Pea Island and the mouth of the Pearl River.

5. The first to report to General Jackson that the British were within nine miles of New Orleans was

   a. Major René Philippe Gabriel Villeré.
   b. Colonel Pierre Denis de La Ronde.
   c. Augustin Rousseau.
   d. Majors Howell Tatum and A.L. Latour.

6. Plauche's Battalion ran to the city from

   a. Fort St. John on Lake Pontchartrain.
   b. four or five miles above the city.
   c. Gentilly Road.
   d. Mississippi Territory.

7. The first troops to march toward the British were

    a. Carroll's Tennesseans.
    b. Hinds's Dragoons and Coffee's Brigade.
    c. Orleans Rifle Company.
    d. Jugeat's Choctaws.

8. The last unit in the march against the British was

    a. Plauche's Battalion.
    b. the 44th Regular U.S. Infantry.
    c. the 7th Regular U.S. Infantry.
    d. Daquin's Battalion.

9. The commander of American naval forces in the New Orleans area was

    a. Captain Henly.
    b. Colonel de La Ronde.
    c. Vice Admiral Cochrane.
    d. Commodore Patterson.

10. Who do you think was in a better position to win a battle at Villeré's plantation? Why?

_____

_____

_____

_____

_____

_____

_____

_____

_____

WILLIAM T. SHERMAN ARRIVES IN CALIFORNIA

by *William T. Sherman*

In chapter II of his memoirs, Sherman describes life in California. Sherman's adventures in California began in January 1847 after a long trip around the Horn to Monterey.

All the necessary supplies being renewed in Valparaiso, the voyage was resumed. For nearly forty days we had uninterrupted favorable winds, being in the "trades," and, having settled down to sailor habits, time passed without notice. We had brought with us all the books we could find in New York about California. We had read them over and over again: Wilkes's "Exploring Expedition"; Dana's "Two Years before the Mast"; and Forbes's "Account of the Missions."

It was generally understood we were bound for Monterey, then the capital of Upper California. We knew, of course, that General [Stephen Watts] Kearny was *en route* for the same country overland; that [John] Frémont was there with his exploring party; that the navy had already taken possession, and that a regiment of volunteers, Stevenson's, was to follow us from New York; but nevertheless we were impatient to reach our destination. About the middle of January the ship began to approach the California coast, of which the captain was duly cautious, because the English and Spanish charts differed some fifteen miles in the longitude, and on all the charts a current of two miles an hour was indicated northward along the coast.

At last we saw a boat coming out to meet us. When it came alongside, we were surprised to find Lieutenant Henry Wise, master of the *Independence* frigate, that we had left at Valparaiso. Wise had come off to pilot us to our anchorage. While giving orders to the man at the wheel, he, in his peculiar fluent style, told to us, gathered about him, that the *Independence* had sailed from Valparaiso a week after us. It had been in Monterey a week. The Californians had broken out into an insurrection. The naval fleet under Commodore Stockton was all down the coast about San Diego. General Kearny had reached the country, but had had a severe battle at San Pascual, and had been worsted, losing several officers and men, himself and others wounded. War was then going on at Los Angeles. The whole country was full of guerrillas. Recently at Yerba Buena the alcalde, Lieutenant Bartlett, United States Navy, while out after cattle, had been lassoed, etc., etc. Indeed, in the short space of time that Wise was piloting our ship in, he told us more news than we could have learned on shore in a week. Being unfamiliar with the great distances, we imagined that we should have to debark and begin fighting at once. Swords were brought out, guns oiled and made ready. Every thing was in a bustle when the old *Lexington* dropped her anchor on January 26, 1847, in Monterey Bay, after a voyage of one hundred and ninety-eight days from New York.

Every thing on shore looked bright and beautiful. The hills were covered with grass and flowers. The live oaks were so serene and homelike. The low adobe houses, with red-tiled roofs and whitened walls, contrasted well with the dark pinetrees behind. All this made a decidedly good impression upon us who had come so far to spy out the land. Nothing could be more peaceful in its looks than Monterey in January, 1847.

We had already made the acquaintance of Commodore Shubrick and the officers of the *Independence* in Valparaiso, so that we again met as old friends. Immediate preparations were made for landing. As I was quartermaster and commissary, I had plenty to do. There was a small wharf and an adobe custom house in possession of the navy; also a barrack of two stories, occupied by some marines, commanded by Lieutenant Maddox. On a hill to the west of the town had been built a two-story block-house of hewed logs. It was occupied by a guard of sailors under command of Lieutenant Baldwin, United States Navy. Not a single modern wagon or cart was to be had in Monterey, nothing but the old Mexican cart with wooden wheels, drawn by two or three pairs of oxen, yoked by the horns. A man named Tom Cole had two or more of these, and he came into immediate requisition.

The United States consul, and most prominent man there at the time, was Thomas O. Larkin. He had a store and a pretty good two-story house occupied by his family. It was soon determined that our company was to land and encamp on the hill at the block-house. We were also to have possession of the warehouse, or custom-house, for storage.

The company was landed on the wharf. We all marched in full dress with knapsacks and arms, to the hill. We relieved the guard under Lieutenant Baldwin. Tents and camp equipage were hauled up. Soon the camp was established. I remained in a room at the custom-house, where I could superintend the landing of the stores and their proper distribution.

I had brought out from New York twenty thousand dollars commissary funds, and eight thousand dollars quartermaster funds. The ship contained about six months' supply of provisions, also a sawmill, grist mill, and almost every thing needed. We were soon established comfortably. We found the people of Monterey a mixed set of Americans, native Mexicans, and Indians, about one thousand all told. They were kind and pleasant. They seemed to have

24

nothing to do, except such as owned ranches in the country for the rearing of horses and cattle. Horses could be bought at any price from four dollars up to sixteen, but no horse was ever valued above a doubloon or Mexican ounce (sixteen dollars). Cattle cost eight dollars fifty cents for the best. This made beef net about two cents a pound, but at that time nobody bought beef by the pound, but by the carcass.

Game of all kinds—elk, deer, wild geese, and ducks—was abundant; but coffee, sugar, and small stores, were rare and costly.

There were some half-dozen shops or stores, but their shelves were empty. The people were very fond of riding, dancing, and of shows of any kind. The young fellows took great delight in showing off their horsemanship. They would dash along, picking up a half-dollar from the ground, stop their horses in full career and turn about on the space of a bullock's hide. Their skill with the lasso was certainly wonderful. At full speed they could cast their lasso about the horns of a bull, or so throw it as to catch any particular foot. These fellows would work all day on horseback in driving cattle or catching wild horses for a mere nothing, but all the money offered would not have hired one of them to walk a mile. The girls were very fond of dancing. They did dance gracefully and well. Every Sunday, regularly, we had a *baile*, or dance, and sometimes interspersed through the week.

1. In which of the following books would you not find information about California?

   a. *Exploring Expeditions*
   b. *The Pathfinder*
   c. *Two Years Before the Mast*
   d. *Account of the Missions*

2. Even before reaching shore, _____ gave Sherman and his friends all the news.

   a. General Stephen Kearny
   b. John Frémont
   c. Lieutenant Henry Wise
   d. Commodore Stockton

3. When did the *Lexington* leave New York?

    a. 1845
    b. 1846
    c. 1847
    d. 1848

4. The *Independence* was commanded by

    a. Commodore Shubrick.
    b. John Frémont.
    c. Lieutenant Henry Wise.
    d. Commodore Stockton.

5. Which lieutenant commanded the marines?

    a. Wise
    b. Bartlett
    c. Maddox
    d. Baldwin

6. Sherman obtained the assistance of Tom Cole to

    a. relieve the guard.
    b. transport supplies.
    c. buy beef.
    d. buy coffee, sugar, and small stores.

7. The quartermaster is responsible for supplying the army with its necessary supplies, equipment, and provisions. The intent of the commissary system is to provide an income benefit through savings or discount purchases on food and household items necessary to subsist and maintain the household of the military member and family. Sherman had been given _____ in commissary funds than in quartermaster funds.

    a. $8,000 more
    b. $8,000 less
    c. $12,000 more
    d. $12,000 less

8. How do you explain the difference in funds described above?

_____

_____

_____

_____

_____

_____

_____

_____

_____

_____

_____

_____

_____

_____

_____

_____

_____

AFTER THE BATTLE

After defeating the British in the Battle of New Orleans on January 8, 1815, some of the Americans wanted to attack them. The Americans had won from behind fortifications. Now they wanted to fight the British in the open. This was prevented by the higher officers. They knew that the British still had many soldiers able to use bayonets. It would be only a waste of lives to try to destroy the rest of their army. There were truces to bury the dead. The usual tedious and tricky negotiations were conducted over such matters as the exchange of prisoners. Between truces, the American artillery annoyed the enemy.

On January 19th, it appeared that the British had gone. This was confirmed when one of their doctors approached the American lines with a letter from General Lambert informing General Jackson that the British had given up the attempt against New Orleans. The letter asked for care for eighty men wounded too badly to be taken home. Several spiked cannon and some other war materials were also left behind.

Meanwhile, a small British fleet began to bombard Fort St. Philip, about sixty miles below New Orleans on a bend in the river. They soon found they could hit the fort and yet stay out of range of its guns. They continued to bombard it at intervals for more than a week. They did little damage and killed only two men. On January 16th, supplies for the fort arrived from New Orleans, including fuses for the thirteen-inch mortars that the defenders had not been able to use. The next day they hit the ships with projectiles from the mortars. On the 18th the British gave up this rather half-hearted attempt.

Still not knowing that the peace treaty had been signed, the British forces showed their determination by attacking Fort Bowyer on Mobile Bay for a second time in this campaign. The fort was weak in comparison with the force now sent against it. It surrendered on February 11th. Two days later, news of the peace reached the fort. The War of 1812 was over. The fighting in America now ended.

After the British departed, Jackson permitted some of the men to return to their homes in New Orleans. An enthusiastic Latin celebration of the victory followed. There were parades and a triumphal arch. As the climax of the celebration, a ceremony was performed at the cathedral. The crowd outside joined in singing hymns of thanksgiving.

Even though Americans celebrated, their troubles were not over when the enemy left. The troops had long been exposed to every kind of weather. Now

28

disease began to take a toll far heavier than the battle. Mrs. Jackson, arriving in February, wrote to a friend that nearly a thousand had thus died.

Jackson's task was not made easier by the rumors of peace that reached the city. Suspecting a ruse, he refused to believe anything until he had a fully confirmed official notice. He kept the militia under arms and New Orleans under martial law. The raising of the blockade boomed prices. Many of the citizen-soldiers were more anxious to speculate than to do irksome duty. Once the immediate danger was past, the governor and the legislature resented Jackson's high-handed ways. Out of this situation grew a series of unpleasant incidents, culminating in a fine of $1,000 imposed on Jackson by a federal judge for contempt of court. Jackson bore himself with dignity in the courtroom, and paid the fine. He quelled a popular demonstration in his favor, advising his friends to recognize the supremacy of the law.

At long last, indubitable news of peace came. Martial law was lifted on March 12th. Jackson began to release the troops.

Many of the fighters in Jackson's temporary army returned to their usual civilian ways. The Tennessee troops marched back over the Natchez Trace to their homes. General Carroll, their commander, later served six terms as governor of his state. Others of Jackson's commanders were later prominent in civil life. John Adair became governor of Kentucky.

Some of the defenders, however, were adventurers with no civil occupation. Among these were the Baratarians. Because of their part in the battle, President Madison pardoned them for their early offenses. They behaved for a while. Dominique Youx tried to be a New Orleans ward politician. He died in poverty. Renato Beluche became an admiral in the Venezuelan Navy. Others returned to piracy. They set up an "establishment" on Galveston Island. It was destroyed by the United States Navy after outrages had been committed by the pirates. Of Jean Lafitte's life after this incident, we can only say that he " . . . sailed away into the legendary realms from which he had come."

The New Orleans campaign cleared the way for a wave of migration and settlement along the Mississippi. The battles helped to advertise the West. Jackson's soldiers, coming and going, marked and built roads and trails. They made people better acquainted with water routes. More important possibly than all was that European and Indian threats to the Mississippi River were now ended. The outlet for Western products was open for good.

Finally, from the smoke and glory of New Orleans, Andrew Jackson emerged as a national hero. For the first time, a Westerner arose to challenge the power of the eastern "aristocracy" which, until then, had dominated the national politics of the United States. Soon after the battle, he was mentioned for the presidency. He became a candidate in 1824. Jackson received a plurality of popular votes in this election. However, he lost in the electoral college in a four-cornered race. His winning of the next election, in 1828, was hailed as a triumph of the people. He served eight years in the White House.

Out of office, the old warrior became an "elder statesman" and adviser to presidents. As such, he was influential in the annexation of Texas. In 1840, he visited New Orleans for the twenty-fifth anniversary of the battle. At that time he laid the cornerstone of the monument to him in downtown New Orleans's Jackson Square, as the old Place D'Armes is now called.

In 1843, Congress refunded with interest the fine that Andrew Jackson had paid in New Orleans in 1815.

1. After the Battle of New Orleans, the British communicated with the Americans about all of the following **except**

   a. a truce to bury the dead.
   b. an exchange of prisoners.
   c. the peace treaty signed in Ghent.
   d. care for their badly wounded.

2. After leaving New Orleans, the British fleet

   a. conquered Fort St. Philip.
   b. conquered Fort Bowyer.
   c. was driven from Fort Bowyer after new forces arrived.
   d. was driven from Fort St. Philip two days after they attacked it.

3. The biggest problem after the battle was

   a. rumors of peace.
   b. maintaining martial law.
   c. rising prices and speculation.
   d. disease.

4. Who became an admiral?

   a. Adair
   b. Beluche
   c. Carroll
   d. You

5. What do you think was the most important effect of the U.S. victory in the Battle of New Orleans? Why?

_____

_____

_____

_____

_____

_____

_____

_____

_____

_____

_____

_____

_____

_____

_____

_____

_____

JACKSON ARRIVES IN NEW ORLEANS

The easy capture of Washington encouraged the British to proceed with the Gulf Coast phase of their offensive. Major General Sir Edward M. Pakenham was chosen to lead the attack. He was sent on a fast frigate to America.

The British Secretary of War, Lord Bathurst, also sent 2,150 reinforcements. This should make sure of the success of this expedition. His Majesty's government attached great importance to its success. West Indies troops would join the force when it reached Jamaica. Friendly Native Americans in the southern United States would also be armed and equipped.

The expedition would first secure the mouth of the Mississippi. This would deprive inland Americans of access to the sea. Bathurst felt that the people of Louisiana wanted to become independent or to return to Spanish rule. Thus it would not be necessary to maintain a large British occupation force there. To keep the white population on the British side, no encouragement was to be given to a slave revolt.

The choice of commander shows the importance the British attached to this invasion. Sir Edward Michael Pakenham was the brother-in-law of the Duke of Wellington. However, he did not owe his prominence to that connection alone. He was known as the "Hero of Salamanca." He had literally fought his way up. Both Pakenham and the parents of Andrew Jackson had been born in Ireland. They were all born not far apart in County Antrim, Ireland.

In 1814, General Pakenham was thirty-six years old and in vigorous health. His opponent was forty-seven years old. He was in poor health. Pakenham had learned the art of war by fighting against the best armies in the world. Jackson had fought only poorly-equipped Native Americans. Pakenham had under him veterans of the wars against Napoleon. Jackson had mainly inexperienced recruits and militia. It seemed there could be only one outcome of a contest between these two.

Jackson had been busy with Creek Indians in the summer of 1814. He began to hear of British activity on the Florida coast. They were landing soldiers and furnishing supplies to Indians hostile to the United States. Jackson was disturbed by these developments. He dictated a treaty to the Creeks. Jackson then marched to the Gulf Coast in August 1814.

At Mobile he learned that the British under Colonel Edward Nicholls had taken Pensacola from the Spaniards. Nicholls issued a proclamation calling on those whom he supposed to be dissatisfied with American rule—Creoles,

32

Kentuckians, and others—to support the British. Jackson replied with his proclamation urging the inhabitants of Louisiana to resist the invaders.

Jackson's forces were scattered. All together he commanded five regiments and three hundred and fifty artillerymen. He appealed to Secretary of War James Monroe for more men and materials. The successful British attack on Washington tied Monroe's hands.

Adding to Jackson's problems were repeated letters from Governor Claiborne requesting more regular troops and a personal visit by the general to New Orleans to boost lagging morale.

The general felt, however, that affairs near at hand needed attention first. He believed that the enemy wanted to seize Mobile. Then they would go to New Orleans by land. Jackson strengthened Fort Bowyer. It was situated at the entrance to Mobile Bay. Fort Bowyer beat off a British attack. Meanwhile, the American commander continued to build up the defenses of Mobile.

His forces there were much strengthened by the arrival of Brigadier General John Coffee's Brigade of Tennessee mounted infantry. In response to a letter from Jackson to the governor of Tennessee, these volunteers had gathered at Fayetteville in that state. From there, they rode through Chickasaw and Choctaw lands and reached Mobile on October 25th.

Now Jackson could take the offensive and give some attention to New Orleans. A quick march to Pensacola in November and a surprise attack drove out the British. Jackson sent an expedition to keep the Seminoles in check. He left another part of his force at Mobile. Jackson at last departed for New Orleans.

Andrew Jackson arrived in New Orleans for the first time on December 2, 1814. In his history of the campaign, Major A. Lacarriere Latour, Jackson's military engineer, said, "It is scarcely possible to form an idea of the change which his arrival produced on the minds of the people." That such a man was needed is shown by these words of Charles E.A. Gayarre, the distinguished Creole historian of Louisiana:

> Where (Jackson) was as chief, there could be . . . but one controlling and directing power. All responsibility would be unhesitatingly assumed. . . . Such qualifications were eminently needed for the protection of a city containing a motley population, which was without any natural elements of cohesion, and in which abounded . . . conflicting opinions, wishes and feelings, and much diffidence as to the possibility of warding off an attack.

Jackson commenced work with a minimum of formalities. He immediately reviewed the Battalion of Uniform Companies of the Orleans Militia. He then chose aides from among the prominent local citizens. He established headquarters at 106 Royal Street. From there he issued orders for the disposition of troops for the defense of New Orleans.

In 1814, the city was almost an island. It lay about one hundred and five miles from the mouths of the Mississippi. It was surrounded by swamps and marshes, lakes, and the river. Most of the firm ground was along the banks of the Mississippi. A mile or so from the river, the almost impenetrable cypress swamps began. These gradually gave way to marshes. These were filled with tall, razor-edged reeds. The marshes became more watery as the shores of shallow lakes were reached. These lakes were Maurepas, Pontchartrain, Borgne, and many smaller ones. Lake Borgne was an arm of the Gulf of Mexico. The only practicable ways from the lakes to the river were along the bayous. The marshes and swamps were criss-crossed by many of these sluggish streams. Some were navigable by small boats. The banks of the bayous were the only partially firm ground in the extensive morass.

It seemed likely that the British would come by way of Lakes Borgne and Pontchartrain, and Bayou St. John, or up the Mississippi itself. Jackson kept some troops on the alert in New Orleans. He sent others to guard the water approaches. A fleet of gunboats watched the entrance to the lakes. Some of the bayous were blocked with logs and earth. These arrangements were completed within forty-eight hours of his arrival. Jackson inspected the defenses down the Mississippi. There he ordered the strengthening of Fort St. Philip. On his return, he inspected the defenses of the lakes, Chef Menteur, and the Plain of Gentilly, these being north and east of the city. With his defenses in order, Jackson awaited the next move by the British.

1. The British hoped that the forces to attack New Orleans would include all of the following **except**

   a. troops from the West Indies.
   b. slaves.
   c. Native Americans.
   d. reinforcements from England.

2. Who was 47 years old and in poor health in 1814?

   a. Sir Edward Pakenham
   b. Duke of Wellington
   c. Lord Bathurst
   d. Andrew Jackson

3. The first British attack on the Gulf Coast was against the _____ in _____.

   a. Americans . . . Mobile
   b. Americans . . . Pensacola
   c. Spanish . . . Pensacola
   d. Spanish . . . Mobile

4. The second British attack was against the _____ in _____.

   a. Americans . . . Mobile
   b. Americans . . . Pensacola
   c. Spanish . . . Pensacola
   d. Spanish . . . Mobile

5. After attacking the British at Pensacola, Jackson sent an expedition against the

   a. Creek.
   b. Chickasaw.
   c. Seminole.
   d. Choctaw.

6. Which of the following **best** defines "bayou"?

   a. a cypress swamp
   b. a razor-edged reed
   c. a shallow lake
   d. a slow-moving stream

7. _____ was connected directly to the Gulf of Mexico.

   a. Lake Maurepas
   b. Lake Borgne
   c. Lake Pontchartrain
   d. Bayou St. John

8. _____ was located on the Mississippi River below New Orleans.
    a. Fort St. Philip
    b. Fort Bowyer
    c. Jackson's headquarters
    d. The Plain of Gentilly

9. Do you think Jackson's choice of aides was a wise one? Why or why not?

PRINCE JERGER OKOKUDEK

Once Zulu Prince, Now Private for Uncle Sam

PRIVATE THOMAS W. TAYLOR of Company H, Twenty-fourth Regiment, U.S.A., is now on duty at Fort Alcatraz.

He is only plain Tommy Taylor to the boys in blue, but he is called Prince by his kith and kin. One day he will be King. And that is why this story is told. It is a true dramatic tale of a royal household.

The royal folk who compose this tale are the children of Jerger, King of the Zulus. The heir apparent to this powerless throne is Prince Jerger Okokudek. One year ago as "Private Taylor" he enlisted in the American army.

He forced his way through the superstitious boundaries of Kafirland. He won medals from Cambridge University. Finally, he joined the gallant Twenty-fourth Regiment that fought so bravely throughout the Santiago campaign.

That Prince Jerger became an American soldier is but the sequel of what the British invasion of the Kafir interior made possible over a score of years ago.

The Prince joined the United States army that he might gain the knowledge of modern warfare to teach his own people. King Jerger, his father, rules over his court. He does not know that his only son and heir apparent is a private soldier in the American army. The Crown Prince of the Zulus risked his life in defense of the flag of the republic while charging up the hills of San Juan.

In the years gone, when Great Britain penetrated beyond their frontier to Zululand, she found a remarkable nation, organized entirely upon a military system and forming a great standing army.

As for the natives, they received the wonderful strangers with true African hospitality. They gave gold and diamonds, the best gifts of their store, to the white men from the north seas. And their unscientific charity cost them their kingdom.

The Hottentots and Zulus became engaged in war and England proved the powerful ally of the former. A number of sharp skirmishes ensued. The Zulu King was captured. His military system was abolished. His territory was divided into districts. His mines were made amenable to the crown of England. Then concessions followed, the King was set free, pensioned and allowed to rule as potentate over the chiefs of his tribe.

And this was not all. It was the last clause of the treaty that affected the Zulu nation more than all else combined—the cause that guaranteed education to the King's heirs—and it will eventually be the keynote to free them from savagery. The ten royal Princesses and the Crown Prince of the house of Okokudek were sent to Cambridge University. It is considered something even for an ambitious mother to graduate one varsity daughter, but it is given to few Queens to graduate ten Princesses of blood royal into the profession of new women.

Two of these ten daughters are practicing physicians in London. Four of them are gold miners in South Africa. Two are expert mathematicians, and two of them are seamstresses. These ten daughters of the King left Cambridge University to fight their battles with the civilized world. One of the royal family remained within the old college walls. That one was Prince Jerger.

The Prince loved the study of mathematics as he loved his own loyal, uncivilized people. But within a year of graduation he discovered another love. And this was his love for a woman. It was the steady growth of an affection that began upon the very first day of his entrance to the university.

Although the civilized world was a wonderland to him and inspired the keenest interest, still he pined for his home and half-savage comrades with a longing only understood by those whose lives are cast among a foreign people. The Saxon language was hard to master. Saxon manners were difficult and insincere. The alien Prince felt the wretchedness that never had been his even when his father's kingdom passed under British rule.

That night Prince Jerger wandered into the college grounds with heart bowed down. The strange religion of the north did not appeal to him. Civilization oppressed him; he would seek consolation from the only God that his people could understand. And so, under the darkening shadows of the trees he prostrated himself upon the earth and offered up his prayer. The Christian God could not understand, but when did the Zulu gods ever fail to hear the far voice of their followers?

His prayer was answered even before finished.

Prince Jerger was so absorbed in his devotions that he did not hear a soft tread on the grass, nor was he aware that a young girl stood regarding him with pity, until her hand was on his shoulder. It was Miss Rosella Williams, fair and French, and the daughter of one of the university teachers. She interrupted his devotions by singing a chant in the Kafir tongue, a song that he had heard in the kraals of his far away home, and it came like a benediction.

Sympathy has only one language the wide world over, and this is the way their courtship began. Like poor Othello, Jerger told her the story of his life, of his ambitions for his people of the battles he and lost, and she loved him for the dangers he had passed and he loved her that she did pity them. So their love grew apace. Together they made plans for the future welfare of his people, and then he boldly announced his intended marriage to the professors. The faculty said [to] him nay; the law of the university forbade the marriage of its students. The professors advised him to consider well. They argued that no man can pursue two idols with success, and that marriage would detract from his studies.

But Cupid obeys no law save its own, and he was not to be vanquished.

If they could not marry with the consent of the faculty they could marry without it, and they did. The Prince and the fair Rosella were wed.

It was a marriage that strengthened his love for his people and concentrated his energies toward their upliftment. He began the study of civil and military tactics and to further his knowledge he came to America to discover the modern arts of war, and soon found that actual experience was the quickest school. So he enlisted in the Twenty-fourth Regiment at Fort Barancas.

He joined the American army, but he kept this fact a secret from his people. It was better for them to think that he was quietly studying our laws of peace and war than to know that he was actually courting the dangers of the battlefield.

> At the battle of San Juan I saw only one feature that reminded me of the last battle that I fought in with my father, and that one was the wild, fierce shrieks and yells of the Americans when we charged upon the enemy. I think this noise had much to do with weakening Spanish nerve, for the enemy thought that we were all alive while their men were dropping everywhere. Of course there is a great contrast between civilized and savage warfare.
>
> Before going to battle the Zulus offer up incantations, make salaams until the forehead touches the ground in front, and then with a yell and a dash strike both ways with their double-headed swords.
>
> I have learned much for the good of my country in the late Spanish-American war. My education in civilization has also strengthened my sense of its injustice toward the uncivilized countries. I would not be afraid to go anywhere in the world with the American soldiers, but I would not fight under the English flag.

Prince Jerger enlisted in the regular army for a term of three years. Rumors are now afloat of trouble in South Africa. They have reached the Prince's ear. He will remain in Uncle Sam's service until the period of his enlistment expires, unless trouble arises or the King, his father, dies. In such an event he will leave this country at once, for Okokudek in English signifies "Death leaves one"—and Prince Jerger will be King.

ANNABEL LEE

San Francisco Call
Sunday, July 2, 1899

1. Prince Jerger is heir to the _____ throne.

    a. Hottentot
    b. Zulu
    c. Kafir
    d. South African

2. The prince served in the American army during the _____ War.

    a. French and Indian
    b. Revolutionary
    c. Mexican-American
    d. Spanish-American

3. Company H was probably _____ unit.

    a. an all-white
    b. an integrated
    c. a black, "Buffalo Soldier"
    d. a cook and support staff

4. The Hottentots were able to defeat the Zulus because the

    a. Hottentots had a superior military system.
    b. Zulus had no standing army.
    c. English helped the Zulus.
    d. English helped the Hottentots.

5. The peace treaty between the Zulus and the English

   a. kept the Zulu king a prisoner.
   b. provided for the education of the king's children at Cambridge University.
   c. exiled the king.
   d. reserved all mining rights to the Zulus.

6. Apparently, the princesses and the prince entered Cambridge

   a. with no education.
   b. with no knowledge of English.
   c. well educated and prepared.
   d. without the intelligence or training to succeed.

7. The author of this article was

   a. prejudiced against educating women.
   b. prejudiced against educating Africans.
   c. prejudiced against mixed marriages.
   d. remarkably broad-minded for her time.

8. Compare this true story with a recent movie. How is it the same? How is it different?

   _____

   _____

   _____

   _____

   _____

   _____

   _____

   _____

   _____

9. What do you think of Prince Jerger? Why?

_____

_____

_____

_____

_____

_____

_____

_____

_____

_____

_____

_____

_____

_____

_____

_____

_____

_____

43

JOHN LORENZO HUBBELL
AND HUBBELL TRADING POST

John Lorenzo Hubbell was born in Pajarito, New Mexico, near Albuquerque, in November 1853. His parents were James Lawrence Hubbell from Connecticut and Julianita Gutierrez of New Mexico. John Lorenzo went to Santa Fe to attend Fraley's Presbyterian Academy. Then he took a clerking job in the post office in Albuquerque. After about a year in the post office, he set off on his own for the Utah Territory.

Hubbell was a clerk for a time at a Mormon trading post at Kanab, Utah. While there, in 1872, he was reportedly seriously wounded in a fight at Panguitch, Utah. Hearsay tells us that the incident may have been about a woman who was the wife of another man. The "fight" may have been nothing more than John Lorenzo getting plugged as he was exiting a bedroom by way of a window. However that may be—a real fight or wounds for the sake of dalliance—the lively young man thought it better to ride out of town. He headed south, which is important for the rest of the story.

Legend tells us, too, that some Paiute Native Americans picked up the wounded John Lorenzo and took care of him until he had regained mobility. We next find him working as an interpreter at Fort Defiance, Arizona. Then he was a clerk at the trading post at Fort Wingate, New Mexico. With some clerking and trading post experience under his belt, John Lorenzo went to Ganado Lake, Arizona, in 1876. Here he finally settled down. He opened his first trading post at what was then called the Hardison place. He operated there until he bought the Leonard Trading Post in 1878. The original Leonard buildings were out in front of the present home and trading post. The Leonard buildings were razed in the 1920s.

J.L. Hubbell had a partner in the early years, C.N. Cotton. During the years of this partnership Cotton assumed much of the day-to-day operation of the trading post while Hubbell pursued a political career. John Lorenzo was sheriff of Apache County. He was a territorial senator during the years before Arizona became a state. His political ambition ended in 1914. He was defeated in an expensive race for the U.S. Senate.

In the 1890s, long before the disastrous political race for the Senate, Hubbell became sole owner of the trading post. He concentrated more of his time on expanding the operations. Cotton moved to Gallup, New Mexico. He opened a warehouse. He provided wholesale merchandise for Hubbell and other Native American traders. He became very important in the marketing of rugs and blankets in many parts of the United States.

44

Hubbell's developed into one of the most successful and influential of the trading posts. During the early decades of the business, the Hubbells branched out considerably. The Hubbells bought out or opened trading posts in other areas. They did freighting for themselves and others. Apparently they even opened a used car business. J.L. Hubbell was a businessman right down to his bone marrow. As he became more influential, people came to know him as "Don" Lorenzo, the "Don" being a Spanish term of respect.

It seems likely that his concern for his Navajo neighbors and customers did surpass the necessity of a purely business relationship. He had true friends among the Navajo. He was of use to them, and of course he needed them. (A trader who was a cheat, who was of no use to the Navajo, would not last long.)

The relationship between the Navajo and the trading post continues to this day. The trading post is still a place for them to buy supplies and to trade crafts. Now that it is a historic site, it brings people and money to the area.

The trading post as it is now could not exist without the support of the Navajo. The trading post needs their crafts. Hubbell Trading Post is considered something of an economic asset in the area. It is in the interest of the tribal council delegates, the Ganado governing body, and the administrators of the trading post to remain on good terms, and to exchange ideas and discuss mutual problems.

Don Lorenzo's influence on the local culture was considerable. Many Navajo rugs look the way they do simply because Hubbell advised the weavers as to which designs would sell and which might not. The "Ganado Red" is a style associated with Hubbell Trading Post. He advised them on farming matters. The farm at the trading post set an example. J.L. Hubbell tried to keep pace with some modern developments. He was a strong, intelligent businessman with a large dose of compassion running through him. He was open to another culture. He was perfectly fluent in Navajo. He was also a frontiersman, so his talents lay in many directions. There aren't many specialists on a frontier.

Donald Scott stayed at the trading post in 1917. In 1958, Scott visited again. Donald Scott described the experience:

> . . . again I was deeply impressed by [Hubbell Trading Post's] historic associations.
>
> As you know it stands head and shoulders above all other trading posts. While its trade has fallen off in these later days it still stands as a unique monument of the early days of the Indian trader and the Navajo economy. It

was founded in 1874 by John Lorenzo Hubbell. He was a man of such character that his reputation soon spread through all the Navajo country.

The great business in wool, piñon nuts and other goods traded for his commercial stock led to the building of a striking adobe compound of warehouses and stores. Because of the danger in an unsettled land, the group of buildings has partly the aspect of a fort. In a way its character is half way between the forts of fur trading days, such as Laramie and Bridger, and the more peaceful posts of today.

I had a long talk with Mrs. Ramon [sic] Hubbell in the dining hall where Roosevelt, Taft and a great many other celebrities have eaten in days gone by. The family which made the name Hubbell, a synonym for honesty and power, has now reached its end. Don Lorenzo's older son, Lorenzo, whom you knew, succeeded his father and established himself as far west as Winslow. On his death the younger son, Ramon, took over. It is his widow who is now managing the post. I found her a woman of exceptional character and charm.

Mrs. Ramon feels she must dispose of the property. . . . It seems to me that some way should be found to perpetuate the post. Its physical character—the great adobe compound, warehouses, stores and patios—and its historic associations are a unique reminder of a colorful and important period in our relations with the native tribes. Much as I wish other monuments of the past preserved, there are many covered bridges, many historic houses and churches, but this trading post is unique as I am sure you would testify.

When I first saw Ganado it was a picturesque spot surrounded by the camp-fires of Navajos who had come by horseback or in farm wagons from near and far to trade. The warehouses were bursting with wool. Don Lorenzo, quiet but powerful, made a deep impression on me. The Navajo are still there in this cedar-dotted, good grazing land.

The Hubbells started farming their land very early in the twentieth century. A system of irrigation ditches was developed for their own land and to get water from Ganado Lake. J.L. Hubbell was a dynamic and interested man. Trader, politician, farmer, and patron of the arts, he was the builder of a unique trading post and business empire. Unfortunately, after his death, it all slowly faded away.

By the early 1950s, only the trading post in Ganado remained. Dorothy and Roman Hubbell lived there and ran the trading post. Roman was J.L.'s son. He cut a dashing figure in his boots and riding britches. By 1957, Roman Hubbell was confined to a wheelchair. Without Roman to help her, Dorothy was beginning to find the trading post operation to be just a little more than she could comfortably handle. She carried on until 1967. Others now operate the business.

1. John Hubbell's father was originally from

    a. New Mexico.
    b. Albuquerque.
    c. Connecticut.
    d. Utah.

2. John Hubbell attended school in

    a. Albuquerque, New Mexico.
    b. Santa Fe, New Mexico.
    c. Pajarito, New Mexico.
    d. Kanab, Utah.

3. John Hubbell worked in the post office in

    a. Albuquerque, New Mexico.
    b. Santa Fe, New Mexico.
    c. Pajarito, New Mexico.
    d. Kanab, Utah.

4. John Hubbell worked in a trading post in

    a. Albuquerque, New Mexico.
    b. Santa Fe, New Mexico.
    c. Pajarito, New Mexico.
    d. Kanab, Utah.

5. John Hubbell was wounded in a fight at

    a. Kanab, Utah.
    b. Panguitch, Utah.
    c. Fort Defiance, Arizona.
    d. Fort Wingate, New Mexico.

6. Hubbell worked as an interpreter, probably translating _____ into English.

    a. Spanish or a Native-American language
    b. French or Portuguese
    c. Italian or Greek
    d. Polish or Russian

7. In 1914, Hubbell lost a race for

    a. sheriff of Apache County.
    b. the territorial senate.
    c. the U.S. Senate.
    d. Leonard Trading Post.

8. The principal focus of this article is

    a. C.N. Cotton's wholesale warehouse business.
    b. Hubbell's used car business.
    c. Hubbell's freight business.
    d. the Hubbell Trading Post at Ganado.

9. The most important relationship Hubbell developed was with

    a. C.N. Cotton.
    b. the Navajo.
    c. the Paiute.
    d. art collectors.

10. What do you think is the most interesting part of Don Lorenzo's story? Why?

_____

_____

_____

_____

_____

_____

_____

_____

_____

_____

THE CAMP JACKSON MASSACRE AND THE BATTLE OF LEXINGTON

For the five years before the Civil War, residents of Missouri and its neighbor to the west, Kansas, waged their own civil conflict. It was characterized by unrelenting and unparalleled brutality. Both sides were lined up along the border, ready to fight for race. War is about armies on the battlefield, but this was personal. More than anywhere else in the nation, the conflict raging in Missouri and Kansas was truly a civil war, whose wounds were a long time in healing.

The first formal military action in Missouri took place in 1861. It was less than a month after the Confederate bombardment of South Carolina's Fort Sumter in April. Missouri's fanatically pro-southern governor, Claiborne Fox Jackson, attempted to force secession. He planned to obtain control of the guns and ammunition stored at the U.S. Arsenal in St. Louis. He ordered the State Guard to meet at Camp Jackson, near St. Louis. Then he planned to march on the arsenal. On May 10th, the "Home Guard" of German troops led by hotheaded Captain Nathaniel Lyon of the unconditional-Union faction converged on Camp Jackson, from several directions. Lyon demanded unconditional surrender, which he received.

Lyon's force, numbering seven thousand men, marched its prisoners through the city. Hostile crowds gathered to shout insults and throw rocks. The troops fired several volleys into the crowd. Members of the crowd then drew their own weapons and returned the fire. Twenty-eight crowd members lay dead or wounded. The incident became known as the "Camp Jackson Massacre." Tensions ran high. Angry newspaper articles deplored the "massacre." Songs were even written about it. One of the songs was called "The Invasion of Camp Jackson by the Hessians." For the next month, St. Louis continued to be subject to chaos and sporadic violent outbreaks. The "massacre" was an ominous beginning to official hostilities.

Ulysses S. Grant had resigned his army commission. Reunited with his family, he began to farm on part of his father-in-law's estate south of St. Louis. Colonel Dent had given Julia the farm and four slaves. Grant's farm went under in the depression of 1857. He moved to St. Louis in search of work. Everything he tried turned out badly. Nonetheless, he freed the only slave he had ever owned in 1859. It was at a time when his fortunes were low. The Grants now had two more children, Nellie and Jesse. In desperation he finally agreed to work for his father in Illinois. However, in 1861 he happened to be back in St. Louis. Both U.S. Grant and William Tecumseh Sherman had been citizen spectators of the taking of Camp Jackson.

Governor Jackson made the following proclamation on June 12, 1861:

> All our efforts toward conciliation have failed. We can hope nothing from the justice or moderation of the agents of the Federal Government in this State. They are energetically hastening the execution of their bloody and revolutionary schemes for the inauguration of civil war in your midst; for the military occupation of your State by armed bands of lawless invaders; for the overthrow of your State government; and for the subversion of those liberties which that Government has always sought to protect. They intend to exert their whole power to subjugate you. . . . Rise, then, and drive out ignominiously the invaders who have dared to desecrate the soil which your labors have made fruitful, and which is consecrated by your homes.

By the end of June, the pro-Southern governor and members of the cabinet and legislature had been driven into exile. A provisional pro-Union government had been created to rule the state. The tide turned on August 10, 1861. A Union army was defeated at the bloody Battle of Wilson's Creek near Springfield. This set the stage for a rebel offensive into the heart of the Missouri River valley. In late August, the commander of the pro-Southern state guard forces, Major General Sterling Price, set his seven thousand men in motion. Their objective was the prosperous and strongly pro-Southern Missouri River town of Lexington.

While Price was advancing on Lexington, a body of two thousand seven hundred Federals built fortifications to protect themselves. They were under the command of Colonel James A. Mulligan. They had fortified themselves inside the grounds of the Masonic College. It was on the northern end of town.

By the first day of the battle, September 18th, Price's army had swelled from ten thousand to twelve thousand men. More recruits were pouring in daily from the surrounding countryside. With the strains of "Dixie" in the air, Price's men marched through Lexington. They completely encircled the college. For the next nine hours, the huddled Unionists received a continuous bombardment of shot and shell. Meanwhile, the Southerners seized the house of Oliver Anderson. It was then serving as a Union hospital. Outraged by what he considered a breach of the etiquette of war, Colonel Mulligan ordered the house to be retaken. In a bloody counter-charge, his men stormed the house and took heavy casualties. Soon after, the house changed hands for a third time as the guardsmen drove the Yankees back to their trenches.

On the second day of the battle, the bombardment was continued. The lines around the college were drawn in and tightened. The entrapped blue coats had run out of water by then. They were suffering greatly from thirst and heat.

The siege ended on the third day in a dramatic and unusual way. The Southerners had discovered a quantity of hemp bales in a nearby warehouse.

50

They arranged these bales in a line on the west side of the Union entrenchments. They then began rolling the bales ever closer to the line of trenches. The panicked Federals unleashed their artillery into the moving breastwork. Their cannonballs had little effect on the dense bales.

By early afternoon, the snakelike line of bales had advanced close enough to the Union trenches for a charge. The defenders of that sector engaged in a brief but bloody hand-to-hand fight. They were driven back into their entrenchments. By now, Mulligan and most of his officers had been wounded. He realized that the time for surrender had come.

The casualty count from the Battle of Lexington was twenty-five killed and seventy-five wounded on Price's side. The Federals had thirty-two killed and one hundred and twenty wounded. Price did experience some immediate gains from the battle. He captured five artillery pieces, three thousand rifles, and seven hundred and fifty horses, all of which were of great help to his under-equipped army. Beyond that, he returned some $900,000 that the Federals had looted from the local bank. He became a hero throughout the South.

The battle, also known as the "Battle of the Hemp Bales," encouraged Southern spirits. It consolidated Confederate control in the Missouri Valley west of Arrow Rock. However, the long-term gains were less significant.

In response to the defeat at Lexington, the Union commander in Missouri, General John C. Fremont, mounted a massive force to drive Price from Missouri. In the face of this threat, Price had little choice but to retreat back to southwest Missouri. Lexington and the Missouri River Valley once again returned to Union control.

1. Armed conflict in Missouri over slavery began about

   a. 1856.
   b. 1861.
   c. 1866.
   d. 1871.

2. Military conflict in Missouri began in _____ 1861.

   a. April
   b. May
   c. June
   d. August

3. The first clash of military forces led to the defeat of the

   a. Home Guard.
   b. German troops.
   c. Hessians.
   d. State Guard.

4. The "Camp Jackson Massacre" took place in

   a. Camp Jackson.
   b. St. Louis.
   c. Springfield.
   d. Lexington.

5. The Battle of Wilson's Creek took place near

   a. Camp Jackson.
   b. St. Louis.
   c. Springfield.
   d. Lexington.

6. When did the Battle of Wilson's Creek take place?

   a. April 1861
   b. May 1861
   c. June 1861
   d. August 1861

7. The commander of the pro-Union forces at Camp Jackson was

   a. Ulysses S. Grant.
   b. William T. Sherman.
   c. Nathaniel Lyon.
   d. Claiborne Fox Jackson.

8. Who was the commander of the pro-Union forces at Lexington?

   a. Ulysses S. Grant
   b. John C. Fremont
   c. Major General Sterling Price
   d. Colonel James A. Mulligan

9. The _____, serving as a _____, changed hands several times.

   a. Anderson house . . . hospital
   b. Anderson house . . . Union fort
   c. Masonic College . . . Union fort
   d. Masonic College . . . hospital

10. What was the decisive element in the Battle of Lexington?

    a. a breach of etiquette
    b. use of hemp bales as shields
    c. the Federal artillery
    d. hunger

11. Why do you think Missourians were so divided before and during the first year of the Civil War?

    _____

    _____

    _____

    _____

    _____

    _____

    _____

    _____

    _____

    _____

    _____

    _____

    _____

DEVELOPMENTS IN MICHIGAN AGRICULTURE

In 1860, a law was passed known as the Free Homestead Act. It gave one hundred and sixty acres of farmland to every U.S. citizen or person declaring his intention to become a citizen. This encouraged both immigrants and farmers whose land in the eastern U.S. had become depleted to travel to Michigan looking for new land.

Several other developments occurred within the state that influenced agriculture both at the state and at the local level. The Industrial Revolution during the mid-nineteenth century was a major influence. It changed farming through labor-saving machines. Among them were the McCormick Reaper, hay loaders, cream separators, manure spreaders, spraying equipment, combines, and many others.

Gradually, agricultural products in Michigan became diversified based upon a wide range of soil and climate conditions in the state. The heaviest concentration of farmland remained in the southern Lower Peninsula. Much of the forest-covered land was cleared for farming. Prairie land and oak openings made the best choices for a farm site.

The first settlers raised grains. Corn was a good choice because the ground did not have to be plowed. Only a hole had to be punched for the corn kernel. Wheat was extensively grown for profit until about 1900. After that the western states provided too much competition. When the fertility of the land was exhausted, farmers went to general farming. They combined livestock (cattle, sheep, and hogs) with cereal growing.

By the 1850s, many farmers had improved their lot by buying more land and increasing the numbers and types of support structures on their farms. Some built larger houses or added to the existing ones. Due to better transportation, mechanization, and scientific methods, the type of farming changed from subsistence to general farming. In addition to general farming, some farmers specialized in dairy farming. Many others sold dairy products to supplement their incomes. A 1940 article on Michigan dairying sums up the progress that was made from the mid-nineteenth to the mid-twentieth centuries:

> The dairy industry was originally a primitive art. The artists were the wives and daughters of pioneer farmers. The barn was a dark, damp stable housing all manner of domestic animals. The creamery was the crowded kitchen of the pioneer's log cabin. The dairy industry in this state has now

grown into a science, employing the genius of highly educated men in all its branches. . . . Michigan's cows are housed in modern, well-ventilated barns, erected especially for dairy cows. These cows have been freed from that great plague, tuberculosis. They are fed scientifically balanced rations. Their milk is handled under the supervision of boards of health, processed in up-to-date plants. In many cases the milk is delivered sweet and fresh to the ultimate customer as far away from the point of production as the distance across the state.

Lenawee County is considered to be the birthplace of commercial dairy farming in Michigan. In the 1860s and 1870s, Michigan's commercial cheese industry took hold. In the mid-nineteenth century, David Boldman of Canton Township had a cheese factory on Canton Center Road. Lenawee County led the way with ten cheese factories in 1874. Wayne County had five. There were four in Genesee.

As the state's population grew, farming became more intensive. Potatoes were more widely grown around 1885. Beans and sugar beets became popular around 1905. Fruit was commercially grown on the western side of the state because of the climate and soil conditions.

The availability of trucks in the 1920s encouraged more farmers to take garden produce to the Detroit and local markets. An article in 1936 in *The Plymouth Mail* stated, "In the immediate vicinity of Plymouth there are probably more roadside stands where fruits and vegetables are sold than in any other place in Michigan." In fact, *The Plymouth Mail* has called the Plymouth road to Detroit "the Market highway of Michigan."

Sweet corn was widely grown. Canton Township became known as the "Sweet Corn Capital." In the 1920s, sweet corn was a labor-intensive crop. Early, medium, and late Golden Bantam corn was planted in April. Two horses and a row cultivator cultivated it. It was picked in the heat of an August day. Two methods were used for picking corn. One was a corn boat (sled) pulled by a horse between forty-two-inch rows. The corn was picked, counted and slid into bags on the boat. The other way was to bag corn in the field. It was then put at the end of the rows to be picked up later by truck. Family members provided most of the labor. Some hired hands were also used.

By the 1930s, trucks and tractor cultivation made farming easier. Of course, life was never "easy" for the farmer. At this time, the European corn borer arrived in Michigan. It made early sweet corn almost unmarketable. Mid-season corn was edible, but the late corn was home to a second infestation of worms. During 1933–1934, all farming was affected by the weather. Those years were the driest on record. Tractors and high-clearance rigs became more efficient at harvesting corn. Michigan State University and the University of Illinois developed the chemical rotenone to control the corn borer.

The 1950s saw improvements in herbicides. Chain stores and shippers were buying from local growers. Instead of crops being taken to market in a truck by the farmer, clients such as Krogers would come to the farm with large trucks to pick up produce to be delivered to their stores. By the mid-twentieth century, only five percent of Michigan's population was engaged in farming. Many of the farmers supplemented their income with other jobs.

More improvements were made in the 1960s, such as hybrid seed corn. (Gold Prairie and Gold Cup were popular.) Better insecticides replaced DDT. Sprayers replaced dusters. Cutting corn early in the day, and then keeping it cool, increased productivity. The 1960s approached the peak of sweet corn production. Michigan farmers sold to markets as far away as Massachusetts, Georgia, and Texas. In the 1970s, U-Pick farms reached a peak with strawberries, beans, and tomatoes sold, in addition to sweet corn.

1. Of the following, which brought more immigrants to Michigan?

   a. the Industrial Revolution
   b. the McCormick Reaper
   c. the Free Homestead Act
   d. combines

2. The first farmers to specialize in one crop in Michigan often chose _____ because it was easiest.

   a. subsistence farming
   b. to grow corn
   c. to grow wheat
   d. dairy farming

3. Wheat farming was **not** profitable in Michigan after 1900 because

   a. the fertility of the land had been depleted.
   b. the cereal companies had moved out of Battle Creek.
   c. livestock ate all the wheat.
   d. western farms could grow it more cheaply.

4. Of the following, which was **not** a factor in improving the Michigan farmer's lot?

    a. increased competition from western states
    b. better transportation
    c. mechanization
    d. scientific methods

5. The most important improvement in dairy farming was

    a. scientifically-balanced rations.
    b. boards of health.
    c. freedom from tuberculosis.
    d. up-to-date plants.

6. The center of the dairy and cheese industry in late 19th-century Michigan was

    a. Canton Township.
    b. Lenawee County.
    c. Wayne County.
    d. Genesee County.

7. What was the principal factor causing farmers to add potatoes, beans, and sugar beets to their crops?

    a. the availability of trucks
    b. population increases
    c. climate and soil conditions
    d. Sweet corn was a labor-intensive crop.

8. Garden farming became popular with farmers because

    a. of the availability of trucks.
    b. of population increases.
    c. of climate and soil conditions.
    d. sweet corn was a labor-intensive crop.

9. What was the worst problem for corn farmers in the 1930s?

    a. trucks and tractor cultivation
    b. family members provided most of the labor
    c. the European corn borer
    d. the weather

10. The 1950s and 1960s saw great improvements in

    a. transportation.
    b. irrigation.
    c. U-Pick farms.
    d. scientific farming.

11. Which crops, if any, do you think will be grown in Michigan fifty years from now? Why?

_____

_____

_____

_____

_____

_____

_____

_____

_____

_____

_____

_____

_____

_____

_____

_____

58

RICHARD HENDERSON, DANIEL BOONE, AND THE TRANSYLVANIA COMPANY

Until the opening of the following spring Kentucky seemed almost deserted. This was because of the Dunmore's recall of the pioneers in the summer of 1774. For seven months silence reigned over the wilderness. No sounds of woodsman's ax or crack of hunter's rifle were heard. No solitary white man had been left in the great domain during this long interval of time. However, preparations were being to change things. In January 1775, Governor Dunmore proclaimed that, "the Shawanees, to remove all ground of future quarrel, have agreed not to hunt on this side of the Ohio River." This gave assurance of safety to all who might wish to settle in the new country.

However, the Cherokee nation, dwelling on the upper waters of Tennessee River, also held a claim to the disputed territory of Kentucky. This tribe of Native Americans had dwelt here a long time ago, but were driven out by the Shawnee. They insisted that their title was older, and therefore more legitimate, than that of the latter.

Judge Richard Henderson, of North Carolina, formed the Transylvania Company. Its bold and ambitious purpose was to purchase title of the Cherokee nation to the vast territory of Kentucky, and to place it under the authority of a government of its own.

Judge Henderson and Nathaniel Hart were fully advised of this claim of the Cherokees to Kentucky, which they had asserted and guarded in their treaties with the whites for many years. Daniel Boone was employed by the company to visit the chiefs of the nation and to open the way for a council meeting. He was successful in his mission. The great council met in the last days of February 1775, at Sycamore Shoals.

Judge Henderson and Boone were present to represent the company. After a discussion, the terms of sale and transfer of title by the Native Americans were agreed upon. The price fixed for the transfer was fifty thousand dollars, to be paid in merchandise, such as suited the tastes and habits of the Native Americans. On March 17, the treaty was signed, and the goods delivered in payment.

The boundaries of the territory were described:

> Beginning at the mouth of Cantuckee, or what the English call Louisa river, thence up said river, and the north fork of same, to the head spring thereof; thence southeast to the top of Powell's mountain; thence westwardly along the

ridge of said mountain, to a point from which a northwest course will strike the head spring of the most southward branch of Cumberland river; thence down said river to the Ohio river; thence up said river as it meanders, to the beginning; which territory of lands was, at the time of said purchase, and time out of mind had been, the land and hunting-grounds of the said Cherokee tribe of Native Americans.

The name given to the territory was that adopted for the company— "Transylvania." It means "the forest beyond." Within this area were as fine hunting grounds as there were in the land, if not the best. Daniel Boone was chosen to pioneer the path of the new enterprise into the wilderness. For these purposes he was chosen by the company, and given full power and discretion. He gathered a party composed of Squire Boone, Richard Callaway, John Kennedy, and eighteen others. It was joined afterwards by Captain Twetty, with eight men, making thirty in all.

Boone began the work of opening a "trace," or road, for the travel of men and packhorses. It began at Holston River. It went over the mountains, to the mouth of Otter creek, and on to the Kentucky River. With axes and hatchets they began the toilsome work of carving their way through the wilderness, cutting down the undergrowth and blazing the sides of the trees with their axes to mark the path in future. In the narrative of one of the party, Felix Walker, says:

> We marked the track with our hatchets until we reached Rockcastle River. Thence for twenty miles we had to cut our way through a country covered with brush. The next thirty miles were through thick cane and reed. As the cane ceased, we began to discover the pleasing and rapturous appearance of the plains of Kentucky. So rich a soil we had never seen before, covered with white clover, in full bloom, while the woods abounded in game. It appeared that nature, in her profusion, had spread a feast for all that lived, both for the animal and rational world.

All went well until March 20, 1775 when the party reached a point fifteen miles south of Boonesborough. Asleep in camp, they were fired on from the brush by Native Americans, just before the dawn of day. Felix Walker and Captain Twetty were badly wounded. A black servant was killed. Boone rallied his men, and drove off the Native Americans. On March 27th, another attack was made on Boone's men. Five were killed and wounded. A hasty stockade cabin was thrown up for protection. The wounded were cared for. Captain Twetty died the next day. It was thought best to bear the wounded with them, and to go on to the place selected for the post. They arrived on the first day of April.

60

This path marked out by the Boone party is known in history as "Boone's Trace." It became the main southern route by which many emigrants from North Carolina and Virginia came into Kentucky. The Ohio River was the main route of those who came from the counties farther north. The trace was in time widened and improved for the passage of vehicles. It became a great highway across the mountains, from Kentucky to Tennessee.

1. Why did the Cherokee become involved in the land dispute?

    a. They claimed to be the rightful and original landowners.
    b. They claimed to have been driven out by the Shawnee.
    c. They claimed to have known the Shawnee the longest.
    d. They wanted to help the Shawnee to drive out the colonists.

2. Which of the following was Boone's role with the Cherokee?

    a. to translate during the meetings
    b. to keep the peace
    c. to locate the Cherokee chiefs
    d. to encourage participation in a discussion of land rights

3. Which of the following events occurred first?

    a. The Transylvania Company was formed.
    b. The Cherokee were run off by the Shawnee.
    c. The Shawnee gave up their land rights.
    d. The Cherokee sold the land to white settlers.

4. What did the Cherokee get in return for their land?

    a. fifty thousand dollars in cash
    b. land west of the river
    c. goods and items worth fifty thousand dollars
    d. the promise of peace and fifty thousand dollars

5. What was the objective of the Transylvania Company?

    a. to venture deeper into the newly-acquired wilderness
    b. to keep the Native Americans at bay
    c. to buy as much land as possible from the natives
    d. to report back to the governors of the eastern colonies

6. Why did Felix Walker write that nature had given them a "feast"?

    a. The Native Americans provided them with a great feast upon their arrival.
    b. They were relieved to have survived the journey.
    c. The game and flora were bountiful.
    d. The plains were beautiful.

7. Which of the following is the reason Boone's Trace was established?

    a. The company carried their wounded with them.
    b. The colonists needed a route from Kentucky to Tennessee.
    c. Emigrants from North Carolina and Virginia needed a route into Kentucky.
    d. The company needed to avert further hostilities.

8. Briefly describe the sequence of events following the recall.

_____

_____

_____

_____

_____

_____

_____

_____

_____

_____

9. Describe the probable emotions of the members of Boone's party both
    before and after March 20th.

    _____

    _____

    _____

    _____

    _____

    _____

    _____

    _____

10. Many settlers and surveyors in Kentucky created detailed maps as they
    explored the wilderness. Explain the importance of those maps.

    _____

    _____

    _____

    _____

    _____

    _____

    _____

    _____

    _____

    _____

TOOLS AND POTTERY AT POVERTY POINT

In a culture that thrived during the first and second millennia B.C.E., hunters used spears; bows and arrows were unknown. Spears were tipped with a variety of stone points. Some points were exclusive Poverty Point styles. Many were forms which had been made for hundreds and even thousands of years before. Spears were thrown with "atlatls," or spear-throwers, which gave added distance and power. Shaped like oversized crochet needles, atlatls were held in the throwing hand with the hooked end inserted into a shallow socket in the butt of the spear. Hurled with a smooth, gliding motion, the spear was cast toward the target while the atlatl remained in the hand.

Atlatl hooks were sometimes made of carved antler, and polished stone weights were attached to the atlatl shaft. The weights helped to transfer the forces of the throwing motion to the spear in flight. Atlatl weights were made in a variety of sizes and shapes, including rectangular, diamond, oval, boat-shaped bars, and a host of unusual forms. Some were quite elaborate with shiny finishes and engraved decorations. Many broken weights have repair holes along the edges.

The hunters and fishermen also used plummets. These objects were ground from heavy lumps of magnetite, hematite, limonite, and occasionally other stones. Shaped like plumb bobs or big teardrops, plummets often had encircling grooves or holes drilled in the small end to aid in attachment. Some archaeologists consider plummets to be bola weights, but they were more likely weights for cast and gill fishing nets.

Other kinds of hunting devices, such as deadfalls, snares, and traps, were probably used by Poverty Point hunters, but because they were made of perishable wood, their use can only be inferred from the presence of bones of nocturnal animals among food remains. The presence of fishbones, ranging from those of tiny minnows to those of giant gar, suggests that fishermen used some technique, such as poisoning or muddying, for mass catches.

Other kinds of tools undoubtedly were used to obtain food, but we cannot identify with certainty which of the many other chipped and ground artifacts may have been used. Gathering plant foods, such as nuts, acorns, seeds, fruits, berries, greens, and vegetables, probably did not require any tools. Digging edible roots would have required some sort of tool, but it need not have been anything other than a convenient pointed stick. Stone hoes have been found at several Poverty Point villages. Some of these objects have coatings which look like melted glass or thick shellac. The coatings are called sickle-sheen and are formed when hoes chopped through sod.

Foods were prepared with a variety of implements. Animals were butchered with heavy chipped stone bifaces (or cleavers) and sharp flakes or blades (knives). Battered rocks, pitted stones, and mortars served to pound nuts, acorns, and seeds into flour and oil.

Food was cooked in open hearths and earth ovens. The earth oven was an ingenious Poverty Point invention. A hole was dug in the ground, hot "clay balls" were packed around the food, and the pit was covered. Ovens efficiently regulated heat and conserved energy. "Clay balls" were hand-molded. Fingers, palms, and sometimes tools were used to fashion dozens of different styles. Although they are often referred to as "clay balls," they are not really balls, and they are made of silt, not clay. These objects are distinguishing hallmarks of Poverty Point culture. They are so common that archaeologists call them Poverty Point objects.

Some archaeologists have cooked in earth ovens, made like those at Poverty Point. They found, if they always put the same number of Poverty Point objects in the oven every time they cooked, that the shapes (cylindrical, biconical, spheriodial, etc.) controlled how hot the pit got and how long it stayed hot. Using different shaped objects was apparently the cooks' means of regulating cooking temperature, just like setting the time and power level in modern microwave ovens.

Poverty Point peoples had a variety of vessels for cooking, storage, and simple containment. They used pots and bowls made of stone and baked clay. Stone vessels were chiseled out of soapstone (a dense soft rock) and sandstone at the rock quarries. Tons of soapstone were imported to the Poverty Point site from quarries in northern Georgia and Alabama. Most stone vessels were plain, but a few had decorations and small handles. One notable soapstone fragment was decorated with a bas-relief of a bird and another with a panther. Holes drilled along the edges of some fragments show that cracked vessels were often repaired by lacing them back together. Broken pieces also were made into beads, pendants, and, sometimes, plummets.

Many other tools were used in the everyday tasks of building houses, doing odd jobs, and making other tools. We know Poverty Point peoples used stone tools for these jobs. They probably also used wood, bone and antler ones, as well. Most of these were very similar to those used by earlier Archaic people. Hammerstones, whetstones, polishers, and other tools required little or no preparation, beyond selecting suitable rocks.

Fabricated tools include gouges, adzes, axes, and drills. These objects were chipped from large pieces of gravel or big flakes. The working edges of these tools often bear polish or tiny scratches. These marks confirm that they were used for chopping, carving, digging, and drilling. Some of these items, especially celts and adzes (cutting tools with the blades set at right angles to the handles), have counterparts made of ground and polished stone. These ground tools were made in combination or singly by chipping, battering, grinding, and polishing.

Another group of chipped stone artifacts is quite abundant at the Poverty Point and Jaketown sites. They also occur in respectable numbers at other Poverty Point villages. These curious objects are called "microliths" (meaning "small stones"). Microliths are made from flakes and blades (specialized flakes at least twice as long as they are wide with parallel sides). One end is expanded. The other is pointed. They look like small car keys. They are presumed to be drills or punches. The end of one microlith was found lodged in the bottom of an unfinished hole in a stone tablet. That suggests that the original assumption was correct.

Poverty Point clay vessels mark the first appearance of pottery in the Lower Mississippi Valley. Archaeologists accord great historical significance to this event. Recent excavations at the Poverty Point site suggest that Poverty Point people started designing pottery independently of the other southern centers of early pottery. This conclusion is based on new archaeological evidence showing that some Poverty Point pottery was made before soapstone containers and eastern-style pottery arrived at the site.

There are site-to-site differences in Poverty Point pottery. Some pottery contains plant fibers, like early ceramics in other parts of the South. Some contains sand and grit, bone particles, concretions, and/or hard lumps of clay. Some contains no additions or impurities. They are made just from pure clay. Some archaeologists think sand, bone, and other things were intentionally added to the wet clay as temper. These are additives designed to prevent breaking when pots were fired. Other archaeologists suspect the included particles are natural and just happened to be in the dirt selected to make the pottery. If the inclusions were natural, it suggests that potters were merely using the handiest supply of suitable material, no matter what it contained. Such a practice seems to be in keeping with the first groping efforts of a new technology.

Most Poverty Point pottery was plain. Decorations sometimes were made by lightly pressing objects or fingernails into the damp clay. Other decorations were made by rocking simple tools back and forth, and by pinching or incising patterns into the surface.

1. "Atlatls," as described in the first paragraph, are

   a. arrows.
   b. bows.
   c. spears.
   d. spear throwers.

2. What is similar in function to an atlatl?

   a. bowling ball
   b. lacrosse stick
   c. baseball glove
   d. basketball net

3. _____ were sometimes made from antlers.

   a. Atlatl hooks
   b. Atlatl weights
   c. Plummets
   d. Snares and traps

4. _____ were made of wood.

   a. Atlatl hooks
   b. Atlatl weights
   c. Plummets
   d. Snares and traps

5. _____ were made in a variety of forms.

   a. Atlatl hooks
   b. Atlatl weights
   c. Plummets
   d. Snares and traps

6. _____ were sometimes beautifully decorated.

   a. Atlatl hooks
   b. Atlatl weights
   c. Plummets
   d. Snares and traps

7. Grooves in plummets were used

    a. as deadfalls.
    b. as snares.
    c. as traps.
    d. to help attach the plummets to fishing nets.

8. Hoes would have been used to

    a. gather plant food.
    b. dig edible plants.
    c. split open nuts.
    d. coat melted glass or thick shellac.

9. Food was cooked in

    a. stone bifaces.
    b. battered rocks.
    c. earth ovens.
    d. mortars.

10. "Clayballs" were made from

    a. clay.
    b. silt.
    c. soapstone.
    d. sandstone.

11. Archaeologists believe that Pottery Point people perfected pottery prior to its creation elsewhere because

    a. there are site-to-site differences in Poverty Point pottery.
    b. some pottery contains plant fibers.
    c. Poverty Point pottery predates the arrival of soapstone containers and eastern-style pottery at the site.
    d. some pottery is made from pure clay.

12. Why would Poverty Point people purposefully add impurities to clay or choose clay with impurities in it when making their pottery?

   a. They helped to prevent the pots from breaking while being hardened by heat.
   b. They helped to decorate the pottery.
   c. They helped to distinguish the pottery from that made in nearby Pottery Point sites.
   d. They helped to distinguish the pottery from that made in faraway southern and eastern sites.

13. Why do you think archaeologists cooked in earth ovens?

_____

_____

_____

_____

_____

_____

_____

_____

_____

_____

_____

_____

_____

_____

QUANAH PARKER

The Comanche Native Americans were a nomadic people. They first were associated with the Shoshone. They were located in the Rocky Mountains near the head of the Missouri River. They became separated from their Shoshone kinsmen about four hundred years ago. At that time, they emerged from the Rocky Mountains into the broad plains west of the Mississippi River. Here they followed the migratory birds as the different seasons approached. They went south for the winter to escape the severe cold and snow. They traveled back north in the spring to escape the heat of the summer and to camp where there were extensive stretches of green pastures. These pastures furnished food for the herds of buffalo, which were the main source of food and clothing for the tribes of the plains. In their migrations, the Comanche often came into contact with other tribes of the plains. There was almost perpetual warfare for the disputed territory.

As the coasts of America were being more thickly settled, the white race began to push toward the interior. It was at this time that the hostile relations between the whites and Native Americans began. Instead of inter-tribal wars, many of the native tribes united to fight a common foe. They did so in an attempt to roll back the tide that threatened their hunting grounds and their very existence. Before their subjugation, the Comanche frequently raided the pioneer American settlements. The frontiersmen never were sure of life or property. Federal troops began to hunt Native Americans down; however, in the skirmishes, their foes never offered battle in the open, but always from ambush. The white enemy was sometimes taken by surprise.

The defeat of a band of Comanche under Chief Peta Nocona by a company of Texas Rangers marked the first step toward the conquering of the tribe. In this battle, the chief was killed. His wife was Cynthia Ann Parker. She was a white woman. She had been captured by the Comanche when she was but nine years old. She was recaptured by the whites after a captivity of twenty-four years. Cynthia Ann Parker had been taken into the tribe. She had become so accustomed to Native-American ways that, when taken back to her white relatives, she pined away and died, broken-hearted, in 1870. At the time of her recapture by the Texas Rangers, Cynthia Ann Parker's two sons escaped. One of these died a year or two later. The remaining one, Quanah, survived.

Quanah was about the age of eleven or twelve when his father died. The chieftainship of the band, which otherwise might have been inherited by him, was seized by other hands. Later, Quanah gained the rank of chief through sheer force of character, courage, and ability. Eventually, when the various bands of the Comanche were merged into one tribe, Quanah became recognized as principal chief of the entire tribe. He was also a trusted counselor of several other western tribes, including the Kiowa and Apache, who were closely affiliated with his own people.

After the loss of his mother and his sister and the death of his brother, Quanah remained sullen. He wished to avenge the wrong. He became a war-chief in his young manhood. He led his braves on many expeditions against the whites. Gradually the iron band of the white man closed in on the freedom of the tribe. It was difficult for the spirit of revenge to find expression. In the spring of 1874, most of the Comanche, Cheyenne, and a part of the Kiowa smoked the war pipe together. The Arapaho refused to join them. The hostilities consisted of raiding ranches and running off stock.

Quanah's last battle came at a trading post called Adobe Walls, on the South Canadian, about sixty miles west of the Oklahoma boundary line, on June 25, 1874. A party of buffalo hunters had taken refuge there. A band of seven hundred Comanche and Kiowa, under the leadership of Quanah, repeatedly charged them. The Native Americans were repulsed with heavy loss. They finally retired in defeat. Quanah himself was badly wounded.

One by one, the Native American tribes surrendered. Quanah and his men held out. A post at Fort Sill had been constructed several years before. It was garrisoned by troops of the United States Army to watch the movements of the Indians. To this fort Quanah began his march to surrender when no alternative was left. The flag of truce was waved. The Comanche under Quanah surrendered to Colonel R.S. McKenzie, at Fort Sill. They were the last Native Americans of the southern plains to make peace with the whites.

Shortly after his surrender, Quanah went to Texas to visit the relatives and grave of his mother. It was at this time that he added "Parker" to his name.

However, even after making a treaty, Quanah was much opposed to the white man's ways. He kept his tribe from adopting civilization and the Christian religion. The plains Native Americans were restricted to reservations. Quanah and a part of his tribe once left the reservation without permission, which had been refused. He went out to the Texas Panhandle country to spend the winter in Palo Duro Canyon. When spring came, a detachment of troops were sent out to find Quanah and bring him in. The troops arrived at the brink of the canyon just as Quanah's party came up from below to start back to the reservation. A fight started before Quanah knew of the presence of the troops. He immediately galloped out between his own people and the troops. He explained that they were not at war. They were peaceably going wherever the army wanted them.

By the Treaty of Medicine Lodge, in 1867, the Comanche and Kiowa were assigned to a reservation. After their subjugation, the Comanche stayed on this reservation until it was opened for settlement in 1901. At that time, each Native American was given an allotment of one hundred sixty acres.

Quanah Parker was allotted a tract of land four miles northwest from Cache, Oklahoma. Here a home had been built for him by S.E. Burnett, the wealthy Texas cattleman and banker, and other cattlemen. The lumber for this house had been hauled from Vernon, Texas. It consisted of twenty-two rooms.

Rooms for each one of Quanah's wives were furnished identically alike, so none of his wives could complain of partiality on this score. During his lifetime, Quanah recognized seven different wives, but he never had more than five at one time. Whenever Quanah Parker went to town or made trips on special occasions, he used a large stagecoach drawn by four mules. He often took all of his wives along and some of the children. At fairs and celebrations, this stagecoach, with all the pomp and pride of its owner, was frequently seen.

In 1892, when the Comanche and Kiowa agreed to accept allotments, the commissioner of Indian Affairs approached Quanah in regard to the number of wives he would be allowed to keep. The commissioner began as follows:

> Quanah, you have agreed to take allotments and sell your surplus lands and let them be settled by white people. When the white people come to be your neighbors it will be the white man's law and the white man's law says one wife. You have too many wives. You will have to decide which one you want to keep and tell the rest of them to go somewhere else to live.

Quanah listened attentively and looked at the commissioner with a very fixed gaze for some moments, and then startled that worthy by saying, "You tell um!" Then he waited several moments until the significance of this had dawned on the commissioner's mind, when he added, "You tell me which wife I love most—you tell me which wife love me most—you tell me which wife cry most when I send her 'way—then I pick um."

The commissioner replied, "Oh, let's talk about something else." In time Parker quarreled with one wife, then another, and "threw them away," to use the Native American phrase for divorce. At the time of his death, he had but two left.

Quanah Parker was a born politician and orator. He could speak English, but not read it. He took many newspapers and had them read to him. Many times he went to Washington, D.C. in the interest of his tribe. On one such trip, he succeeded in having passed a congressional appropriation of $1,000. It was to be used to exhume the body of his mother, Cynthia Ann Parker, from a Texas cemetery and brought to Post Oak Mission, near Indiahoma, Oklahoma, where many of his fellow tribesmen lie buried. This appropriation also included a large granite monument and high iron fence. Parker himself selected the burial plot for his mother. He was to be buried at her side when he died. This lot is set a little apart from the rest of the cemetery on an elevation which can be seen for miles. When his mother's remains were re-buried at this place on December 4, 1910, Parker gave a great feast, inviting both whites and Native Americans. The address that he gave shows his change of attitude since his last surrender, a change from hostility to white men to that of friendliness and adoption. He spoke, in English, as follows:

> Forty years ago my mother died. She captured by Comanche, nine years old. Love Indian and wild life so well no want to go back to white folks. All same people any way, God say. I love my mother. I like white people. Got great heart. I want my people follow after white way, get educate, know work, make living when payments stop. I tell um they got to know pick cotton, plow corn. I want um know white man's God. Comanche may die tomorrow, or ten years. When end come then they all be together again. I want to see my mother again. That's why when Government United States give money for new grave I have this funeral and ask white folks to help bury. Glad to see so many my people here at funeral. That's all.

Shortly after the funeral, the great granite monument was erected and the iron fence placed around the lots.

On February 11, 1911, word was sent by telephone that the great chief had taken sick among the Cheyenne, where a great medicine feast had been under way, and that he was returning by train to his home. Arriving at Cache, he was taken to his ranch, four miles distant. At his home, he was helped to a couch. Tau-pay, one of his wives, asked him if he had any objection to a white doctor, to which he replied, "No, it's good. I'm ready."

The Native American women seemed to know that death was near and soon motioned the white doctor away. As a last resort, they had one of their own medicine men minister to him. The chief asked the medicine man to pray to God. He began, "Father in heaven, this our brother is coming." Placing his arms about the chief's body, he flapped his hands and imitated the call of the great eagle, the messenger of the Great Father. Water was given to the chief. He died just twenty minutes after his arrival. The wailing of the women was taken up by others. Soon the message of his death was carried by messengers and telephone. After his death, the government denied the Comanche the right of another chief.

Parker's death and funeral attracted attention all over the United States. Almost two thousand whites and Native Americans gathered at the mission. They came in every imaginable conveyance, making a funeral cortege of almost two miles. The body of the dead chief was decked in the regalia of a Comanche warrior and a suit of buckskin. He had gold band rings on every finger, a sparkling brooch pin, and a silver dollar over each eye. It was rumored that many other valuables, even a large sum of money, was buried with him.

A watch was kept over the grave for almost a week. It was not until four years after his death that ghouls entered the grave and robbed it of many of its valuables. One Sunday, one of the chief's wives came to mourn over the grave. When she saw the partially filled grave with bits of the casket and bones lying here and there, she fainted away. Other Native Americans hurried toward her. They found what was wrong and spread the news rapidly. The tribe was much aroused with indignation that, even in death, their beloved chief could not rest undisturbed. An all-night vigil was kept over the grave after the discovery of the desecration of the grave. The following day, his remains were picked up one by one by the men and reverently placed in a new casket. Once more the funeral orations, the sobbing, and the cries of the Native Americans were heard as it was placed in the same grave, thus enacting again the event of four years before.

1. When and where did the Comanche hunt buffalo?
   a. in the summer in the Rocky Mountains
   b. in the winter in the south
   c. in the winter in green pastures of the plain
   d. in the summer in green pastures of the plain

2. Quanah Parker was probably born a few years before
   a. 1850.
   b. 1860.
   c. 1870.
   d. 1880.

3. Cynthia Ann Parker was _____ years old when she was taken away from the Comanche.
   a. 9
   b. 24
   c. 33
   d. 57

4. How did Cynthia Ann react when she was taken from the Comanche tribe?

   a. She was excited because she knew she was being released from captivity.
   b. She was afraid that the Comanche would come after her and start a war.
   c. She was devastated because she had come to love the Comanche way of life.
   d. She was sure that the Comanche were deceiving her white relatives.

5. As mentioned in the fifth paragraph, what is likely to have happened when the Native American tribes gathered to "smoke the war pipe together"?

   a. They agreed upon peace-making endeavors with white men.
   b. They traded goods for tobacco products.
   c. They chose a new tribal leader.
   d. They discussed going to war as allies.

6. Quanah surrendered at _____ after losing his last battle at _____.

   a. Fort Sills . . . Adobe Walls
   b. Adobe Walls . . . Fort Sill
   c. Adobe Walls . . . Palo Duro Canyon
   d. Palo Duro Canyon . . . Fort Sill

7. The Treaty of Medicine Lodge

   a. brought peace between warring tribes.
   b. assigned the Kiowa and Comanche to a reservation.
   c. was never signed.
   d. was drafted by Quanah Parker, but left at the reservation when he escaped.

8. Who built Quanah Parker's home?

   a. Quanah Parker
   b. Comanche Native Americans
   c. a group of cattlemen
   d. the owner of a lumbermill

9. What is ironic about Quanah's statement to the commissioner of Indian Affairs regarding his many wives?

   a. Quanah did not have as many wives as the commissioner suspected.
   b. The commissioner was mistaken; white settlers would not be bothered by Quanah's lifestyle.
   c. The commissioner was jealous of Quanah's many wives and his large home and family.
   d. Quanah eventually "threw away" all but two of his wives.

10. In your own words, rewrite Quanah Parker's speech delivered over his mother's new gravesite in 1910.

   _____

   _____

   _____

   _____

   _____

   _____

   _____

   _____

   _____

   _____

   _____

   _____

   _____

   _____

   _____

11. This article mentions that Quanah Parker "was much opposed to the white man's ways [and] kept his tribe from adopting civilization and the Christian religion." However, when he is lying on his death bed, the chief "asked the medicine man to pray to God." What do you think caused Parker to change his behavior so radically?

_____

_____

_____

_____

_____

_____

_____

_____

_____

_____

_____

_____

_____

_____

_____

_____

THE DISCOVERY OF GOLD IN CALIFORNIA

by General John A. Sutter

It was in the first part of January, 1848, when the gold was discovered at Coloma, where I was then building a sawmill. The contractor and builder of this mill was James W. Marshall, from New Jersey. In the fall of 1847, after the mill seat had been located, I sent up to this place Mr. P.L. Wimmer with his family, and a number of laborers, from the disbanded Mormon Battalion. A little later I engaged Mr. Bennet from Oregon to assist Mr. Marshall in the mechanical labors of the mill. Mr. Wimmer had the team in charge, assisted by his young sons, to do the necessary teaming. Mrs. Wimmer did the cooking for all hands.

I was very much in need of a new sawmill, to get lumber to finish my large flouring mill, of four run of stones, at Brighton, which was commenced at the same time, and was rapidly progressing; likewise for other buildings, fences, etc., for the small village of Yerba Buena, (now San Francisco). In the City Hotel, (the only one) at the dinner table this enterprise was unkindly called "another folly of Sutter's," as my first settlement at the old fort near Sacramento City was called by a good many, "a folly of his." They were about right in that, because I had the best chances to get some of the finest locations near the settlements; and even well stocked rancho's [*sic*] had been offered to me on the most reasonable conditions; but I refused all these good offers, and preferred to explore the wilderness, and select a territory on the banks of the Sacramento.

It was a rainy afternoon when Mr. Marshall arrived at my office in the Fort, very wet. I was somewhat surprised to see him, as he was down a few days previous; and then, I sent up to Coloma a number of teams with provisions, mill irons, etc., etc.

He told me then that he had some important and interesting news which he wished to communicate secretly to me. He wished me to go with him to a place where we should not be disturbed, and where no listeners could come and hear what we had to say. I went with him to my private rooms. He requested me to lock the door. I complied. I told him at the same time that nobody was in the house except the clerk, who was in his office in a different part of the house. After requesting of me something which he wanted, which my servants brought and then left the room, I forgot to lock the doors. It happened that the door was opened by the clerk just at the moment when Marshall took a rag from his pocket, showing me the yellow metal. He had about two ounces of it. How quick Mr. M. put the yellow metal in his pocket again can hardly be described.

The clerk came to see me on business, and excused himself for interrupting me, and as soon as he had left I was told, "now lock the doors; didn't I tell you that we might have listeners?" I told him that he need fear nothing about that, as it was not the habit of this gentleman; but I could hardly convince him that he need not to be suspicious. Then Mr. M. began to show me this metal, which consisted of small pieces and specimens, some of them worth a few dollars; he told me that he had expressed his opinion to the laborers at the mill, that this might be gold; but some of them were laughing at him and called him a crazy man, and could not believe such a thing.

After having proved the metal with aqua fortis, which I found in my apothecary shop, likewise with other experiments, and read the long article "gold" in the *Encyclopedia Americana*, I declared this to be gold of the finest quality, of at least twenty-three carats. After this Mr. M. had no more rest nor patience. He wanted me to start with him immediately for Coloma; but I told him I could not leave as it was late in the evening and nearly supper time. It would be better for him to remain with me till the next morning, and I would travel with him, but this would not do. He asked me only "will you come tomorrow morning?" I told him yes. Off he started for Coloma in the heaviest rain, although already very wet, taking nothing to eat.

I took this news very easy, like all other occurrences good or bad, but thought a great deal during the night about the consequences which might follow such a discovery. I gave all my necessary orders to my numerous laborers, and left the next morning at seven o'clock, accompanied by an Indian soldier, and vaquero, in a heavy rain, for Coloma. About half way on the road I saw at a distance a human being crawling out from the brushwood. I asked the Indian who it was: he told me "the same man who was with you last evening." When I came nearer I found it was Marshall, very wet; I told him that he would have done better to remain with me at the fort than to pass such an ugly night here but he told me that he went up to Coloma, (fifty-four miles) took his other horse and came half way to meet me; then we rode up to the new Eldorado.

In the afternoon the weather was clearing up, and we made a prospecting promenade. The next morning we went to the tail race of the mill, through which the water was running during the night, to clean out the gravel which had been made loose, for the purpose of widening the race. After the water was out of the race we went in to search for gold. This was done every morning. Small pieces of gold could be seen remaining on the bottom of the clean washed bedrock. I went in the race and picked up several pieces of this gold, several of the laborers gave me some which they had picked up, and from Marshall I received a part. I told them that I would get a ring made of this gold as soon as it could be done in California. I have had a heavy ring made, with my family's coat of arms engraved on the outside, and on the inside of the ring is engraved, "The first gold, discovered in January, 1848." Now if Mrs. Wimmer possesses a piece which has been found earlier than mine Mr. Marshall can tell, as it was probably received from him. I think Mr. Marshall could have hardly known himself which was exactly the first little piece, among the whole.

1. Who came from the disbanded Mormon Battalion?

   a. James W. Marshall
   b. P.L. Wimmer
   c. laborers
   d. Mr. Bennet

2. Who was responsible for hauling?

   a. James W. Marshall
   b. P.L. Wimmer
   c. laborers
   d. Mr. Bennet

3. John Sutter needed lumber

   a. for his flour mill at Yerba Buena.
   b. to sell to builders and settlers in Brighton.
   c. to sell to builders and settlers in Yerba Buena.
   d. to build his flour mill at Coloma.

4. Sutter's sawmill was called a folly like his decision to

   a. buy land near the settlements.
   b. buy a well-stocked ranch.
   c. settle in Yerba Buena.
   d. settle in the wilderness.

5. Why was Sutter surprised to see Marshall?

   a. He was very wet.
   b. He had been to the fort very recently.
   c. Sutter had sent him supplies.
   d. Sutter had sent him mill irons.

6. When Marshall asked Sutter to lock the doors, Sutter

    a. forgot to.
    b. forgot to at first, but later locked them.
    c. locked them, but later forgot to relock them.
    d. locked them immediately, and relocked them after the servants came.

7. What did Sutter **not** do with the yellow metal Marshall gave him?

    a. Consult an assessor.
    b. Consult an encyclopedia.
    c. Test it with aqua fortis.
    d. Test it with other experiments.

8. Sutter decided that the yellow metal was really the finest quality gold after

    a. meeting Marshall at 7:00 the next morning.
    b. riding to Coloma with Marshall.
    c. picking up several pieces of gold from the mill race.
    d. completing his experiments and research.

9. Who do you think was more excited by the gold: Marshall or Sutter? Why? Point out details and specifics to support your argument.

_____

_____

_____

_____

_____

_____

_____

_____

_____

_____

10. Why do you think Sutter refers to Mrs. Wimmer's piece of gold? What does he say about it?

_____

_____

_____

_____

_____

_____

_____

_____

_____

_____

_____

_____

_____

_____

_____

MADAM C.J. WALKER

"I had to make my own living and my own opportunity! But I made it! Don't sit down and wait for the opportunities to come. Get up and make them!"

Madame Walker was born Sarah Breedlove in December 1867, in Delta, Louisiana. She was the third child of Minerva and Owen Breedlove. The Breedloves were former slaves. They worked as sharecroppers on a cotton plantation. They lived in a one-room cabin. By the time she was five years old, Sarah had learned to carry water to field hands and drop cotton seed into plowed furrows. For a dollar a week, she washed white people's clothes with strong lye soap, wooden sticks, and washboards.

In 1874, Sarah was left an orphan. She moved in with her older sister, Louvenia. A few years later, after a failure of the cotton crop, the sisters moved across the river to Vicksburg, Mississippi. There they worked as washerwomen and domestic servants. At fourteen years old, Sarah married Moses McWilliams. At seventeen years old, she bore her only child, a daughter named Lelia. Her husband died in 1887. Sarah was nineteen years old. Not willing to live with her sister again, Sarah set off for St. Louis. She was told that laundress jobs were plentiful there and fairly well paid.

For the next seventeen years, Sarah supported herself and her daughter as a washerwoman. She went through a second, brief marriage. She became active in the St. Paul African Methodist Episcopal (AME) Church. It was there that she encountered prosperous, well-educated African Americans.

She began to consider how to improve her appearance. Only in her thirties, she found her hair was falling out. She experimented with hair products already on the market. Nothing helped. Finally, as she told a reporter, God "answered my prayer, for one night I had a dream, and in that dream a big black man appeared to me and told me what to mix up for my hair. Some of the remedy was grown in Africa. I sent for it, mixed it, put it on my scalp, and in a few weeks my hair was coming in faster than it had ever fallen out. I tried it on my friends. It helped them. I made up my mind. I would begin to sell it."

Because St. Louis already had several cosmetic companies, Walker decided to move to another city to set up her own business. She chose Denver because her brother's widow and four children lived there. Her own daughter was by then at college in Tennessee. The one special friend she truly regretted leaving was Charles Joseph (C.J.) Walker, a sales agent for a local African-American newspaper.

Walker arrived in Denver in 1905 with $1.50 savings. She rented an attic room. She joined the local AME church. She found a job as a cook. She saved her money. Before long, she was able to quit that job. She took in laundry two days a week to pay her rent. She spent the rest of her time mixing her hair products and selling them door to door. Wonderful Hair Grower, Glossine, and Vegetable Shampoo were well accepted by the African-American women of Denver. By 1906, C.J. Walker moved to Denver. The two soon married. From then on, Sarah began calling herself Madam (sometimes spelled Madame) C.J. Walker, a name she thought would give her products more appeal.

At first, Madam Walker used all her profits for materials and advertising in papers such as Denver's *Colorado Statesman*. C.J. Walker was familiar with newspaper promotion campaigns. He helped develop a marketing plan. He designed advertisements and organized a mail order business for his wife's products. He was not as ambitious as his wife. As Madam Walker described:

> When we began to make $10 a day, he thought that was enough. He thought I ought to be satisfied. But I was convinced that my hair preparation would fill a long-felt want. And when we found it impossible to agree, due to his narrowness of vision, I embarked on business for myself.

She later divorced Walker. She put twenty-one-year-old Lelia in charge of the mail-order branch of the business. Meanwhile, she traveled around the country promoting the products. The business grew. In 1908, Walker and Lelia settled in Pittsburgh where they established Lelia College. It was a training facility for the Walker System of Hair Culture.

Walker continued to tour the country, promoting her business and hiring hairdressers and door-to-door sales representatives. She recruited and trained a national sales force that included schoolteachers, housewives, cooks, and washerwomen. Walker's traveling agents taught these women to set up beauty shops in their homes, keep business records, and make their customers feel pampered and valued.

In February 1910, Walker visited Indianapolis, Indiana. She was very impressed with what she saw. The city had become the country's largest inland manufacturing center because of its access to eight major railway systems. This would be a major asset for a mail-order business. The city also was home to a substantial African-American community. Its main thoroughfares were lined with cafes, offices, and other thriving businesses.

Madam Walker decided to move her entire operation to Indianapolis. She built a factory, a hair and manicure salon, and another training school. After intensive training in hair and beauty culture, graduates of the school were ready to give scalp treatments, restyle hair, and give manicures and massages. She soon had five thousand agents throughout the country. Her company was making $7,000 per week.

In 1913, her daughter, who would later change her name to A'Lelia, persuaded Madam Walker to buy a house in Harlem as the New York base of the business. The house contained living quarters, a beauty salon, and a school for training salon operators. Walker soon began to spend at least half her time in New York. She moved there permanently in 1916. She left the day-to-day management of her manufacturing operation in Indianapolis to F.B. Ransom, her attorney and general manager, and Alice Kelly, the factory forewoman. Later that year, she built her dream house, a mansion in Irvington-on-Hudson, a wealthy community north of New York City.

By 1917, Walker agents were holding yearly conventions, learning new techniques and sharing experiences. One agent wrote in 1913: "You opened up a trade for hundreds of colored women to make an honest and profitable living where they make as much in one week as a month's salary would bring from any other position that a colored woman can secure." These employed women now were able to educate their children, buy homes, and support various charitable organizations.

By the time she died in 1919, the fifty-one-year-old former laundress had become one of the wealthiest businesswomen of her day. She was mourned by many, including W.E.B. DuBois. He wrote an obituary for *The Crisis*, the magazine of the National Association for the Advancement of Colored People (NAACP). "It is given," he said, "to few persons to transform a people in a generation. Yet this was done by the late Madam C.J. Walker. . . . [She] made and deserved a fortune and gave much of it away generously."

Walker left one unfulfilled dream. The dream grew out of an experience that enraged her. After she had been in Indianapolis for some time and was already a wealthy woman, she went one afternoon to the Isis Movie Theater. She gave the ticket seller a dime, standard admission at the time. The agent pushed the coin back across the counter, saying that the price had gone up to 25¢, but only for "colored persons." Madam Walker, an enthusiastic moviegoer, immediately asked her attorney to sue the theater. She hired an architect to draw up plans for a new building to house the Walker business. The building, covering a whole city block, was also intended to serve as a social and cultural center for the African-American community in Indianapolis. An elegant theater in the new building would welcome African Americans.

Madam Walker's business was carried on by her daughter. It is still in operation, although no one in the Walker family is currently associated with the firm. In 1927, A'Lelia Walker Robinson completed the Walker Building in Indianapolis in memory of her mother. It is a fitting tribute to a woman who once proclaimed, "Perseverance is my motto!"

1. Madam Walker's parents were _____ until shortly before she was born.

   a. slaves
   b. sharecroppers
   c. clothes washers
   d. domestic servants

2. Sarah's parents died when she was _____ years old.

   a. four or five
   b. six or seven
   c. fourteen
   d. seventeen

3. Sarah was married to Moses McWilliams for _____ years.

   a. two
   b. three
   c. five
   d. seven

4. Sarah worked as a washerwoman for 17 years in

   a. Vicksburg.
   b. St. Louis.
   c. St. Paul.
   d. Denver.

5. Madam Walker claimed she got the idea for her first cosmetic formula

   a. from her second husband.
   b. from her brother's widow.
   c. in a dream.
   d. from C.J. Walker.

6. Madam Walker moved away from St. Louis to

    a. be near her brother's widow.
    b. be near C.J. Walker.
    c. get away from C.J. Walker.
    d. get away from too much competition.

7. Madam Walker moved to Denver to

    a. be near her brother's widow.
    b. be near C.J. Walker.
    c. get away from C.J. Walker.
    d. be near her second husband.

8. C.J. Walker was familiar with newspaper promotion because he had

    a. organized a mail order business.
    b. developed a marketing plan.
    c. published a newspaper.
    d. been a sales agent for a newspaper.

9. Lelia College was named for Madam Walker's

    a. sister.
    b. daughter.
    c. mother.
    d. factory forewoman.

10. In 1913, Madam Walker's manufacturing operations

    a. moved to Pittsburgh.
    b. moved to Denver.
    c. moved to Harlem.
    d. remained in Indianapolis.

11. In 1916, Madam Walker

    a. moved to Pittsburgh.
    b. moved to Denver.
    c. built a house in Irvington-on-Hudson.
    d. bought a house in Harlem.

12. What factors do you think helped the Walkers' business to be so
    successful?

    _____

    _____

    _____

    _____

    _____

    _____

    _____

    _____

13. Write a biography of A'Lelia Walker Robinson. Include a discussion of
    the relationship between her and her mother. Also address why you
    think A'Lelia wanted to move to Harlem.

    _____

    _____

    _____

    _____

    _____

    _____

    _____

_____

_____

_____

_____

_____

_____

14. What do you think was Madam Walker's greatest accomplishment?
    Why?

_____

_____

_____

_____

_____

_____

_____

_____

_____

_____

_____

89

MISSOURI RIVER CLEANUP

Two hundred years ago, Meriwether Lewis and William Clark explored the Missouri River. Treacherous rapids, rattlesnakes, and pictographs left by American Indians greeted them. Rapids, snakes and some of the Indian art work remain. However, modern-day adventurers are as likely to encounter rusted bed springs, mountains of beer cans and the all-too-common discarded snow tire. Sometimes the snow tire comes complete with a less-than-shiny wheel.

Area residents set out to reverse the river's descent into a garbage dump recently. On a bright Saturday in October, hundreds of volunteers descended upon the Big Muddy. Their goal was to remove a hundred years of junk that had accumulated along her banks, sandbars, roads and trails.

"A lot of people think the Missouri is just a big, dirty, dangerous river," said Steve Johnson, project manager for Missouri River Communities Network. "We want to promote the idea that it's one of the most beautiful natural resources in Missouri. It's worth taking care of."

Four agencies got together to sponsor the clean-up. Missouri River Communities was one of the agencies. It teamed up with the Missouri Departments of Natural Resources and Conservation and the U.S. Army Corps of Engineers to conduct the river cleanup. Chad Pregracke of East Moline, Illinois, led the groups. He has directed cleanups of the Mississippi and Illinois rivers. Pregracke's nonprofit organization, Living Lands and Waters, towed a barge up the Missouri River to Easley. Easley is approximately twenty-five miles northwest of Jefferson City. The barge served as the floating headquarters of a mammoth effort. The clean-up extended thirty-four miles from Hartsburg to Rocheport.

It was a trip that almost did not happen.

Documentary filmmaker Jim Karpowicz of Columbia first conceived of the river cleanup a year earlier. He approached Pregracke and requested the help of Living Lands and Waters. Pregracke agreed. During the ensuing months, Karpowicz enlisted the aid of Missouri River Communities, state and federal agencies, and other interested groups.

Pregracke purchased a tugboat at a river-bottom price in January 2001. The old tug required extensive work. That included a new engine, transmission, lights and propeller shaft. The overhaul took place in Minneapolis. Completion was scheduled for June. However, two weeks before the planned

Missouri River cleanup, the tug had only just been finished. The tug had a long trip ahead of it. It had approximately one thousand miles to travel down the Mississippi River at speeds of up to ten miles per hour. Then it had to go up the Missouri at top speeds of four miles per hour. It literally was a race to Easley for the refurbished tug and its unwieldy barge.

"Do you know how much we were sweating that barge?" Karpowicz said.

In the weeks before the cleanup, Karpowicz could only cross his fingers as he anxiously tracked the barge's progress. Meanwhile, scouts took to the water to plot locations of trash along the river. With almost no rain, the river level dropped. Evidence of years of dumping surfaced.

The morning of the event, Pregracke's barge was safely anchored at the midway point of Easley. Volunteers arrived there and at Rocheport, Eagle Bluffs Wildlife Area, and Hartsburg. Conservation boats ferried volunteers to the flagged trash locations. There, they loaded johnboats with propane bottles, tires, car fenders, a gutted refrigerator, televisions—even a pool table. The junk-laden crafts returned to the barge. The boats were emptied before embarking on other trash collection excursions.

On the barge, more volunteers clad in work boots, sturdy gloves and life vests sorted and washed the junk. Aluminum cans were placed in one stack. Bottles went in another. Pregracke used a Bobcat to haul scrap metal from one end of the barge to the other. An oversized dumpster was filled with old bicycles, plastic drums and cables. It bore a tongue-in-cheek sign reading, "Positively No Swimming Allowed." The barge's final destination was a St. Louis recycling center.

Meanwhile, another team on bicycles and on foot patrolled Katy Trail State Park. They collected debris along the route. They placed it in trash bags for pick-up.

As the day progressed, the volunteers gathered for a group photograph. They wanted to commemorate the Missouri River Relief and to celebrate their accomplishment. They cited different reasons for their involvement.

Karpowicz, an avid climber, frequents the Missouri River bluffs. He said he grew tired of looking at the litter. Johnson said his group hopes to work with small communities along the river to develop their riverfronts in advance of Lewis and Clark bicentennial celebrations.

Others, like Lori Thweatt of Columbia, simply love the river. "We don't realize that there is this incredible wilderness right here. We go to Colorado, we go to the ocean, and here it is, right in our own backyard."

1. A boat is going to be most helpful for cleaning up junk on Missouri River

   a. roads.
   b. trails.
   c. banks.
   d. sandbars.

2. Steve Johnson believes the Missouri River is

   a. dirty.
   b. dangerous.
   c. a beautiful natural resource.
   d. not worth taking care of.

3. Of the following, which is an agency of the national government?

   a. Army Corps of Engineers
   b. Department of Natural Resources
   c. Missouri River Communities
   d. Department of Conservation

4. Of the following, which is a part of the Missouri state government?

   a. Army Corps of Engineers
   b. Living Land and Waters
   c. Missouri River Communities
   d. Department of Conservation

5. Which of the following coordinated the cleanup?

   a. Army Corps of Engineers
   b. Living Land and Waters
   c. Missouri River Communities
   d. Department of Conservation

6. Whose idea was it to clean up the river?

    a. Steve Johnson
    b. Chad Pregracke
    c. Jim Karpowicz
    d. Lori Thweatt

7. The key ingredient in the cleanup, which almost did not make it on time,

    a. were the conservation boats.
    b. were the johnboats.
    c. was the tugboat.
    d. was the barge.

8. Volunteers were ferried to trash locations by

    a. conservation boats.
    b. john boats.
    c. tugboat.
    d. barge.

9. Of the following, which was the most common item found among the junk?

    a. pool table
    b. gutted refrigerator
    c. snow tire with wheel
    d. tire

10. No swimming was allowed in the

    a. river.
    b. dumpster.
    c. barge.
    d. Bobcat.

11. The project was called

    a. Missouri River Relief.
    b. Missouri River Communities
    c. Living Lands and Water
    d. Lewis and Clark Bicentennial

12. Draw up plans for a cleanup project in your area. Make them as detailed as possible (who, what, when, where, why, how much, etc.).

_____

_____

_____

_____

_____

_____

_____

_____

_____

_____

_____

_____

_____

_____

_____

_____

_____

_____

_____

_____

BILL ANDERSON AND
THE JAMES BROTHERS

Bill Anderson's quarrels with Quantrill led him to form a fierce band of his own. It included Frank James and his sixteen-year-old brother, Jesse. The oath of allegiance was "I swear to defend the Constitution of the Confederate States, obey orders and kill Yankees."

Bill Anderson had grown up in Huntsville, Missouri. Hometown allegiance, however, apparently did not deter him from raiding the place on July 15, 1864. He robbed merchants and a bank of $45,000. He shot a passerby imprudent enough to try to stop the raiders. (Anderson did, at least, make his boys return money stolen from people with whom he had gone to school.) Two days later, he led thirty-five followers into nearby Rocheport. They did great damage to the town and terrified its inhabitants. On July 23rd, one hundred of his raiders gutted the railroad station in Renick. The next day, the Bushwhackers ambushed and dispersed a pursuing company of the 17th Illinois Cavalry. Two slain Federals were even found scalped.

Following that engagement, Anderson's men moved north into Shelby County. There they destroyed the Salt River railroad bridge. They torched depots at Shelbina and Lakenan. Then in August, Anderson attacked the riverboat *Omaha* near Glasgow. He raided Rocheport again, shooting up more boats and snarling all the river traffic. Another band, led by Todd and Thrailkill moved to Keytesville on September 20th. They captured the Union garrison and burned the courthouse. During the same month, Anderson's men robbed thirteen stagecoaches in Howard County. On September 23rd, Todd's forces joined Anderson's. The three hundred guerrillas then wiped out a twelve-wagon Federal train near Rocheport. They captured eighteen thousand rounds of ammunition and killed fifteen Union troops.

These forces were briefly joined by Quantrill. Together they attacked Fayette. Federal soldiers barricaded in the courthouse repulsed them. Seeking revenge for this setback, Anderson's guerrillas raided Centralia on September 27th. They prowled the village for three hours, looting stores and terrorizing citizens. Drunken Bushwhackers burned the depot. The arrival of a stagecoach from Columbia gave them an opportunity for more plunder. Then a westbound train from St. Charles provided unexpected bounty: twenty-five unarmed Union soldiers. The command was given to have them "mustered out." The helpless Federals were lined up on the platform, stripped of their uniforms, and shot.

After the Centralia Massacre, a Union detachment chased the fleeing guerrillas. They turned outside Centralia and killed one hundred and fourteen of their pursuers. On October 11th, Anderson's Bushwhackers sacked Boonville. Meanwhile their leader joined Quantrill to capture Glasgow.

George Todd was killed by a Union sharpshooter just outside Independence a few days before the Battle of Westport. Anderson was killed in a charge on Union troops in Ray County a few days after that battle. Quantrill, who had been in hiding for several months, gathered some of his most trusted men, including Frank James. They left Missouri for Kentucky. Some say he was planning to assassinate Lincoln in Washington, D.C. On May 10, 1865, Captain Edwin Terrell's Federal rangers surprised them in a Spencer County barn. Quantrill was shot in the back. He lay paralyzed and in agony at a Louisville military prison for nearly a month before he died.

Jesse James lasted longer. After recovering from a serious wound, he and his brother, Frank, began making plans to form an outlaw gang. Joined by several other former guerrillas, including the Younger brothers, Cole and Jim, they went on in the late 1860s to apply Quantrill's hit-and-run tactics to bank and train robbery. Missouri, to the dismay of state boosters, gained the reputation of being the "Outlaw State." Pinkerton agents and the law had tried to find Jesse. Finally, in 1882—living as Thomas Howard in St. Joseph, Missouri—he was murdered. Jesse James was shot in the back in his own home by a new member of his own gang. Robert Ford was out for the governor's reward.

> It was Robert Ford, that dirty little coward,
> I wonder how he does feel;
> For he ate of Jesse's bread and slept in Jesse's bed
> And laid poor Jesse in the grave.
>
> Poor Jesse had a wife to mourn for his life.
> His children they were brave;
> But that dirty little coward shot Mr. Howard
> And laid poor Jesse in the grave!
>
> —from a ballad "made by Billy Gashade"

1. The first raid by Anderson's bands was

   a. in Shelby County.
   b. on his hometown, Huntsville.
   c. on Rocheport.
   d. on Renick.

2. Anderson's men attacked Rocheport on July _____, 1864.

    a. 15
    b. 17
    c. 23
    d. 24

3. Anderson's men ambushed a Federal cavalry unit on July _____, 1864.

    a. 15
    b. 17
    c. 23
    d. 24

4. Anderson and Todd's bands combined to destroy a Federal wagon train

    a. in Shelby County in July 1864.
    b. near Rocheport in August.
    c. near Rocheport on September 23rd.
    d. in Howard County.

5. Of the following, which came directly after the destruction of the Salt River bridge?

    a. the attack on the riverboat, Omaha
    b. the capture of Union forces in Keytesville
    c. the robbery of 13 stagecoaches in Howard County
    d. the burning of depots in Shelbina and Lakenan

6. Anderson's worst atrocity occurred in

    a. Centralia.
    b. Columbus.
    c. St. Charles.
    d. Fayette.

7. Anderson was killed

    a. outside Independence.
    b. before the Battle of Westport.
    c. during the Battle of Westport.
    d. after the Battle of Westport.

8. Why do you think many people make outlaws like Jesse James into folk heroes?

_____

_____

_____

_____

_____

_____

_____

_____

_____

_____

_____

_____

_____

_____

_____

_____

_____

_____

_____

FREMONT'S SECOND EXPEDITION TO CALIFORNIA

by John Bidwell

In the autumn of 1845 [John] Frémont came on his second exploring expedition to California. This time he divided his party east of the Sierra Nevada. He sent the greater portion to come in through a gap supposed to exist farther to the south. He followed substantially what is now the emigrant road, or Truckee route. He came direct to Sutter's Fort with about eight or nine men.

At that time I was in charge of Sutter's Fort and of Sutter's business, he being absent at the bay of San Francisco. Frémont camped on the American River about three miles above the fort. The first notice of his return to California was his sudden appearance, with Kit Carson, at the fort. He at once made known to me his wants, namely, sixteen mules, six pack saddles, some flour and other provisions, and the use of a blacksmith's shop to shoe the mules, to enable him to go in haste to meet the others of his party. I told him precisely what could and could not be furnished. I said that we had no mules, but could let him have horses, and could make the pack saddles; that he might have the use of a blacksmith's shop, but we were entirely out of coal. He became reticent, and, saying something in a low tone to Kit Carson, rose and left without saying good day, and returned to his camp.

As they mounted their horses to leave, Frémont was heard to say that I was unwilling to accommodate him, which greatly pained me. Of course, we were always glad of the arrival of Americans, and especially of one in authority. Besides, I knew that Captain Sutter would do anything in his power for Frémont. So I took with me Dr. Gildea, a recent arrival from St. Louis, across the plains, and hastened to Frémont's camp and told him what had been reported to me. He stated, in a very formal manner, that he was the officer of one government and Sutter the officer of another; that difficulties existed between those governments; and hence his inference that I, representing Sutter, was not willing to accommodate him. He reminded me that on his first arrival here, in 1844, Sutter had sent out and in half an hour had brought him all the mules he wanted. I protested my willingness to do anything in my power, but was obliged to plead inability to do more than stated, telling him that in 1844 Sutter was in far better circumstances; that on that occasion a man (Peter Lassen) had just arrived with a hundred mules, of which Sutter had bought what Frémont needed. But he had not been able to pay for them, because Frémont's drafts had to go East before Sutter could realize on them the money which had been promised to Lassen.

In a few days Sutter returned, but could not furnish anything more than I had offered. Then Frémont concluded to go down to the bay and get supplies. He went with his little party of eight or nine men, including Kit Carson, but without success; so he sent the men back to Sutter's Fort to go, as best they could, to find the main party. Meanwhile he himself had made his way Monterey to see the American consul, Thomas O. Larkin. After several weeks Frémont and his entire party became united in the San Joaquín Valley. While at Monterey he had obtained permission from Jose Castro, the commandant general, to winter in the San Joaquín Valley, away from the settlements, where the men would not be likely to annoy the people. He had in all in the exploring party about sixty well-armed men. He also had permission to extend his explorations in the spring as far south as the Colorado River.

His men in the mountains had suffered considerably. Frémont had given positive orders for them to wait at a certain gap or low divide till he should meet them with supplies, but the place could not be found. The men got out of provisions and bought from the Indians. The kind they most relished was a sort of brown meal, which was rich and spicy, and came so much into favor that they wanted no other. After a while the Indians became careless in the preparation of this wonderful meal, when it was discovered to be full of the broken wings and legs of grasshoppers! It was simply dried grasshoppers pounded into a meal. The men said it was rich and would stick to the mouth like gingerbread, and that they were becoming sleek and fat. But after the discovery they lost their appetites. How hard it is sometimes to overcome prejudice!

1. Who was away from the fort?

   a. John Frémont
   b. Kit Carson
   c. John Sutter
   d. John Bidwell

2. Who did Frémont think was unwilling to accommodate him?

   a. Dr. Gildea
   b. Kit Carson
   c. John Sutter
   d. John Bidwell

3. To whom did Frémont probably first say that he was being mistreated?

   a. Dr. Gildea
   b. Kit Carson
   c. John Sutter
   d. John Bidwell

4. What government did Frémont believe Sutter represented?

   a. American
   b. Russian
   c. British
   d. Mexican

5. Frémont went to Monterey to see

   a. Thomas Larkin.
   b. Jose Castro.
   c. Peter Lassen.
   d. Kit Carson.

6. The Native Americans were careless in preparing the brown meal in that

   a. they had not kept out the grasshopper's wings.
   b. they had not cleaned out the grasshopper's legs.
   c. they had not pounded it sufficiently.
   d. it was a kind of gingerbread.

7. Write a story about someone who is in a situation similar to the hungry soldiers.

   _____

   _____

   _____

   _____

   _____

   _____

NIGHT ON THE BATTLEFIELD

The following are excerpts from two articles that appeared in the *Cleveland Herald* in April 1863.

NIGHT ON THE BATTLE FIELD OF STONE'S RIVER—THE OLD YEAR OUT—THE NEW YEAR'S RIDE

Carefully, driver, carefully! Let the hard iron of the wheels roll slowly over the pounded stone of the [Nashville] pike. The young soldier still lives. His breath is short, but we may yet reach the hospital ere he dies. Guide steadily past the shattered wagons—round the heaps of dead horses—through the long rows of corpses; watch that no foot of a horse jars against the fallen dead—the heroes of the last day of 1862—resting now, where they fell, or where friends have laid them. Here they lie in rows of miles, sleeping out the old year. On the last day of Sixty-two they stood for their country and for Freedom. At its midnight hour they sleep, no more to awake to war's ringing bugle call.

Well might thoughts of the old year and of eternity crowd upon the mind of the soldier whose duty to the wounded living brought him across that vast field of the ghastly dead—this night so clear and frosty—the last of December.

The story, as he told it—he, a private . . . —let me tell it.

That awful night! Words will not paint it, yet may give some faint idea of what sad experience a day of carnage brings.

At 9 o'clock of the evening of December 31st, an ambulance left one of the hospitals of Rosecrans' army, moving in the direction of Nashville. Two soldiers lay upon the carriage. The life blood of one, following the passage of a minnie ball through the breast, was oozing out from the right lung, staining the blankets beneath. The other, suffering from a crushing shot through the left leg . . . [was] scarcely conscious. Along with the carriage walked [the] private—going to care for his wounded companions.

Three miles along the stony pike . . . lay their route. Here an artillery wagon had been swept by a bursting shell—its gun dismounted, its wheels shattered, the horses and men fallen together, lay mixed as they had gone down. Still tangled in the harness hitched to the caissons, lay the hind parts of a horse, his breast and forelegs swept away, while the lifeless body of an artillerist rested with an arm over the dismounted gun. . . .

Yonder a cavalryman had fallen, his drawn saber reflecting in the moonlight against the dark earth where he lay; and beside him his comrade and his horse, all keeping the same silent watch of death.

The sharp frost of a clear night spread its white drapery over the clothes of the dead—on the locks [of hair] . . . gathered its icy breath, offering alike to all a common shroud. . . .

All along the road for more than two miles, were these scenes of horror met by the weary soldier. Still on rolled the ambulance—past broken wagons—lost muskets and dismounted artillery, to the great general hospital of the fourth division.

Here after midnight lay the wounded and dying, covering an acre of ground . . . of which every room was filled, every outhouse crowded, the very floor wet with blood. Close by lay a man with an arm gone—next to him one with a leg smashed—there a part of a face was shot away. . . . Yet all those hundreds living, many waiting the dressing of their wounds with patience.

Our two soldier boys were taken from the ambulance into the building, and with hundreds of others closed no eyes to sleep that last December night.

The morning sun of Jan. 1st, 1863 rose upon a day as clear as ever dawned. Surgeons came that morning, and looked upon the one wounded in the breast, . . . whispering to the private that "He will die."

At 9 o'clock that morning [another] soldier and the one wounded through the breast were put into a strong army wagon . . . and, with the private and . . . driver, started over the pike for Nashville. Just as they reached the bridge the enemy, sweeping round our right, had brought a battery to bear upon the bridge.

Fearfully whirled our driver on, as if careless of the dying men in his charge, and only seeking safety in flight. Full three miles the race continued, when on came dashing a battalion of the rebel Wheeler's cavalry . . . yelling and firing on the teamster and the wounded. The breast-wounded soldier lay gasping, and ordering the other soldier, who held his footless leg in one hand . . . , to shoot the driver if he did not stop, that they might surrender, before they were murdered by the now near foe. But on, on heedless alike of threats and enemy, dashed the driver. . . . Nine miles over the stony road had the race continued. The determined driver had brought his team through, and escaped with the suffering load.

At 9 o'clock that evening they were taken from the wagon . . . and placed upon good cots, receiving close attention at the hands of skillful surgeons.

104

Charles Stansell, the driver, and the soldiers he transported survived their ordeal at Stones River. Later, Stansell was killed in a fight. He is buried at the Hazen Brigade Monument on the battlefield at the request of those he saved. The soldier who had been wounded in the breast at Stones River wrote the following tribute for the *Cleveland Herald*:

DEATH OF A BRAVE SOLDIER

The untimely death of Charles Stansell, Co. G 41st Ohio, deserves from me more than a passing notice.

Charles Stansell was the fearless driver of a four horse team from Murfreesboro to Nashville . . . when Lieut. Wolcott and myself were being conveyed to a hospital. . . . He . . . would not stop, but rushed on, heedless of our protests and threats . . . thus saving our team, our wagon, and our lives, all of which would have been sacrificed had we fallen into the hands of the rebels.

1. What is another word for "ere" as it is used in the first paragraph of the first exerpt?

   a. when
   b. as soon as
   c. before
   d. here

2. A soldier who had to tend to wounded soldiers, according to the author, would

   a. probably cry.
   b. act very bravely.
   c. leave the military.
   d. think about his past and future.

3. The author would most likely agree that the aftereffects of the battle were

   a. gruesome.
   b. soothing.
   c. everlasting.
   d. marvelous.

4. How was the author able to relate the events in such great detail?

    a. He was a soldier.
    b. He had spoken to a private.
    c. Journalists know everything.
    d. He started the battle.

5. After leaving the division hospital, what happened to the ambulance and its occupants?

_____

_____

_____

_____

_____

_____

_____

_____

_____

_____

_____

_____

_____

_____

6. Why do you think the soldier felt compelled to write a tribute to Charles Stansell after his death?

_____

_____

_____

_____

_____

_____

_____

_____

_____

_____

_____

_____

_____

_____

_____

_____

_____

_____

_____

_____

_____

THE HISTORY OF TRANSPORTATION IN MICHIGAN

While Michigan was under French and then British control, little was done to foster settlement or to improve transportation. Those Europeans who lived in the territory were mainly involved in the lucrative fur trade or were with the military. They used native trails and waterways as a means of transportation. After the War of 1812, the British finally relinquished both Detroit and Mackinac. With the British gone and the Indian threat under control, the U.S. government began to take steps to attract settlers. A survey was commissioned in order to offer land for sale. Steps were initiated to improve transportation.

The Erie Canal was inaugurated in 1825. It opened the floodgates to settlement of the Michigan Territory. Settlers from New York, in particular, traveled the new waterway to Buffalo. From there they boarded sail and steamships that carried them to Detroit and Monroe in Michigan. Here they found the routes to the interior primitive and muddy. Often they were little more than native trails.

The Chicago Road also encouraged westward migration north into Michigan. Father Gabriel Richard, a Roman Catholic priest and a member of Michigan Territory's delegation to Congress, lobbied for federal appropriations. He understood the importance of the road to settlement. Congress was concerned with keeping the natives under control. It commissioned a military road to carry troops from Detroit to Chicago. It was the second road to be funded by the U.S. Congress.

In 1824, Congress earmarked $3,000 for survey of the road. Orange Risdon and his crew began in Detroit with plans to cut a new route straight west. Within the first mile, they realized that the funds would not be sufficient to build a new road. They abandoned their plans. Instead, they followed the pre-existing Sauk Trail. They surveyed the route to Fort Dearborn in present-day Chicago. This road became a main "thoroughfare," carrying thousands of settlers to the interior of Michigan.

The "road" cut through the forest was just wide enough for a wagon. Often tree stumps were left in place. Primitive bridges were laid across streams and rivers. During rains, the road was muddy, and it became rutted and bumpy when dry. Logs were often placed over the worst of the mud holes. Although this primitive route was almost impassable at times, by 1830 a twice-weekly stage was running along the route. This soon increased to daily stages so crowded that reservations had to be made in advance. The *State Gazetteer* reported, in 1840, that "travel on this road (was) . . . immense, equal to, if not more, than any other of the United States." With so many on the road a need arose for accommodations for travelers. Inns and taverns were opened along with other businesses.

These roads with their stage and wagon traffic were the farmer's contacts with civilization. He used them to take crops to markets in Detroit or Ypsilanti. On them he traveled to churches, schools, and villages. Transportation was still difficult. The settler seldom strayed far from his own community.

Efforts were made to improve the road system. In 1848, the Michigan state legislature passed the Plank Road Act. Companies received charters to build roads. They were granted the right to charge a toll to finance the road's construction and maintenance. In 1851, the Detroit–Saline Road was chartered. Planking was placed along fifty miles of the Chicago Road at a cost of $66,795. Eventually, these "plank roads" were surfaced in gravel. They continued to operate as toll roads into the twentieth century. By 1900, eighteen miles between Detroit and Wayne were still in operation with five tollgates. Five gatekeepers were employed at $29 per month. A superintendent was paid $55 a month.

Although an improvement, these roads were not the answer to the need for rapid, year-round transportation. Many were not profitable. In 1900, gross income for the Chicago Road was $1,200. Maintenance cost $1,200. Periods of wet weather and the need for constant maintenance frequently rendered the roads impassable. Settlers looked to other means of transportation. Area residents saw the railroads as the answer.

On December 24, 1834, a convention was called in Detroit. Its purpose was to petition Congress for an appropriation of land to build a railroad across the peninsula. The convention was successful in its petition. The new railroad was to be laid out along a route surveyed earlier by Lieutenant Berrien of the War Department. According to Lieutenant Berrien, "our line follows the course of the Chicago turnpike . . . (and) varies but little from it until it approaches the Huron River at Ypsilanti." This became the Michigan Central. It is now Amtrak. A second railroad was built in 1878. It was the Holly, Wayne & Monroe. The railroad has changed ownership several times over the years. Today it is operated as part of the Chesapeake & Ohio. These roads gave farmers ready access to both local and national markets. Today along the routes, industrial development attests to the continuing importance of these railroads.

Railroads did not prove to be the definitive answer to the area's transportation dilemma, however. Although of great importance for long-distance shipping and travel, they were not economically as advantageous as the toll roads. On the road the farmer could haul his goods to market at a rate of 10¢ a mile. The railroads charged 25¢ a mile.

Another means of transportation rose to fill the gap between the expensive railroads and the inconvenient, often impassable, but cheap toll roads. The interurban or street railroad played a short-lived, but important role in the development of transportation in Michigan. The Detroit, Jackson & Chicago line was inaugurated in 1898. Its route ran down Michigan Avenue with stops to the west and east. Along this route, farmers delivered milk and other produce to be taken to markets in Detroit and Ypsilanti. Rural residents were able—for very little money—to travel to Detroit and Ypsilanti and even as far as Toledo. Originally, the charge was 1¢ per mile. The interurban carried rural young people to high school in Plymouth, Wayne, and Ypsilanti, resulting in a high percentage of high school graduates for farming communities. The ride to school cost as little as 9¢. The easy access to large communities both to the east and west helped preserve rural communities.

1. The British abandoned Detroit after the

    a. French and Indian War.
    b. Revolutionary War.
    c. War of 1812.
    d. Mexican War.

2. In order to offer land for sale, the government had to

    a. threaten the Native Americans.
    b. survey the land.
    c. build the Erie Canal.
    d. build the Chicago Road.

3. Most travelers on the Erie Canal took a boat from

    a. Monroe to Detroit.
    b. Detroit to Buffalo.
    c. Buffalo to Detroit or Monroe.
    d. Detroit to Monroe.

4. Congress approved financing for the Chicago Road because

    a. Father Gabriel Richard had lobbied for it.
    b. the Erie Canal had opened in 1825.
    c. the roads from Detroit to Monroe were poor.
    d. they wanted to be able to move troops from Detroit to Chicago.

5. Father Gabriel Richard helped convince Congress to fund the Chicago Road because he

    a. was concerned about the defense of Chicago.
    b. knew a road would bring settlers to Michigan.
    c. was worried about British attacks.
    d. wanted Chicago to grow.

6. Which of the following statements about the Chicago Road is **true**?

    a. It followed the Sauk Trail.
    b. It headed straight west from Detroit to Fort Dearborn.
    c. It was never completed.
    d. It received its first appropriation before the Erie Canal was completed.

7. Daily stages were running on the Chicago Road through Michigan

    a. before 1830.
    b. by 1830.
    c. shortly after 1830.
    d. after 1840.

8. The Plank Road Act

    a. was passed in 1851.
    b. required all communities to improve their roads with planks.
    c. required all communities to charge tolls.
    d. permitted companies to receive charters to build roads and charge tolls.

9. Gravel replaced planks

    a. only after tolls were no longer charged.
    b. along fifty miles of the Chicago Road.
    c. in 1851.
    d. before the end of the nineteenth century.

10. The second railroad in Michigan was the

    a. Michigan Central
    b. Amtrak
    c. Holly, Wayne & Monroe.
    d. Chesapeake & Ohio.

11. The principal problem with shipping by railroads for farmers was that

    a. they could not ship long distances.
    b. the railroads were too expensive.
    c. the railroads were unreliable.
    d. the railroads would not carry agricultural products.

12. Which do you think contributed the most to Michigan's development: roads, canals, railroads, or interurban transportation? How and why?

_____

_____

_____

_____

_____

_____

_____

_____

_____

_____

_____

GEORGE ROGERS CLARK
RECAPTURES VINCENNES

George Rogers Clark and his rag-tag army were now on high ground two miles from Vincennes. Two or three French hunters were taken captive. From them Clark learned that no one in Vincennes knew of his approach. They reported, however, that, although the *habitants* were tired of the "Hair-Buyer's" presence and would gladly return to American allegiance, some two hundred Indians had just arrived at the fort. The *Willing* had not been heard from. However, an immediate attack seemed the proper course. The young colonel planned and carried it out with the curious mixture of bravery and *braggadocio* of which he was a past master.

First he drew up a lordly letter, addressed to the inhabitants of the town, and dispatched it by one of his French prisoners. It ran:

> Gentlemen, being now within two miles of your village with my army . . . and not being willing to surprise you, I take this step to request such of you as are true citizens, and willing to enjoy the liberty I bring you, to remain still in your houses. And those, if any there be, that are friends to the King, will instantly repair to the fort and join the Hair-Buyer General and fight like men.

Having thus given due warning, he led his "army" forward, marching and counter-marching his meager forces among the trees and hills to give an appearance of great numbers. He and his captains helped keep up the illusion by galloping wildly here and there on horses they had confiscated, as if ordering a vast array. At nightfall the men advanced upon the stockade and opened fire from two directions.

Not until a sergeant reeled from his chair with a bullet in his breast did the garrison realize that it was really under attack. The *habitants* had kept their secret well. There was a beating of drums and a hurrying to arms. Throughout the night a hot fusillade was kept up. By firing from behind houses and trees, and from rifle pits that had been dug before the attack began, the Americans virtually escaped loss. Hamilton's gunners were picked off as fast as they appeared at the portholes of the fort. Clark's ammunition ran low, but the *habitants* furnished a fresh supply. They also brought a hot breakfast for the men.

In a few hours the cannon were silenced. Parleys were opened. Hamilton insisted that he and his garrison were "not disposed to be awed into an action unworthy of British subjects," but they were plainly frightened. Clark finally sent the commandant back to the fort from a conference in the old French church with the concession of one hour's time in which to decide what he would do. To help him make up his mind, the American leader caused half a dozen Indian allies of the British, who had just returned from the forests with white men's scalps dangling at their belts, to be tomahawked and thrown into the river within plain view of the garrison.

Surrender promptly followed. Hamilton and twenty-five of his men were sent off as captives to Virginia. There the commandant languished in prison. In 1780, he was paroled at the suggestion of Washington. On taking an oath of neutrality, the remaining British sympathizers were set at liberty. For a second time the American flag floated over Indiana soil, not to be lowered again.

Immediately after the capitulation of Hamilton, a scouting-party captured a relief expedition which was on its way from Detroit. That placed in Clark's hands ten thousand pounds' worth of supplies. He used it for distribution as prize-money among his deserving men. The commander's cup of satisfaction was filled to the brim when the *Willing* appeared with a long-awaited messenger from Governor Henry. He brought to the soldiers the thanks of the legislature of Virginia for the capture of Kaskaskia and also the promise of more substantial reward.

The whole of the Illinois and Indiana country was now in American hands. Tenure, however, was precarious so long as Detroit remained a British stronghold. Clark now broadened his plans to embrace the capture of that strategic place. He left Vincennes in charge of a garrison of forty men. He returned to Kaskaskia with the *Willing* and set about organizing a new expedition. Kentucky pledged three hundred men. Virginia promised to help. However, in midsummer when the commander returned to Vincennes to consolidate and organize his force, he found the numbers to be quite insufficient. From Kentucky there came only thirty men.

Disappointment followed disappointment. He was ordered to build a fort at the mouth of the Ohio. That was a project of which he had himself approved. When at last he had under his command a force that might have been adequate for the Detroit expedition, he was obliged to use it in meeting a fresh incursion of Indians. They had been stirred up by the new British commandant on the lakes.

Thomas Jefferson succeeded Henry as governor of Virginia in 1779. He was deeply interested in the Detroit project. At his suggestion Washington gave Clark an order on the commandant of Fort Pitt for guns, supplies, and such troops as could be spared. On January 22, 1781, Jefferson appointed Clark "brigadier-general of the forces to be embodied on an expedition westward of the Ohio." Again Clark was doomed to disappointment. One obstacle after another interposed. Yet as late as May 1781, the expectant conqueror wrote to Washington that he had "not yet lost sight of Detroit." Suitable opportunity for the expedition never came. When peace was declared the northern stronghold was still in British hands.

Clark's later days were clouded. Virginia gave him six thousand acres of land in southern Indiana and presented him with a sword. However, peace left him without employment. He was never able to adjust himself to the changed situation. For many years he lived alone in a little cabin on the banks of the Ohio. He spent his time hunting, fishing, and brooding over the failure of Congress to reward him in more substantial manner for his services. He was land-poor, lonely, and embittered. In 1818, he died a paralyzed and helpless cripple.

The finest statue of George Rogers Clark stands in Monument Circle, Indianapolis. It is of an athletic figure, scarcely past youth, tall and sinewy, with a drawn sword, in an attitude of energetic encouragement, as if getting his army through the drowned lands of the Wabash.

1. The "Hair-Buyer" was probably _____, who paid for the scalps of his enemy.

    a. an Indian chief
    b. a French officer
    c. an American officer
    d. a British officer

2. The *Willing* was probably _____ boat full of soldiers.

    a. an American
    b. a French
    c. a British
    d. an Indian

3. The "creoles" were the _____ Vincennes.

    a. French soldiers at
    b. French inhabitants of
    c. British inhabitants of
    d. British soldiers at

4. The *habitants* were _____ Vincennes.

    a. French soldiers at
    b. French inhabitants of
    c. British inhabitants of
    d. British soldiers at

5. Hamilton was the

    a. sergeant first to die in the attack.
    b. leader of the American attack.
    c. "Hair Buyer."
    d. captain of the *Willing*.

6. Why did Clark **not** attack the British at Detroit?

    a. He had been fired for tomahawking captured Indians at Vincennes.
    b. Governor Patrick Henry opposed the project.
    c. Governor Thomas Jefferson opposed the project.
    d. He never had enough men available.

7. What happened to Detroit?

    a. It was never conquered.
    b. It was conquered by George Rogers Clark.
    c. It was conquered by another American officer.
    d. It was conquered by a French and Indian force.

8. Do you think George Rogers Clark was treated fairly? Why or why not? If not, what do you think should have been done for him?

_____

_____

_____

_____

_____

_____

_____

_____

_____

_____

_____

_____

_____

_____

_____

_____

_____

_____

_____

_____

_____

_____

117

DRED SCOTT TRAVELS TO AND FROM MISSOURI

Dred Scott was born to slave parents in Virginia sometime around the turn of the nineteenth century. His parents may have been the property of Peter Blow. Blow may have purchased Scott at a later date.

By 1830, Peter Blow had settled his family of four sons and three daughters in St. Louis. With him he had six slaves. In St. Louis, Peter Blow undertook the running of a boarding house, the Jefferson Hotel. Within a year, though, his wife Elizabeth died. On June 23, 1832, Peter Blow passed away.

The Blow children remained in St. Louis after the deaths of their parents. They became well established in the city's society through marriage to prominent families. Charlotte Taylor Blow married Joseph Charless, Jr., in November 1831. His father had established the first newspaper west of the Mississippi River. The father had been a leading opponent of slavery while editor. Charless, Jr., operated a wholesale drug and paint store. It was called Charless & Company. It later became Charless, Blow, & Company when brothers-in-law Henry Taylor Blow and Taylor Blow became partners.

Martha Ella Blow married attorney Charles Drake in 1835. Drake is better known for his role in the creation of Missouri's 1865 constitution. As a leader of the Radical Republican Party after the Civil War, he was determined to punish those considered Southern sympathizers. The constitution he helped author took away many of their rights, including enfranchisement.

Peter Ethelrod Blow married Eugenie LaBeaume in 1833. She was from an old French banking family. Her oldest brother was a wealthy businessman. He and Peter Blow formed Peter E. Blow & Company. She had two other brothers. One was the St. Louis County sheriff for a time in the 1840s. The other, Charles Edmund LaBeaume, was a St. Louis attorney who played an important role in Dred Scott's freedom suits. All of these St. Louis connections proved helpful to Dred Scott.

At sometime after the Blows arrived in St. Louis in 1830—it was before Dr. Emerson reported to Fort Armstrong in Illinois on December 1, 1833—Dred Scott was sold to Dr. John Emerson. There is no record of the sale. Peter Blow apparently sold Dred Scott to Emerson before his death. On June 30, 1847, Henry Taylor Blow testified in Dred Scott's circuit court trial for freedom that Peter Blow sold Scott to Dr. Emerson.

118

John Emerson came to St. Louis sometime before August 1831. He served as a civilian doctor at Jefferson Barracks for a time. On October 25, 1833, he received his appointment as an assistant surgeon in the United States Army. He left St. Louis on November 19th. He was accompanied by Dred Scott. He reported for duty at Fort Armstrong, Illinois. The stay there is referred to in court documents as being at Rock Island.

Emerson's assignment lasted for nearly three years. Under the conditions of the Northwest Ordinance of 1787, this entitled Dred Scott to his freedom. That ordinance prohibited slavery in regions between the Mississippi and Ohio Rivers and the Great Lakes, except as punishment for crimes. In addition, when the state of Illinois was created from part of the Northwest Ordinance territory in 1818, its state constitution prohibited slavery.

Living at Rock Island presented Dred Scott's first chance to sue for his freedom. He did not sue, though. In May 1836, he traveled with Dr. Emerson to Fort Snelling. Emerson had been transferred there. Fort Snelling was located in the newly-created Wisconsin Territory on the west bank of the Mississippi River. The journey and the residence at Fort Snelling offered Dred Scott a second chance to sue for freedom. Now he resided in a territory that was governed by the 1820 Missouri Compromise. It prohibited slavery north of 36° 30' except within the boundaries of the state of Missouri. Again, though, he did not pursue his opportunity to sue for freedom based on this residence.

In either 1836 or 1837, Dred Scott married Harriet Robinson. She was a teen-aged slave. She was owned by Major Lawrence Taliaferro. He was the Indian agent for the territory. Unusual for slave weddings was the fact that an actual civil ceremony took place. Taliaferro was a justice of the peace. He performed the wedding. At some point, ownership of Harriet was transferred to Emerson.

On October 20, 1837, Emerson left Fort Snelling for assignment to St. Louis. He had repeatedly requested the transfer. He traveled from the fort by canoe because the upper Mississippi River was already frozen. Steamboats could not make the trip. Due to the mode of travel, he left behind most of his possessions, including Dred and Harriet Scott. The Scotts were left in the care of someone else. They were to be hired out until Emerson could make arrangements to send for them. They had the opportunity to escape slavery by running away in his absence. However, they did not leave. Nor did they attempt to sue for their freedom during this time.

Almost immediately upon arriving in St. Louis, Emerson was transferred to Fort Jesup, Louisiana. He arrived there on November 22, 1837. The assignment lasted less than a year. During that time in Louisiana he met Eliza Irene Sanford (known as Irene) of St. Louis. She was visiting her sister Mary. Emerson married Irene on February 6, 1838. In April 1838, at Emerson's request, Dred and Harriet Scott traveled to Louisiana. They thus voluntarily returned to a slave state.

That September, the Emersons and the Scotts returned to St. Louis for a brief stay. Then they traveled back to Fort Snelling in October. On that October trip back to Fort Snelling, Eliza Scott, named for her mistress, was born on the steamer, *Gipsey,* north of the boundary of 36° 30', in free territory. The group remained at Fort Snelling until May 1840.

On May 29, 1840, Emerson was transferred to Florida. The Seminole War was being fought there. He left his wife and slaves in St. Louis. Dred and Harriet Scott were hired out to various people during that time. Emerson was honorably discharged from the United States Army in August 1842. He returned to St. Louis. He was unable to maintain a successful private practice in the city. He settled permanently in Davenport, Iowa, on land he purchased in 1835. He began a practice there in the summer of 1843. Irene Emerson joined him. She gave birth to their daughter, Henrietta, in November 1843.

On December 29, 1843, Emerson died suddenly. He was forty years old. An inventory of his Iowa estate mentioned slaves. The inventory is no longer extant, so it is impossible to determine whether or not this reference was to the Scott family. In Emerson's Missouri estate inventory, there is no mention of any slaves although it is likely that Dred and Harriet Scott were living in or around St. Louis, hired out. After Emerson's death, Irene Emerson returned to St. Louis with her daughter and lived with her father. His proslavery sentiments probably influenced many of her decisions after Dred and Harriet Scott filed for freedom.

By March 1846, Dred and Harriet Scott were hired out to Samuel Russell. He was the owner of a wholesale grocery, Russell & Bennett. It was located on Water Street in St. Louis. At some prior point, Dred Scott had been in the service of Irene Emerson's brother-in-law, Captain Henry Bainbridge. Later reports claim that he traveled with Bainbridge to Corpus Christi, Texas, but returned to St. Louis at the outbreak of the Mexican War. No mention of this travel is made in official court documents. There is no mention of where Harriet and Eliza Scott were living during the time that Dred Scott was with Bainbridge.

On April 6, 1846, Dred and Harriet Scott each filed separate petitions in suits against Irene Emerson in the St. Louis Circuit Court to obtain their freedom from slavery. These documents were identical in nature. They stated that the petitioners were entitled to their freedom based on residences in the free state of Illinois (Rock Island) and the free Wisconsin Territory (Fort Snelling).

1. Dred Scott was born in Virginia some time around

   a. 1800.
   b. 1850.
   c. 1900.
   d. 1950.

2. All together, Peter Blow's household, family, and slaves totalled _____ people.

   a. six
   b. seven
   c. thirteen
   d. fifteen

3. Of the following, who did **not** go into business with his brother-in-law?

   a. Henry Taylor Blow
   b. Taylor Blow
   c. Peter Ethelrod Blow
   d. Charles Edmund LaBeaume

4. Who married an attorney?

   a. Charlotte Taylor Blow
   b. Martha Ellen Blow
   c. Eugenie LaBeaume
   d. Charles Edmund LaBeaume

5. Whose brother was a sheriff?

   a. Charlotte Taylor Blow
   b. Joseph Charless, Jr.
   c. Eugenie LaBeaume
   d. Charles Drake

6. Elizabeth Blow's name before she was married was probably

    a. Taylor.
    b. Emerson.
    c. Blow.
    d. Charless.

7. Peter Blow sold Dred Scott to Dr. John Emerson

    a. before 1830.
    b. between August 1831 and June 1832.
    c. on December 1, 1833.
    d. on June 30, 1847.

8. Fort Armstrong was located in

    a. St. Louis.
    b. the Wisconsin Territory.
    c. Rock Island, Illinois.
    d. the Jefferson Barracks.

9. While living in Fort Snelling, Dred Scott could have sued for freedom based on the

    a. Northwest Ordinance.
    b. Illinois state constitution.
    c. Missouri Compromise.
    d. Missouri state constitution.

10. In September 1838, the Scotts traveled to St. Louis from

    a. Fort Snelling.
    b. Fort Jesup.
    c. Fort Armstrong.
    d. Florida.

11. In October 1838, the Scotts traveled from St. Louis to

    a. Fort Snelling.
    b. Fort Jesup.
    c. Fort Armstrong.
    d. Florida.

12. There is no definite evidence that Dred Scott ever visited

    a. Illinois.
    b. Wisconsin.
    c. Louisiana.
    d. Texas.

13. Dr. Emerson moved to _____ after being unable to make a living in St. Louis.

    a. Florida
    b. Iowa
    c. Louisiana
    d. Texas

14. Describe all the chances Dred Scott and his family had to claim their freedom. Why do you think they failed to do so?

_____

_____

_____

_____

_____

_____

_____

_____

_____

_____

_____

_____

123

15. Do you think the fact that Dred and Harriet Scott were earning wages in 1846 and not working for the Emerson family had something to do with their filing suit in April 1846? Why or why not?

_____

_____

_____

_____

_____

_____

_____

_____

_____

_____

_____

_____

_____

_____

_____

_____

_____

_____

"WHO IS GOVERNOR OF CALIFORNIA?"
by *William T. Sherman*

We heard occasionally from Yerba Buena and Sutter's Fort to the north, and from the army and navy about Los Angeles at the south. We also knew that a quarrel had grown up at Los Angeles, between General Kearny, Colonel Frémont, and Commodore Stockton, as to the right to control affairs in California. Kearny had with him only the fragments of the two companies of dragoons, which had come across from New Mexico with him. They had been handled very roughly by Don Andreas Pico, at San Pascual. Captains Moore and Johnson, and Lieutenant Hammond, were killed. Kearny himself was wounded.

Frémont had marched down from the north with a battalion of volunteers. Commodore Stockton had marched up from San Diego to Los Angeles, with General Kearny, his dragoons, and a battalion of sailors and marines. They was soon joined there by Frémont. They jointly received the surrender of the insurgents under Andreas Pico. We also knew that General R.B. Mason had been ordered to California. Colonel John D. Stevenson was coming out to California with a regiment of New York Volunteers. Commodore Shubrick had orders also from the Navy Department to control matters afloat. General Kearny, by virtue of his rank, had the right to control all the land forces in the service of the United States. Frémont claimed the same right by virtue of a letter he had received from Colonel Benton. Benton was then a Senator, and a man of great influence with Polk's Administration. So that among the younger officers the query was very natural, "Who the devil is Governor of California?"

One day I was on board the *Independence* frigate. I was dining with the wardroom officers, when a war vessel was reported in the offing, which in due time was made out to be the *Cyane*, Captain DuPont [commanding]. After dinner, we were all on deck, to watch the new arrival. The ships meanwhile exchanged signals, which were interpreted that General Kearny was on board. As the *Cyane* approached, a boat was sent to meet her, with Commodore Shubrick's flag officer, Lieutenant Lewis, to carry the usual messages, and to invite General Kearny to come on board the *Independence* as the guest of Commodore Shubrick. Quite a number of officers were on deck, among them Lieutenants Wise, Montgomery Lewis, William Chapman, and others, noted wits and wags of the navy. In due time the *Cyane* anchored close by. Our boat was seen returning with a stranger in the stern sheets, clothed in army-blue. As the boat came nearer, we saw that it was General Kearny with an old dragoon coat on, and an army cap, to which the general had added the broad *visor*, cut from a full-dress hat, to shade his face and eyes against

126

the glaring sun of the Gila region. Chapman exclaimed: "Fellows, the problem is solved; there is the grand vizier (visor) by G–d! He is Governor of California."

All hands received the general with great heartiness. He soon passed out of our sight into the commodore's cabin. Between Commodore Shubrick and General Kearny existed from that time forward the greatest harmony and good feeling, and no further trouble existed as to the controlling power on the Pacific coast. General Kearny had dispatched from San Diego his quartermaster, Colonel Swords, to the Sandwich Islands, to purchase clothing and stores for his men, and had come up to Monterey. He was delighted to find a full strong company of artillery, subject to his orders, well supplied with clothing and money in all respects. Much to the disgust of our Captain Tompkins, he took half of his company clothing and part of the money held by me for the relief of his worn out and almost naked dragoons left behind at Los Angeles.

In a few days General Kearny moved on shore. He took up his quarters at Larkin's house. He established his headquarters, with Captain Turner as his adjutant-general. One day Turner and Warner were at my tent. Seeing a store box full of socks, drawers, and calico shirts, of which I had laid in a three years' supply, and of which they had none, made known to me their wants. I told them to help themselves, which Turner and Warner did. The latter, however, insisted on paying me the cost. From that date to this Turner and I have been close friends. Warner, poor fellow, was afterward killed by Indians.

Things gradually came into shape, a semi-monthly courier line was established from Yerba Buena to San Diego. We were thus enabled to keep pace with events throughout the country. In March Stevenson's regiment arrived. Colonel Mason also arrived by sea. P. St. George Cooke's battalion of Mormons reached San Luis Rey. They were assigned to the company of dragoons at Los Angeles. All these troops and the navy regarded General Kearny as the rightful commander.

Frémont still remained at Los Angeles, styling himself as Governor, issuing orders and holding his battalion of California Volunteers in apparent defiance of General Kearny. Colonel Mason and Major Turner were sent down by sea with a paymaster, with muster-rolls and orders to muster this battalion into the service of the United States, to pay and then to muster them out; but on their reaching Los Angeles Frémont would not consent to it. The controversy became so angry that a challenge was believed to have passed between Mason and Frémont, but the duel never came about.

Frémont traveled to Monterey. He camped in a tent about a mile out of town. He called on General Kearny. It was reported that the latter threatened him very severely and ordered him back to Los Angeles immediately, to disband his volunteers, and to cease the exercise of authority of any kind in the country.

The younger officers had been discussing what the general would do with Frémont, who was supposed to be in a state of mutiny. Some thought he would be tried and shot, some that he would be carried back *in irons*. All agreed that if any one else than Frémont had put on such airs, and had acted as he had done, Kearny would have shown him no mercy, for he was regarded as the strictest sort of a disciplinarian.

We had a pleasant ride across the plain which lies between the seashore and Los Angeles, which we reached in about three hours, the infantry following on foot.

General Kearny ordered me to call on Frémont to notify him of his arrival, and that he desired to see him. I walked round to the house which had been pointed out to me as his. I inquired of a man at the door if the colonel was in. I was answered "Yes," and was conducted to a large room on the second floor. Very soon Frémont came in, and I delivered my message. As I was on the point of leaving, he inquired where I was going. I answered that I was going back to Pryor's house, where the general was. He remarked that if I would wait a moment he would go along. Of course I waited. He soon joined me, dressed much as a Californian, with the peculiar high, broad brimmed hat, with a fancy cord. We walked together back to Pryor's, where I left him with General Kearny.

We spent several days very pleasantly at Los Angeles, then, as now, the chief *pueblo* of the south, famous for its grapes, fruits, and wines. There was a hill close to the town, from which we had a perfect view of the place. The surrounding country is level, utterly devoid of trees, except the willows and cottonwoods that line the Los Angeles Creek and the *acequias*, or ditches, which lead from it. The space of ground cultivated in vineyards seemed about five miles by one, embracing the town. Every house had its enclosure or vineyard, which resembled a miniature orchard. The vines were very old, ranged in rows, trimmed very close, with irrigating ditches so arranged that a stream of water could be diverted between each row of vines. The Los Angeles and San Gabriel Rivers are fed by melting snows from a range of mountains to the east, and the quantity of cultivated lands depends upon the amount of water. This did not seem to be very large; but the San Gabriel River, close by, was represented to contain a larger volume of water, affording

128

the means of greatly enlarging the space for cultivation. The climate was so moderate that oranges, figs, pomegranates, etc., were generally to be found in every yard or enclosure.

1. In a battle at San Pascual, _____ was wounded.

   a. Captain Moore
   b. Captain Johnson
   c. Lieutenant Hammond
   d. General Kearny

2. Andreas Pico fought against the

   a. Russians.
   b. Mexicans.
   c. Americans.
   d. Spanish.

3. Who was **not** yet in California in February?

   a. General Kearny
   b. Commodore Stockton
   c. Colonel Frémont
   d. Colonel Stevenson

4. What right did Benton have to authorize Frémont to be in charge of California?

   a. He was a colonel.
   b. He was a senator.
   c. He was a man of great influence in the Polk administration.
   d. none

5. William Chapman joked that _____ was governor because he had a grand vizier.

   a. Commodore Shubrick
   b. General Kearny
   c. Colonel Frémont
   d. Colonel Swords

6. Who offered to pay for socks, drawers, and shirts?

   a. Lewis
   b. Chapman
   c. Turner
   d. Warner

7. Who was already in California in February?

   a. Stevenson
   b. Mason
   c. Turner
   d. Cooke

8. Kearny tried to assert his authority by

   a. putting Frémont in irons.
   b. mustering out Frémont's forces.
   c. ordering Frémont to Monterey.
   d. arriving in force in Los Angeles.

9. William T. Sherman in his description of Los Angeles mentions a possible problem. What do you think it is?

   _____

   _____

   _____

   _____

   _____

   _____

   _____

   _____

WASH DAY

by Guadalupe Vallejo

There was a group of warm springs a few miles distant from the old adobe house in which we lived. It made us children happy to be waked before sunrise to prepare for the "wash-day expedition" to the Agua Caliente. The night before the Indians had soaped the clumsy carretas' great wheels. Lunch was placed in baskets, and the gentle oxen were yoked to the pole. We climbed in, under the green cloth of an old Mexican flag which was used as an awning. The white-haired Indian ganan, who had driven the carreta since his boyhood, plodded beside with his long garrocha, or ox goad. The great piles of soiled linen were fastened on the backs of horses, led by other servants. The girls and women who were to do the washing trooped along by the side of the carreta. All in all, it made an imposing cavalcade, though our progress was slow.

It was generally sunrise before we reached the spring. The oxen pulled us up the slope of the ravine, where it was so steep that we often cried, "Mother, let us dismount and walk, so as to make it easier." The steps of the carreta [were] so low that we could climb, in, or out without stopping the oxen. The watchful mother guided the whole party, seeing that none strayed too far after flowers, or loitered too long talking with the others. Sometimes we heard the howl of coyotes, and the noise of other wild animals in the dim dawn. Then none of the children were allowed to leave the carreta.

A great dark mountain rose behind the hot spring. The broad, beautiful valley, unfenced, and dotted with browsing herds, sloped down to the bay. Columns of white steam rose among the oaks. The precious waters, which were strong with sulphur, were seen flowing over the crusted basin, and falling down a worn rock channel to the brook. Now on these mountain slopes for miles are the vineyards of Josiah Stanford, the brother of Senator Leland Stanford. The valley below is filled with towns and orchards.

We watched the women unload the linen and carry it to the upper spring of the group, where the water was best. Then they loosened the horses, and let them pasture on the wild oats. The women put home made soap on the clothes. They dipped clothes in the spring, and rubbed them on the smooth rocks until they were white as snow. Then they would spread out to dry on the tops of the low bushes growing on the warm, windless, southern slopes of the mountain. There was sometimes a great deal of linen to be washed, for it was the pride of every Spanish family to own much linen. The mother and daughters almost always wore white.

I have heard strangers speak of the wonderful way in which Spanish ladies of the upper classes in California always appeared in snow-white dresses, and certainly to do so was one of the chief anxieties of every household. Where there were no warm springs the servants of the family repaired to the nearest arroyo, or creek, and stood knee-deep in it, dipping and rubbing the linen, and enjoying the sport. In the rainy season the soiled linen sometimes accumulated for several weeks before the weather permitted the house mistress to have a wash day. Then, when at last it came, it seemed as if half the village, with dozens of babies and youngsters, wanted to go along too and make a spring picnic.

The group of hot sulphur springs, so useful on wash days, was a famed resort for sick people, who drank the water, and also buried themselves up to the neck in the soft mud of the slope below the spring, where the waste waters ran. Their friends brought them in litters and scooped out a hole for them. Then they put boughs overhead to shelter them from the hot sun. They placed food and fresh water within reach, leaving them sometimes thus from sunrise to sunset.

The Paso Robles and Gilroy Springs were among the most famous on the coast in those days. After the annual rodeos people often went there to camp and to use the waters. But many writers have told about the medicinal virtues of the various California springs, and I need not enlarge upon the subject. To me, at least, one of the dearest of my childish memories is the family expedition from the great thick-walled adobe, under the olive and fig trees of the Mission, to the Agua Caliente in early dawn, and the late return at twilight, when the younger children were all asleep in the slow carreta, and the Indians were singing hymns as they drove the linen-laden horses down the dusky ravines.

1. The warm springs were called

    a. carreta.
    b. garrocha.
    c. Agua Caliente.
    d. ganan.

2. The instrument used to control the oxen was called a

    a. carreta.
    b. garrocha.
    c. Agua Caliente.
    d. ganan.

3. The Native Americans probably soaped the wheels to

    a. clean them.
    b. remove any smells that would attract bears.
    c. allow them to turn more easily.
    d. improve traction.

4. Who was in charge of the expedition?

    a. mother
    b. father
    c. Indian ganan
    d. women who were to do the washing

5. When did the children get out of the carreta?

    a. when they heard coyotes or other wild animals howl
    b. when going downhill
    c. when going uphill
    d. never

6. How was the dirty linen carried?

    a. in baskets
    b. on the oxcart
    c. on mules
    d. on horses

7. The valley below the Agua Caliente, at the time this passage was written (1899), was occupied by

    a. the vineyards of Josiah Stanford.
    b. towns and orchards.
    c. a great dark mountain.
    d. browsing herds.

8. There was sometimes a huge amount of linen to wash because

    a. the mother and daughter of every Spanish family always wore white linen.
    b. every Spanish family took pride in how much linen they had.
    c. the washmistress sometimes had to wait until the end of rainy season to do awash.
    d. all of the above.

9. Sulphur springs were not used for

    a. swimming.
    b. washing.
    c. drinking.
    d. mud baths.

10. What fond memories do you have of family expeditions? How are they like the author's? How are they different?

_____

_____

_____

_____

_____

_____

_____

_____

_____

_____

_____

_____

_____

_____

CLEARING THE GREAT AMERICAN FOREST

When the Europeans first came to the New World, they encountered forests larger than any they had ever known. As the settlers pushed west, it seemed that the forests would never end. When the Lincolns moved into southern Indiana in the early nineteenth century, they found it "covered with heavy timber . . . three to four feet in diameter with trunks fifty to sixty feet high." It was a land of boundless opportunities but, also, of endless challenges.

Among the first challenges that faced the pioneer was the clearing of the forested land for his new home. For this, the indispensable tool was the axe. The felling axe used by the American pioneer was a prime example of a tool that had been in existence for centuries, but had been modified for the unique conditions of the frontier.

Unlike its European predecessor, the American axe had a heavy poll on the head opposite the blade that added weight, which made it more effective when swung to chop down a tree. Abraham Lincoln became especially skilled in the use of the felling axe. One of his companions stated, "If you heard him felling trees in a clearing, you would say there were three men at work."

The task of clearing the land of trees was difficult and many pioneers worked at it for years. According to one early settler, the "first clearing was done in a 'hurry-up-and-get-in-a-crop' style." Underbrush and trees under eighteen to twenty inches were cut and piled around larger trees for burning. Sometimes larger trees were girdled, which consisted of cutting a ring through the bark of the tree. This cut the lifeline of the tree and led to its death. Walnut, hickory, elm, and beech never put out leaves again after being girdled while in full leaf, but hackberry and ash had to be piled around with brush and burned deeply. Some farmers set fire to the dead trees the following winter, otherwise the trees were simply left standing until they fell on their own. Dead beech and sugar maples would begin to fall about the third year, but oak, poplar, and walnut would stand for several years.

One aspect of the timber clearing process developed into an important social event for the pioneers as well. Once the trees had been chopped down, neighbors gathered together for the "log rolling" that was necessary to put the dead trees into piles for burning. Often they took advantage of the occasion to visit, eat and enjoy one another's company. The children played and the women cooked and prepared the food. The men organized into teams and, armed with handspikes, which were tough, seasoned saplings about six feet long and three inches wide, proceeded to carry and drag the logs to the piles. Often, contests would take place among the teams to determine which was faster or stronger. Sometimes the rivalry could be intense, although it was nearly always good-natured. Usually the "rolling" was concluded with a big dinner.

When the log piles were ready, they were set on fire. In some instances, these fires could be quite large and would burn for days. Often the pungent, eye-stinging smoke of the burning woodpiles filled the settlements. It would make any other work in the area impossible for a while. One Indiana pioneer later related his memories of log rolling in the 1820s:

> It was a purty sight to see all them big piles of logs a burnin', especially at night. Such a poppin' and a crackin' and a shootin' of flames and sparks high in the air! The big fires would throw out so much light it would turn darkness into daylight. The heat and smoke would be so bad you couldn't go near for a day or so. When the fires did die down enough, we went in with our handspikes and righted the heaps by pryin' and pushin' the logs together so they would keep burnin'. Log heaps would burn and smolder for several days. In fact, there was nearly always a burnin' or smoldern' log heap around a settler's cabin when he was clearin' land. It was a good place to get live coals if the fire went out in the fireplace.

Of course, clearing the land of the trees was not all that had to be done in order for pioneer agriculture to be successful. Often the early plowing was done around the stumps. They remained firmly in place despite the trees having been cut down. Eventually, once they were old and dry, these stumps could be burned out.

1. The American ax was different from older axes because the _____ was _____.

   a. head . . . heavier
   b. head . . . lighter
   c. handle . . . longer
   d. handle . . . shorter

2. Americans needed a different kind of ax because

   a. they were not as strong as Europeans.
   b. they were not as tall as Europeans.
   c. American trees were bigger than European trees.
   d. American trees were further from cities than European trees.

3. The slower, easier way to fell trees was to

   a. cut them down.
   b. burn them down.
   c. cut a ring through the bark.
   d. pile brush around them.

4. When trees were cut down, they were usually

   a. burned in place.
   b. cut up for lumber.
   c. cut up for firewood.
   d. put in a pile and burned.

5. Which of the following statements is **correct**?

   a. Iron handspikes were used to drag logs to the fire and keep the fire burning.
   b. Wooden handspikes were used to drag logs to the fire and keep the fire burning.
   c. Iron handspikes were used to drag and carry logs to the fire and wooden handspikes were used to keep the fire burning.
   d. Wooden handspikes were used to drag and carry logs to the fire and iron handspikes were used to keep the fire burning.

6. Why did farmers get together for log rolling?

   _____

   _____

   _____

   _____

   _____

   _____

   _____

   _____

HISTORY OF MINGO SWAMP

Twenty-five thousand years ago, the Mississippi River ran between the Ozark Mountains and Crowley's Ridge. Then, approximately eighteen thousand years ago, the river shifted. It sliced its way through Crowley's Ridge. It now joined the Ohio River further north. The abandoned river bed developed into a rich and fertile swamp.

Native Americans were attracted to the swamp by the abundant wildlife. Most likely, Native American occupation was seasonal. They visited the swamp only to hunt. Water-loving animals, such as beaver, river otter, raccoons, and rabbit thrived. White-tailed deer, wild turkey, ruffed grouse and timber wolves were common on the edges of the swamp.

In 1803, the Louisiana Purchase acquired this territory for the United States. At that time, the population of the entire Missouri Bootheel around the swamp was sparse. The swamp area was considered inaccessible. When Missouri became a state in 1821, all of the counties in southeast Missouri had settlers, except Stoddard and Dunklin Counties. Cape Girardeau was the largest town in the area. It was one of the most important river towns in Missouri.

Settlers first came to the swamp because of the vast cypress and tupelo forests. The giant cypress trees were the first to be used. They were ideal for railroad ties and building lumber. The T.J. Moss Tie Company was a large Bootheel lumbering operation. Its headquarters were in Puxico. By 1888, T.J. Moss was the largest tie contractor in the state. Many of their ties were cut from trees taken from the swamp. A large mill was operated just north of Puxico on land now within Mingo National Wildlife Refuge. Local sources claim that, at one time, the mill was the largest bandsaw mill in America.

The lumber industry reached peak production in the Bootheel between 1900 and 1910. During its peak, the Bootheel was consistently the leading lumber-producing area of Missouri. However, by 1935 most of the large operations had ceased. The giant trees had all been cut down. It was necessary to find lumber in other places.

If the land could be drained it would again become an important source of revenue. The State Legislature passed an act that allowed the formation of drainage districts, financed by long-term bonds. Many drainage districts were created in the Bootheel.

138

In 1914, more than twenty drainage districts existed in Stoddard County. One of them was the Mingo Drainage District. It was a small district in the Advance Lowlands near Puxico. More than $1 million was spent to make Mingo Swamp suitable for farming. A system of seven major north–south ditches was constructed to drain water from the swamp into the St. Francis River. The river flowed about ten miles south of Puxico.

During the Great Depression, land values plummeted. Many of the large landholders (lumber companies) defaulted on payment of taxes rather than continuing to maintain unprofitable investments in the land. Throughout the Bootheel, many drainage districts were unable to meet financial obligations and defaulted on bond payments. They couldn't absorb the loss of revenue created by the large landholders. Mingo District was one of these.

Drainage attempts at Mingo had not been completely successful, at least in part because of the overflow from the St. Francis River. Also, the soil was not as productive as it was in other areas of the Bootheel. During the 1930s, Mingo District became insolvent.

The remaining timber was cut by anyone without regard to ownership. The area was open range country. Cattle and hogs ran over the entire swamp. To maintain it in a grassy condition, the land was burned, often several times a year. Hogs and cattle became so numerous that they overflowed into the small towns near the swamp. Indiscriminate shooting of waterfowl was common. Other wildlife species were also not faring so well. Beaver and deer had disappeared. Wild turkey were nearly all gone from the swamp.

In 1945, the U.S. Fish and Wildlife Service purchased 21,676 acres of the Mingo Swamp. It established the Mingo National Wildlife Refuge. The Mingo Drainage District's boundary and the Mingo National Wildlife Refuge boundary are essentially the same. The ditches constructed by the district are used today by the refuge for water control and management.

The condition of the land was deplorable. In the previous fifty years, man had reduced a beautiful swamp, lush with the growth of plants and alive with animals, into a burnt and eroded wasteland.

Through careful management, most of the natural plants and animals were restored. Native trees have replaced much of the brush and briers. A canoe trip down the Mingo River will now reveal little to the casual observer of the abuses to this land in years past. Deer, wild turkey, bobcat and beaver have returned and are plentiful. The 21,676-acre refuge is now able to accomplish its primary objective. It provides food and shelter for migratory waterfowl.

1. Mingo Swamp is located between _____ and the _____.

    a. the Mississippi River . . . Ohio River
    b. Crowley's Ridge . . . Ohio River
    c. Crowley's Ridge . . . Ozark Mountains
    d. the Ozark Mountains . . . Ohio River

2. Of the following, which was **not** likely to be found in the middle of the swamp?

    a. beaver
    b. river otter
    c. raccoons
    d. ruffed grouse

3. The T.J. Moss Tie Company made

    a. railroad ties from tupelo trees.
    b. railroad ties from cypress trees.
    c. bandsaws from cypress trees.
    d. men's ties from cypress trees.

4. _____, Mingo Swamp was drained so that it could be used for farming.

    a. After the Louisiana Purchase
    b. After Missouri became a state
    c. Beginning in 1914
    d. After most lumber operations had ceased

5. The way the Mingo Swamp was drained was by

    a. building ditches to the St. Francis River.
    b. building bridges to the St. Francis River.
    c. cutting down cypress and tupelo trees.
    d. having the St. Francis River flow into Puxico.

6. The Mingo Drainage District failed because

    a. the Great Depression caused land values to fall.
    b. the soil was not good for farming.
    c. the swamp never was fully drained.
    d. all of the above.

140

7. Who controlled the Mingo Swamp area during the 1930s?

    a. the Mingo Drainage District
    b. Stoddard County
    c. the U.S. Fish and Wildlife Service
    d. no one

8. Who purchased the Mingo Swamp in 1945?

    a. the Mingo Drainage District
    b. Stoddard County
    c. the U.S. Fish and Wildlife Service
    d. a lumber company

9. In 1945, the country was fighting and paying for a massive world war, World War II. Is it surprising that Mingo Swamp was purchased at the same time? Why or why not?

_____

_____

_____

_____

_____

_____

_____

_____

_____

_____

_____

EARLY NATIVE AMERICAN TRADITIONS

It was notable that the early hunting parties often found Native Americans, but they came upon no Native American villages in Kentucky. The great tribal wars had driven the Shawanee Native Americans north of the Ohio to build their lodges on the Scioto, the Miami and the Muskingum Rivers. The wars had left Kentucky to become the common hunting ground of those tribes and the Wabash, on the north, and of the Chickasaw, Cherokee and Choctaw of the Tennessee valley, on the south. From these opposite abodes would often come forth bands of Native Americans to hunt. These parties were always painted and armed to act the part of warriors when hostile tribes met. These warriors would meet and re-enact the bloody tragedies for which Native American warfare has ever been noted. From these scenes of strife and its past traditions, Kentucky came to be known as the "Dark and Bloody Ground."

The earliest historians of Kentucky—John Filson, Humphrey Marshall, and Mann Butler—in writing the word, "Shawanee," retained the accent on the second syllable, rather than using the modern "Shawnee." (Please note: From this point in the text, the modern "Shawnee" will be used.) The English custom of rudely changing Native American names and words has not always been true to nature and to history, nor fortunate for the language we speak. We have a few Native American names preserved, as "Kan-tuck-ee," "Tan-nas-see," "Ohio," applied to some of our rivers. We might have had Wausioto Mountains and Shawanee River, instead of the foreign and meaningless word, "Cumberland," applied to both.

The Native Americans had names, rhythmical in sound and poetical in meaning, for all our rivers, mountains and notable objects. These we have changed into the homely and practical names of Big Sandy, Licking, Tug Fork, Green, Barren, Tradewater, and a hundred others. They are useful, perhaps, but not pleasing to the ear. In Tennessee, Ohio, and other regions, where Native American nations had their dwellings when the white men came, many Native American names were retained. No Native Americans dwelt in Kentucky. Therefore the white men gave names to all objects at will and with little regard to traditions or poetic sentiment.

Another people dwelt here before the modern Native Americans. They were more advanced in the arts and useful industries than the modern Native Americans were. Many mound works, ancient graves and strange relics of an extinct people have been found in Kentucky. These remains are found in sixty-five counties of the state. Included in these are temple mounds, burial and altar mounds, stone graves and caves where human skeletons and mummies have been preserved.

142

In early days, an old Native American related to Colonel James Moore of Kentucky said that the ancient inhabitants of this state had perished in war with the Native Americans. The last great battle was fought at the Falls of Ohio. The Native Americans drove the army of the Mound Builders onto an island below the rapids, where they destroyed them. George Rogers Clark and others asserted that there was a great ancient burying ground on the north side of the river near the falls.

The Native American chief, Tobacco, at Vincennes fort told Clark that the battles at the Falls of Ohio decided the conquest of Kentucky by the Native Americans many centuries before. Cornstalk, the old Shawnee chief, related that Kentucky and the Ohio valleys were long ago settled by a people like the whites, who knew the arts and many things the Native Americans did not, but the latter conquered and drove them out of the land. The mounds and forts had been built by this long-ago people. The old Native Americans often expressed surprise that white people could live in "Kan-tuck-ee," where so many wars had been carried on, and so much blood had been shed. Said they, "It is filled with the ghosts of slaughtered people."

The old Native Americans related to the pioneer whites some of the traditions handed down to them by their fathers for generations. These legends have been common to the ruder races in all ages. We must not always regard them as mere stories of fancy, because they are given us by oral recitation, and many times repeated. The Native American tribes selected young men. The older sachems formed them into a school. There they repeated the traditions of their fathers until they were committed to memory.

The most important one is the "Delaware Tradition." It was preserved by a missionary to that tribe. This recites that their ancestors, the Algonkin and the Iroquois Native Americans, resided many hundred years ago in the far West. They migrated eastward, the former, after long journeys, reaching the Mississippi, near the mouth of the Missouri River, and the latter higher up. They wished to continue eastward in search of a country that pleased them. The spies of the Algonkin discovered that numerous and powerful nations, who had many towns on the great rivers, were settled to the east of the Mississippi. These people called themselves Allegewi, and had great strongholds fortified, from which they would sally forth to battle. The Algonkin requested permission to cross over and settle in the country. This was refused. They then asked permission to pass east through their country to find a place to settle. They began to cross, when the Allegewi resisted. The Algonkin then allied with the Iroquois. They agreed to divide the country between them. They went forward.

War was waged for many years. Many great battles were fought. Many were slain. At last the Allegewi were driven back. Fearing destruction, they sent their women and children south across the Ohio. They then made a last stand in a great battle at the Falls of Ohio, but were defeated, and their army destroyed. A remnant escaped. The entire nation fled southward. They crossed the Mississippi, and never returned. The conquered country had been divided. The Iroquois chose the lands on the eastern lakes and the St. Lawrence River. The Algonkin took possession of the Ohio valley and east to the Atlantic. The Allegewi gave to the Alleghany Mountains and River the name which they yet bear.

1. Kentucky came to be known as "Dark and Bloody Ground" as a result of

    a. the French and Indian War.
    b. the war between settlers and Native Americans.
    c. the number of buffalo that were killed.
    d. numerous tribal wars.

2. Why were the original Native American names for rivers and mountains retained in Ohio and Tennessee, but not in Kentucky?

    a. Native Americans themselves did not dwell in Kentucky.
    b. Pioneers did not settle in Ohio and Tennessee.
    c. Pioneers did not like the sound of the Kentucky names.
    d. Native American names were hard to pronounce.

3. Which of the following **best** describes how the author feels about the renaming of Kentucky's rivers and mountains?

    a. It was a good and wise decision.
    b. It was shameful and unfortunate choice.
    c. The author has no feelings about the subject.
    d. All similar sites throughout the country should also be renamed.

4. Why are Native American legends known to be accurate depictions of history?

    a. They were repeated again and again until completely memorized.
    b. They were engraved into the bark of trees and the inner walls of caves.
    c. They are not considered accurate depictions of history.
    d. All legends are true because they are historical records.

5. According to legend and archeological finds, who inhabited the land before the Native Americans?

   a. white settlers
   b. backwoodsmen
   c. a mysterious people similar to the white settlers
   d. Algonkin and Iroquois tribes

6. One of the most important oral traditions affirms that

   a. Delaware was founded by the Algonkins.
   b. Native Americans frequently migrated throughout the country.
   c. Algonkin and Iroquois tribes joined forces to defeat the white settlers.
   d. Algonkin and Iroquois tribes joined forces to defeat the Allegewi.

7. The Native American name for the mountains was "Wausioto." The settlers renamed them "Cumberland." The author of this passage states that while the settlers' names may be practical, the native names sound much better. If you had the responsibility of deciding between the two names, which would you choose? Tell why.

_____

_____

_____

_____

_____

_____

_____

_____

_____

_____

SIMON KENTON, EXPLORER

Simon Kenton was a legendary character. He truly embodied the ideal of the frontier hero. He was wise in the ways of the wilderness. He was a loyal friend and a dreaded enemy. Even in the company of scoundrels, he stuck to his principles. Despite his fame, he remained modest and good-natured.

Simon Kenton's transformation from an ordinary teenaged farm boy into a famous frontiersman started in the spring of 1771. At the age of sixteen, Kenton got into an impassioned fight with a man who stole away his sweetheart. Simon beat the man senseless. He thought that he had killed his romantic rival. He fled into the wilderness without money, food, or provisions. Simon finally reached a distant settlement. He adopted the alias of Simon Butler for a time. He went to work for the local miller to purchase the essentials for survival. After several weeks, he resumed his travels.

Simon was a remarkably strong and tall youth. He adapted well to the rigors of life in the wilderness. His status as a fearful fugitive quickly faded from memory as he pursued a dream to find and explore the fabled "Can-tuc-kee" lands. They were incredibly rich hunting grounds jealously guarded by the Native Americans.

In the fall of 1771, Simon caught his first glimpse of the beautiful Ohio River and the intriguing land beyond. He was traveling with a pair of fur traders. A few miles below Little Beaver Creek, the group put ashore. They paid a friendly visit to Chief Logan's Mingo village on nearby Yellow Creek. Simon must have made quite an impression. Chief Logan would later intervene to save Simon's life.

Simon and his two companions drifted down the uncharted Ohio for more than five hundred miles. They did not find the dense fields of cane that they were seeking. They became convinced that they had somehow passed them.

For the next two years, Simon and his friends would travel up and down the river. They explored streams and rivers along the way between the Ohio and the legendary great lakes. Simon knew that he was an intruder in hostile territory. He became particularly adept at finding and interpreting the subtle signs in the woods that Native-American hunting parties had come this way and may still be in the area. He was eager to assist the trappers and traders who occasionally drifted by. He earned a widespread reputation as an outstanding wilderness scout.

146

In the spring of 1774, Chief Logan's family, who had so graciously welcomed Simon three years before, was brutally murdered by a party of malicious frontier explorers. The grief-stricken Logan took his revenge against settlements in the Virginia territory. This escalated the clashes between settlers and Indians dramatically. Simon decided to exercise prudence. He headed for the relative safety of the large secured settlement at Fort Pitt.

At Fort Pitt, Simon met and befriended Simon Girty. Girty was a scout and translator. Girty was mistrusted by many for his close association with Indians. Simon also met George Rogers Clark, the Virginia militia leader. Clark's brother, William Clark, would later lead the famous expedition to explore the interior of the continent with Meriwether Lewis.

Simon was recruited to serve in the campaign led by Lord Dunmore. Dunmore was governor of the colonies of New York and Virginia. The king of England had appointed him to quell the Indian threats to pioneers on the frontier. After a week's deliberation, Simon joined them as a spy and scout alongside his new friend, Simon Girty.

During Lord Dunmore's War, Simon crisscrossed the Ohio territory. He served as a courier between Lord Dunmore's troops and the backwoods volunteers under the command of Captain Andrew Lewis. Lewis's camp was at Point Pleasant. It had been set up at the point where the Great Kanawha River empties into the Ohio. Simon had just left when the Shawnee chief, Cornstalk, led his surprise attack. After a vigorous fight, Cornstalk eventually retreated. The colonists claimed victory, although they suffered much greater casualties than the Shawnee.

A few weeks later, Dunmore set up temporary headquarters, which he dubbed Camp Charlotte, on the outskirts of Cornstalk's town on the Scioto River. Dunmore invited the Shawnee leaders and Chief Logan to negotiate a peace treaty. Logan, who was still depressed over the murders of his family and his own bloody revenge, had retreated to a small camp of his own on nearby Congo Creek. He refused to take part in the treaty negotiations.

Dunmore sent Simon Kenton and Simon Girty to Logan's camp to bring back a message from Logan. Simon witnessed Logan's outpouring of emotion. Girty translated the heart-rending speech. It concluded with the immortal lines, "Who is there to mourn for Logan? Not one."

Under the Camp Charlotte Treaty in October 1774, the Shawnee agreed to allow settlement by pioneer families in the "Can-tuc-kee" (Kentucky) lands south of the Ohio River. They also agreed to allow boats to navigate the Ohio

River unmolested. Soon, Simon was living his dream of exploring and settling in the canelands where the wild game was as rich and plentiful as he had hoped.

1. Simon Butler was

    a. the man Kenton beat senseless.
    b. the miller Kenton worked for.
    c. the name Kenton adopted for a while.
    d. a scout and translator.

2. Simon Girty was

    a. the man Kenton beat senseless.
    b. the miller Kenton worked for.
    c. the name Kenton adopted for a while.
    d. a scout and translator.

3. Simon Kenton first glimpsed the Ohio River—and met Chief Logan—when he was about _____ years old.

    a. 16
    b. 19
    c. 21
    d. 24

4. Simon Kenton spent the years _____ exploring Ohio and scouting for trappers and traders.

    a. 1771–1772
    b. 1772–1773
    c. 1773–1774
    d. 1774–1775

5. Simon Kenton met _____ in Fort Pitt.

    a. Lord Dunmore
    b. Meriwether Lewis
    c. William Clark
    d. George Rogers Clark

148

6. During Lord Dunmore's War, Simon Kenton carried messages between Lord Dunmore's troops and

   a. Chief Cornstalk.
   b. Chief Logan.
   c. Andrew Lewis.
   d. Meriweather Lewis.

7. Simon Kenton just missed Chief Cornstalk's attack

   a. at Point Pleasant.
   b. on Fort Pitt.
   c. on Camp Charlotte.
   d. at Congo Creek.

8. Who translated Chief Logan's speech?

   a. Simon Kenton
   b. Simon Girty
   c. Simon Butler
   d. Lord Dunmore

9. Why do you think this historian never says that Simon Kenton ever fought against the Native Americans—because he never did or because the writer did not want to mention it? Explain the reasoning behind your answer.

_____

_____

_____

_____

_____

_____

_____

_____

WILLIAM T. SHERMAN AND THE DISCOVERY OF GOLD

by William T. Sherman

I remember one day, in the spring of 1848. Two men, Americans, came into the office. They inquired for the Governor. I asked their business. One answered that they had just come down from Captain Sutter on special business. They wanted to see Governor Mason *in person*. I took them in to the colonel, and left them together. After some time the colonel came to his door and called to me. I went in. My attention was directed to a series of papers unfolded on his table, in which lay about half an ounce of *placer*-gold. Mason said to me, "What is that?" I touched it and examined one or two of the larger pieces, and asked, "Is it gold?"

Mason asked me if I had ever seen native gold. I answered that, in 1844, I was in Upper Georgia. There I saw some native gold, but it was much finer than this, and it was in phials, or in transparent quills. I said that, if this were gold, it could be easily tested, first, by its malleability, and next by acids. I took a piece in my teeth. The metallic lustre was perfect. I then called to the clerk, Baden, to bring an axe and hatchet from the backyard. When these were brought I took the largest piece and beat it out flat. Beyond doubt it was metal, and a pure metal. Still, we attached little importance to the fact. Gold was known to exist at San Fernando, at the south, and yet was not considered of much value.

Colonel Mason then handed me a letter from Captain Sutter, addressed to him. It stated that he (Sutter) was engaged in erecting a sawmill at Coloma, about forty miles up the American Fork, above his fort at New Helvetia, for the general benefit of the settlers in that vicinity. He had incurred considerable expense. He wanted a "preëmption" to the quarter-section of land on which the mill was located, embracing the tail race in which this particular gold had been found.

Mason instructed me to prepare a letter, in answer, for his signature. I wrote off a letter, reciting that California was yet a Mexican province, simply held by us as a conquest. No laws of the United States yet applied to it, much less the land laws or preëmption laws, which could only apply after a public survey. Therefore it was impossible for the Governor to promise him (Sutter) a title to the land. As there were no settlements within forty miles, the letter said he was not likely to be disturbed by trespassers. Colonel Mason signed the letter. He handed it to one of the gentlemen who had brought the sample of gold, and they departed.

That gold was the *first* discovered in the Sierra Nevada. It soon revolutionized the whole country, and actually moved the whole civilized world.

As the spring and summer of 1848 advanced, the reports came faster and faster from the gold mines at Sutter's sawmill. Stories reached us of fabulous discoveries. They spread throughout the land. Everybody was talking of "Gold! gold!!" until it assumed the character of a fever. Some of our soldiers began to desert. Citizens were fitting out trains of wagons and pack mules to go to the mines. We heard of men earning fifty, five hundred, and thousands of dollars per day. For a time it seemed as though somebody would reach solid gold. Some of this gold began to come to Yerba Buena [San Francisco] in trade. It disturbed the value of merchandise, particularly of mules, horses, tin pans, and articles used in mining.

As yet we had no regular mail to any part of the United States. Mails had come to us at long intervals, around Cape Horn, and one or two overland. I well remember the first overland mail. It was brought by Kit Carson in saddlebags from Taos in New Mexico. We heard of his arrival at Los Angeles, and waited patiently for his arrival at headquarters. His fame then was at its height, from the publication of Frémont's books. I was very anxious to see a man who had achieved such feats of daring among the wild animals of the Rocky Mountains, and with wilder Indians of the Plains. At last his arrival was reported at the tavern at Monterey. I hurried to hunt him up. I cannot express my surprise at beholding a small, stoop-shouldered man, with reddish hair, freckled face, soft blue eyes, and nothing to indicate extraordinary courage or daring. He spoke but little, and answered questions in monosyllables. I asked for his mail. He picked up his light saddlebags containing the great overland mail. We walked together to headquarters. There he delivered his parcel into Colonel Mason's own hands.

Toward the close of June, 1848, the gold fever being at its height, by Colonel Mason's orders, I made preparations for his trip to the newly discovered gold mines at Sutter's Fort. I selected four good soldiers. With Aaron, Colonel Mason's black servant, and a good outfit of horses and pack mules, we started by the usually traveled route for Yerba Buena. There Captain Folsom and two citizens joined our party.

At that time there was not the sign of a habitation there or thereabouts, except the fort, and an old adobe house, east of the fort, known as the hospital. The fort itself was one of adobe walls. It was about twenty feet high, rectangular in form, with two-story blockhouses at diagonal corners. The entrance was by a large gate. It was open by day and closed at night, with two iron ship's guns near at hand. Inside there was a large house, with a good shingle roof, used as a storehouse. All round the walls were ranged rooms, the fort wall being the outer wall of the house. The inner wall also was of adobe. These rooms were used by Captain Sutter and by his people. He had a blacksmith's shop, carpenter's shop, etc., and other rooms where the women made blankets.

Sutter was monarch of all he surveyed, and authority to inflict punishment even unto death, a power he did not fail to use. He had horses, cattle, and sheep, and of these he gave liberally and without price to all in need. He caused to be driven into our camp a beef and some sheep, which were slaughtered for our use. Already the gold mines were beginning to be felt. Many people were then encamped, some going and some coming, all full of gold stories, and each surpassing the other.

We found preparations in progress for celebrating the Fourth of July, then close at hand. We agreed to remain over to assist on the occasion. Of course, being the high officials, we were the honored guests. People came from a great distance to attend this celebration of the Fourth of July. After a substantial meal and a reasonable supply of *aguardiente* [brandy] we then began the toasts. All that I remember is that Folsom and I spoke for our party. Others, Captain Sutter included, made speeches. Before the celebration was over Sutter was enthusiastic, and many others showed the effects of the *aguardiente*.

The next day (namely July 5, 1848) we resumed our journey toward the mines, and, in twenty-five miles of as hot and dusty a ride as possible, we reached Mormon Island. I have heretofore stated that the gold was first found in the tail race of the sawmill at Coloma, forty miles above Sutter's Fort, or fifteen above Mormon Island, in the bed of the American Fork of the Sacramento River. It seemed that Sutter had employed an American named Marshall, a sort of millwright, to do his work for him, but Marshall afterward claimed that in the matter of the sawmill they were co-partners. At all events, Marshall and the family of Mr. Wimmer were living at Coloma, where the pine trees afforded the best material for lumber. As Marshall himself was working in the mill race, he observed particles of yellow metal which he gathered up in his hand, when it seemed to have suddenly flashed across his mind that it was *gold*.

After picking up about an ounce, he hurried down to the fort to report to Captain Sutter his discovery. Captain Sutter himself related to me Marshall's account, saying that, as he sat in his room at the fort one day in February or March, 1848, a knock was heard at his door, and he called out, "Come in." In walked Marshall, who was a half-crazy man at best, but then looked strangely wild. "What is the matter, Marshall?" Marshall inquired if any one was within hearing, and began to peer about the room, and look under the bed, when Sutter, fearing that some calamity had befallen the party up at the sawmill, and that Marshall was really crazy, began to make his way to the door, demanding of Marshall to explain what was the matter. At last he revealed his discovery and laid before Captain Sutter the pellicles of gold he had picked up in the ditch.

At first, Sutter attached little or no importance to the discovery, and told Marshall to go back to the mill, and say nothing of what he had seen to Mr. Wimmer, or any one else. Yet, as it might add value to the location, he dispatched to our headquarters at Monterey, as I have already related, the two men with a written application for a preëmption to the quarter-section of land at Coloma. Marshall returned to the mill, but could not keep out of his wonderful ditch, and by some means the other men employed there learned his secret. They then wanted to gather the gold, and Marshall threatened to shoot them if they attempted it. These men had sense enough to know that if *placer*-gold existed at Coloma, it would also be found farther down stream. They gradually "prospected" until they reached Mormon Island, fifteen miles below, where they discovered one of the richest placers on earth. These men revealed the fact to some other Mormons who were employed by Captain Sutter at a grist mill he was building still lower down the American Fork, and six miles above his fort. All of them struck for high wages. Sutter yielded, until they asked ten dollars a day, which he refused. The two mills on which he had spent so much money were never built, and fell into decay.

1. The acting governor of California was

    a. Sherman.
    b. Captain Sutter.
    c. Colonel Mason.
    d. Baden.

2. How many people were in the room when William T. Sherman tested the gold with his teeth?

    a. 1
    b. 2
    c. 3
    d. 4

3. The gold they examined had been discovered

    a. in Upper Georgia.
    b. at the sawmill at Coloma.
    c. at New Helvetia.
    d. at San Francisco.

4. The governor could **not** grant Sutter any rights to the land around the sawmill because

    a. California was still technically part of Mexico.
    b. California had not yet been conquered by the United States.
    c. there were no settlements within 40 miles.
    d. Sutter was unlikely to be disturbed by trespassers.

5. William T. Sherman recognized the significance of the gold-find

    a. never.
    b. as soon as he saw it.
    c. in paragraph 4 of the passage.
    d. in paragraph 5 of this passage.

6. The first overland mail came to California

    a. over the Rocky Mountains.
    b. around Cape Horn.
    c. from Taos, New Mexico.
    d. directly to Monterey.

7. Kit Carson's first stop in California was

    a. Taos.
    b. Los Angeles.
    c. Monterey.
    d. Yerba Buena.

8. Sherman was surprised because Kit Carson had

    a. reddish hair.
    b. a freckled face.
    c. soft blue eyes.
    d. no indication of unusual courage.

9. How many people traveled in Sherman's party from Yerba Buena to Sutter's Fort?

    a. 4
    b. 5
    c. 8
    d. 9

10. The iron guns at Sutter's Fort were near the

    a. gate.
    b. block-house.
    c. hospital.
    d. storehouse.

11. According to John Bidwell, who wrote the contract between the men, Marshall and Sutter were partners. Sherman probably got his information about the relationship from

    a. Bidwell.
    b. Marshall.
    c. Sutter.
    d. Wimmer.

12. What do you think happened in San Francisco as "gold fever" hit?

    _____

    _____

    _____

    _____

    _____

    _____

    _____

    _____

13. Do you think Sutter should have paid the higher wages the grist mill workers sought? Why or why not?

_____

_____

_____

_____

_____

_____

_____

14. Do you think it was necessary or appropriate for Sutter to have and use such absolute power over his colony as he did? Why or why not?

_____

_____

_____

_____

_____

_____

_____

ULYSSES S. GRANT AND CAMP JACKSON

The Illinois legislature authorized the governor to accept the services of ten additional regiments. I had charge of mustering these regiments into the state service. They were assembled at the most convenient railroad centres in their respective congressional districts. I detailed officers to muster in a portion of them, but mustered three in the southern part of the state myself. One of these was to assemble at Belleville, some eighteen miles south-east of St. Louis. When I got there I found that only one or two companies had arrived. There was no probability of the regiment coming together under five days. This gave me a few idle days which I concluded to spend in St. Louis.

There was a considerable force of state militia at Camp Jackson, on the outskirts of St. Louis, at the time. There is but little doubt that it was the design of Governor Claiborne Jackson to have these troops ready to seize the United States arsenal and the city of St. Louis. Why they did not do so I do not know. There was but a small garrison, two companies I think, under Captain N. Lyon at the arsenal, and but for the timely services of the Honorable F.P. Blair, I have little doubt that St. Louis would have gone into rebel hands, and with it the arsenal with all its arms and ammunition.

Blair was a leader among the Union men of St. Louis in 1861. There was no State government in Missouri at the time that would sanction the raising of troops or commissioned officers to protect United States property, but Blair had probably procured some form of authority from the President to raise troops in Missouri and to muster them into the service of the United States. At all events, he did raise a regiment and took command himself as colonel. With this force he reported to Captain Lyon and placed himself and regiment under his orders. It was whispered that Lyon thus reinforced intended to break up Camp Jackson and capture the militia. I went down to the arsenal in the morning to see the troops start out. I had known Lyon for two years at West Point and in the old army afterwards. Blair I knew very well by sight. I had heard him speak in the canvass of 1858, possibly several times, but I had never spoken to him. As the troops marched out of the enclosure around the arsenal, Blair was on his horse outside forming them into line preparatory to their march. I introduced myself to him and had a few moments' conversation and expressed my sympathy with his purpose. This was my first personal acquaintance with the Honorable—afterwards Major-General—F.P. Blair. Camp Jackson surrendered without a fight and the garrison was marched down to the arsenal as prisoners of war.

Up to this time the enemies of the government in St. Louis had been bold and defiant, while Union men were quiet but determined. The enemies had their head-quarters in a central and public position on Pine Street, near Fifth—from which the rebel flag was flaunted boldly. The Union men had a place of meeting somewhere in the city, I did not know where, and I doubt whether they dared to enrage the enemies of the government by placing the national flag outside their head-quarters. As soon as the news of the capture of Camp Jackson reached the city the condition of affairs was changed. Union men became rampant, aggressive, and, if you will, intolerant. They proclaimed their sentiments boldly, and were impatient at anything like disrespect for the Union. The secessionists became quiet but were filled with suppressed rage. They had been playing the bully. The Union men ordered the rebel flag taken down from the building on Pine Street. The command was given in tones of authority and it was taken down, never to be raised again in St. Louis.

I witnessed the scene. I had heard of the surrender of the camp and that the garrison was on its way to the arsenal. I had seen the troops start out in the morning and had wished them success. I now determined to go to the arsenal and await their arrival and congratulate them. I stepped on a car standing at the corner of Fourth and Pine Streets, and saw a crowd of people standing quietly in front of the headquarters, who were there for the purpose of hauling down the flag. There were squads of other people at intervals down the street. They too were quiet but filled with suppressed rage, and muttered their resentment at the insult to, what they called, "their" flag. Before the car I was in had started, a dapper little fellow—he would be called a dude at this day—stepped in. He was in a great state of excitement and used adjectives freely to express his contempt for the Union and for those who had just perpetrated such an outrage upon the rights of a free people. There was only one other passenger in the car besides myself when this young man entered. He evidently expected to find nothing but sympathy when he got away from the "mud sills" engaged in compelling a "free people" to pull down a flag they adored. He turned to me, saying, "Things have come to a ——— pretty pass when a free people can't choose their own flag. Where I came from if a man dares to say a word in favor of the Union we hang him to a limb of the first tree we come to."

I replied that "after all we were not so intolerant in St. Louis as we might be; I had not seen a single rebel hung yet, nor heard of one; there were plenty of them who ought to be, however." The young man subsided. He was so crestfallen that I believe if I had ordered him to leave the car he would have gone quietly out, saying to himself: "More Yankee oppression."

By nightfall, the late defenders of Camp Jackson were all within the walls of the St. Louis arsenal, prisoners of war. The next day, I left St. Louis for

Mattoon, Illinois, where I was to muster in the regiment from that congressional district.

1. Grant decided to go to St. Louis because

    a. he was assigned to muster soldiers there.
    b. he was nearby and had a few free days.
    c. it was a railroad center.
    d. the legislature met there.

2. The original U.S. garrison at the U.S. arsenal in St. Louis was _____ the state militia at Camp Jackson.

    a. larger than
    b. the same size as
    c. smaller than
    d. protected by

3. The commander of the Union forces was

    a. Claiborne Jackson.
    b. Captain Lyon.
    c. Colonel Blair.
    d. Grant.

4. Who favored the Union in the "car" Grant was in?

    a. the "dude"
    b. the other young man
    c. Grant
    d. all of the above

5. How do readers know that this passage was written from a first person point of view?

    a. The author provides many specific details.
    b. The author acts very involved in the events.
    c. The author speaks using the words, "I," "my," and "me."
    d. The author is describing the events as if he is learning of them for the first time.

6. Grant doesn't mention the fact that some of the prisoners from Camp Jackson were killed on the way to the arsenal in what came to be known as the "Camp Jackson Massacre." Why do you think this is so?

_____

_____

_____

_____

_____

_____

_____

_____

_____

_____

_____

_____

_____

_____

_____

_____

_____

160

RUSSIAN SETTLEMENT AT FORT ROSS

The first significant contact between the Russians and the Spanish came in April 1806. Nikolai Resánov had arrived in Sitka the previous year as an "imperial inspector and plenipotentiary of the Russian-American Company." He found the colony on the verge of starvation. He decided to sail southward to Spanish California in hopes of obtaining relief supplies for the beleaguered Alaskan colony. On April 5th, he and his scurvy-stricken crew passed through the Golden Gate. Rezánov knew that foreign ships were not allowed to trade in California. Nevertheless, he sailed his ship, the *Juno*, boldly past the Spanish guns at the harbor mouth.

For the next six weeks, the *Juno* lay at anchor in San Francisco Bay. A battle of wits went on between the Russians and the Spanish. The impasse was broken when Rezánov proposed to marry Concepción Argüello, the teenage daughter of the Spanish commander at San Francisco. The *Juno* was soon being loaded with grain for the starving settlement to the north. On May 21st, it passed again through the Golden Gate.

Rezánov brought back two ideas from his venture into Spanish California. One was the desire to establish permanent trade relations. The second was the wish to found a trading base on what the Russians referred to as the "New Albion." It was the California coast north of Spanish territory. Rezánov convinced Alexander Baranov of the value of his ideas. Ivan Kuskov was a company employee of long standing. Baranov sent Kuskov on a voyage to locate a site suitable for the planned settlement. Moving southward on the ship, *Kodiak*, Kuskov arrived at Bodega Bay on January 8, 1804. He remained there until late August. He and his party of forty Russians and one hundred and fifty Alaskan natives explored the entire region. They brought back more than two thousand sea otter pelts.

By November 1811, Kuskov was ready to head south again. This time he intended to build a colony on the New Albion shore. He arrived at Bodega Bay in early 1812 aboard the *Chirikov*. He then decided that the most suitable location for the colony was the site of a Kashaya Indian village, eighteen miles to the north. The spot was called "Meteni" by the local Indians. According to one account, the entire area was acquired from the natives for "three blankets, three pairs of breeches, two axes, three hoes, and some beads."

The land offered a harbor of sorts, plentiful water, good forage. Nearby was a supply of wood for the necessary construction. It was also relatively distant from the Spanish. They were to be unwilling neighbors for the next twenty-nine years. The fort was completed in a few weeks. It was formally dedicated on August 13, 1812. The name, "Ross," is generally considered to be a shortened version of "Rossiya," the Russia of Tsarist days.

The structures were built of redwood. The builders used joinery techniques that were typical of maritime carpentry in those days. A wooden palisade surrounded the site. It included two blockhouses. One was on the north corner. One was to the south. They were complete with cannons that could command the entire area. The Russian-American Company flag, with its double-headed eagle, flew over the stockade.

The interior of the stockade contained the two-story house of the manager and the officials' quarters. There were barracks for the Russian employees, and various storehouses as well as lesser structures. The chapel was added in 1824. A well in the center provided the colonists with water. Outside the walls were the homes of company laborers and a native Alaskan village. The dwellings of the local native Americans, whom we refer to today as the Kashaya Pomo, were nearby.

In the early years, life at the colony under Kuskov revolved around the hunting of sea otter. Their pelts were extraordinarily valuable in the China trade. Most of the hunting was done by Kodiak Islanders in the service of the company. They would go out to sea in their "bidarkas" (hunting kayaks). There they would use the "atlatl" (a throwing board for darts). These hunters and their families had their own village. It was just west of the stockade, on the bluff above the ocean. The Alaskans and their Russian overseers ranged the coast from Baja California to Oregon, in search of marine mammals.

Only a small number of Russians actually lived at Ross. Very few Russian women (usually wives of officials) lived there. However, intermarriage between Russians and the natives of Alaska and California was commonplace. Natives and people of mixed ancestry as well as lower-ranking company men lived in a village complex. There were some sixty to seventy buildings that gradually grew up outside the stockade walls.

By 1820, extensive sea otter hunting had depleted the otter population. Agriculture and stock raising became the main occupation of the colony. The company's Alaskan outposts still needed supplies but, try as they might, the Russian colony in northern California never fulfilled their agricultural goals. Coastal fog, gophers, mice and lack of genuine interest on the part of men who thought of themselves primarily as hunters all combined to thwart the agricultural effort. Ranches and farms were established at inland sites. One was at Willow Creek on the "Slavyanka" (now known as the Russian River). Others were near the towns of Bodega and Graton. Still, the colonists could not produce enough to make a profit.

In 1839, the Russian-American Company signed an agreement with the Hudson Bay Company to supply Sitka with provisions from its settlements in present-day Washington and Oregon. Soon afterward, the Russian-American Company decided to abandon the Ross Colony. First, they tried to sell it to the Mexican government. When that failed, they approached Mariano Vallejo and others. In December 1841, they reached an agreement with John Sutter of Sutter's Fort in the Sacramento Valley. Within a few months, the Russians were gone. Sutter sent his trusted assistant, John Bidwell, to Fort Ross. He came to gather up the arms, ammunition, hardware, and other valuables. There were herds of cattle, sheep, and other animals. He transported them all to Sutter's Fort in the Sacramento Valley.

1. _____ obtained grain for Sitka by marrying the Spanish commander's daughter.

    a. Ivan Kuskov
    b. Alexander Baranov
    c. Nikolai Rezánov
    d. Concepción Argüello

2. The leader of the Russian settlement in Alaska was

    a. Ivan Kuskov.
    b. Alexander Baranov.
    c. Nikolai Rezánov.
    d. Concepción Argüello.

3. Kuskov's party gathered about _____ pelts a month.

    a. 100
    b. 200
    c. 250
    d. 400

4. Kuskov's gathered about _____ pelts each.

    a. 10
    b. 20
    c. 30
    d. 40

5. The name, Fort Ross, comes from

    a. local Native American tribe.
    b. Native American village's name.
    c. the boat which brought the settlers.
    d. a short version of the word for "Russia."

6. *Chirikov* was the

    a. local Native American tribe.
    b. Native American village's name.
    c. boat which brought the settlers.
    d. expedition's leader, 1811–1812.

7. Which of the following is **not** a ship that sailed from Alaska to California?

    a. *Juno*
    b. *Kodiak*
    c. *Meteni*
    d. *Chirikov*

8. Who hunted with bidarkas?

    a. the native Alaskans living in a village just outside the stockade walls
    b. the Kodiak Islanders living on a bluff above the ocean
    c. the Kashaya Pomo
    d. people of mixed ancestry

9. During the period from 1820 to 1839, where did the Russians in Alaska probably get most of their supplies?

    a. Slavyanka and other farms in northern California
    b. trading with John Sutter
    c. trading with the Hudson Bay Company
    d. trading with southern California

10. Why did the Russians stay in Alaska if they had to get their supplies from outside? Why did they have to go elsewhere to get supplies?

_____

_____

_____

_____

_____

_____

_____

_____

_____

_____

_____

_____

_____

_____

_____

_____

_____

_____

_____

_____

_____

INDIAN WARS OF THE 1790s

A stream of emigration flowed into the Ohio region after the organization of the Northwestern Territory in 1787. General Arthur St. Clair had been a worthy officer of the Continental Army. He was appointed its governor. He soon found serious trouble brewing there. The British, in violation of the treaty of 1783, still held Detroit and other western posts. British traders were jealous of the hardy settlers who were gathering in communities north of the Ohio. British agents were inciting the Indians to make war on the settlers. They were encouraged to do so by Sir John Johnson, the former Indian agent in the Mohawk Valley, and Guy Carleton (then Lord Dorchester), again governor of Canada.

In September 1790, General Harmar led more than a thousand troops, regulars, and volunteers from Fort Washington (now Cincinnati) into the Indian country around the headwaters of the Maumee River to chastise the Indians. Instead of humbling them by spreading desolation over their fair land, Harmar—in two battles near the present village of Fort Wayne, Indiana—was defeated with considerable loss. He abandoned the enterprise.

In May of the following year, General Scott of Kentucky, with eight hundred men, penetrated the Wabash country almost to the site of the present town of Lafayette, Indiana. He destroyed several villages. At the beginning of August, General Wilkinson, with more than five hundred men, pushed into the same region. He destroyed some Kickapoo villages. He then made his way to the Falls of the Ohio, near Louisville. But the Indians, instead of being humbled by these scourges, were urged by these and the false representations of British emissaries to fight desperately for their country and lives.

Congress now prepared to plant fortifications in the heart of the Indian country. In September 1791, two thousand troops were gathered at Fort Washington. They marched northward. They were under the immediate command of General Butler. General St. Clair was in overall charge. Twenty miles from Fort Washington, they built Fort Hamilton on the Miami River. Forty-two miles further on they built Fort Jefferson.

At length the little army of invaders halted. They encamped on the borders of a tributary of the Upper Wabash in Darke County, Ohio. They were near the Indiana line, a hundred miles from Cincinnati. The wearied soldiers went to rest early. All night long the sentinels fired upon prowling Indians. Before sunrise on the morning of the 4th of November, 1791, while the army were preparing for breakfast, they were surprised by the horrid yells of a body of Indians. The Indians fell upon them with great fury. The troops made a gallant defense, but the slaughter among them was dreadful. General Butler was killed. Most of his officers were slain or wounded. The smitten army fled in confusion. St. Clair had three horses killed under him. It was with great difficulty that he escaped on a pack-horse. That evening Adjutant-General Winthrop Sargent wrote in his diary: "The troops have all been defeated. Though it is impossible, at this time, to ascertain our loss, yet there can be no manner of doubt that more than half the army are either killed or wounded."

This defeat spread dismay over the frontiers, and hot indignation throughout the land. Washington was powerfully moved by wrath. For a few minutes he was swayed by a tempest of anger. He paced the room in a rage. "It was awful," wrote Mr. Lear, his private secretary, who was present. "More than once he threw his hands up as he hurled imprecations upon St. Clair. 'O God! O God!' he exclaimed, 'he is worse than a murderer! How can he answer to his country? The blood of the slain is upon him—the curses of widows and orphans—the curse of Heaven!' "

His wrath soon subsided. "This must not go beyond this room," he said; and in a low tone, as if speaking to himself, he continued, "St. Clair shall have justice. I will hear him without prejudice—he shall have full justice." And when, a while afterward, the veteran soldier, bowed with infirmities and the burden of public obloquy, sought the presence of his old commander, Washington extended his hand and gave him a gracious reception. "Poor old St. Clair," said Custis, who was present, "hobbled up to his chief. He seized the offered hand in both of his, and gave vent to his feelings in copious sobs and tears."

Fortunately for the frontier settlers, the Indians did not follow up the advantage they had gained. Hostilities ceased for a while. Commissioners were appointed to treat with hostile tribes. Through the interference of British officials, the negotiations were fruitless. In the meantime General Anthony Wayne, the bold soldier of the war for independence, had been appointed St. Clair's successor in military command. Apprehending that the failure of the negotiations would be immediately followed by hostilities against the frontier settlements, Wayne marched into the Indian country with a competent force in the autumn of 1793. He spent the winter at Greenville, not far from the place of St. Clair's defeat. He built a stockade there and gave it the significant name of Fort Recovery. The following summer he pushed forward to the Maumee River. At its junction with the Auglaize he built Fort Defiance. On the St. Mary's he had erected Fort Adams as an intermediate post. In August he pushed down the Maumee with about three thousand men. He encamped within a short distance of a British military post at the foot of the Maumee Rapids called Fort Miami.

With ample force to destroy the Indiana's power in spite of their British allies, and to desolate their country, Wayne offered the Indians peace and tranquillity if they would lay down the hatchet and musket. They madly refused, and sought to gain time by craftiness. "Stay where you are ten days," they said, "and we will treat with you; if you advance, we will give you battle." Wayne did advance to the head of the Maumee Rapids. At a place called The Fallen Timbers, not far above the present Maumee city, he attacked and defeated the Indians on the 20th of August, 1794. By the side of almost every dead warrior of the forest lay a musket and bayonet from British armories.

Wayne then laid waste the country. By the middle of September he had moved up the Maumee to the junction of the St. Mary's and St. Joseph's that form that stream. There he built a strong fortification. It was named Fort Wayne. The little army went into winter-quarters at Greenville. The next summer the sachems and warriors of the Western tribes, about eleven hundred in all (representing twelve cantons), met (August 3, 1795) commissioners of the United States. They formed a treaty of peace. They ceded about twenty-five thousand square miles of territory in the present states of Michigan and Indiana, besides sixteen separate tracts, including lands and forts. In consideration of these cessions, the Indians received goods from the United States of the value of $20,000, as presents. They were promised an annual allowance valued at nearly $10,000, to be equally distributed among all the tribes who were parties to the treaty. These were the Chippewa, Ottawa, Pottawatomie, Wyandot, Delaware, Shawnee, Miami and Kickapoo, who then occupied the ceded lands.

At the close of the council, on the 20th, Wayne said the following to the Indians:

> Brothers, I now fervently pray to the Great Spirit that the peace now established may be permanent, and that it will hold us together in the bonds of friendship until time shall be no more. I also pray that the Great Spirit above may enlighten your minds, and open your eyes to your true happiness, that your children may learn to cultivate the earth and enjoy the fruits of peace and industry.

By a special treaty made with Great Britain at about that time, the Western military posts were soon afterward evacuated by the British. An immense impetus was given to emigration into that region. The country northwest of the Ohio was now rapidly filled with a hardy population.

1. After the Revolutionary War, the British governor of Canada, _____, continued to stir up trouble in the Northwestern Territory.

   a. Arthur St. Clair
   b. John Johnson
   c. Guy Carleton
   d. General Harmar

2. The first expedition against the Native Americans of Ohio in the 1790s was led by

   a. General St. Clair.
   b. Sir John Johnson.
   c. Lord Dorchester.
   d. General Harmar.

3. The first expedition to be soundly defeated by the Indians of Ohio in the 1790s was led by General

   a. St. Clair.
   b. Scott.
   c. Wilkinson.
   d. Harmar.

4. Of the following, which did General Butler's troops build?

   a. Fort Washington
   b. Fort Jefferson
   c. Fort Adams
   d. Fort Miami

5. Who died in the attack of November 4, 1791?

   a. General Butler
   b. General St. Clair
   c. General Sargent
   d. General Wilkinson

6. Who did Washington first blame, and then forgive, for the disaster of November 4, 1791?

   a. General Butler
   b. General St. Clair
   c. General Sargent
   d. General Wilkinson

7. Of the following, which forts did General Anthony Wayne **not** build?

    a. Fort Recovery
    b. Fort Defiance
    c. Fort Adams
    d. Fort Miami

8. Wayne's great victory was at

    a. Fort Miami.
    b. Fort Wayne.
    c. Greenville.
    d. Fallen Timbers.

9. Why do you think the Native Americans were forced to cede lands in Michigan and Indiana, but not in Ohio?

_____

_____

_____

_____

_____

_____

_____

_____

_____

_____

_____

BUSHWHACKERS AND JAYHAWKERS

The anti-slavery pro-Union Jayhawkers were undisciplined, unprincipled, murderous thieves. They roamed around Kansas and Missouri in guerrilla bands. The term, "Jayhawking," became a widely used synonym for stealing. Still, Jayhawking carried no social stigma. Kansas teams still proudly use the word today. Some prominent, influential and highly regarded leaders were associated with Jayhawking. Among them was James Henry Lane. He called himself the "Grim Chieftain." He served in both the U.S. House of Representatives and the Senate. He was a consummate politician. He had a penchant for fiery oratory. He had some experience in military matters. He also had a tendency not to repay his debts. He was also a notorious womanizer. He was violent, paranoid, and highly unbalanced.

Another Jayhawker was New England-born David Anthony. He was an ardent abolitionist. He was the brother of suffragette Susan B. Anthony. The most active Jayhawker of all was Charles R. "Doc" Jennison. He was originally from New York. He practiced medicine briefly in Wisconsin before coming to Kansas. There he found that horse stealing was more lucrative than medicine. He was so successful that for years the lineage of many good horses in Iowa and Illinois was said to be "out of Missouri by Jennison." His abolitionist sympathies were clear. In 1860 he headed a posse that hanged two unfortunate Missourians. They were caught trying to return fugitive slaves to their masters.

One of the most notorious individual units operating in the state of Kansas was known as "Jennison's Jayhawkers." The unit was mustered into U.S. service on October 28, 1861. Jennison served as colonel. David R. Anthony was lieutenant colonel. Jennison referred to the regiment as "self-sustaining." That meant simply that every foray into Missouri liberated more supplies than were carried into the state. Horses, livestock and wagonloads of agricultural products were seized from Southern sympathizers. Only a minuscule fraction of those goods found their way to the Federal commissary. Slaves, too, trooped westward to freedom in Kansas. If other items found their way into the Jayhawkers' possession—furniture, silverware and money—such was the bitter price paid for secession. It is no wonder the 7th Kansas Volunteer Cavalry Regiment was sometimes called "The Forty Thieves."

A new low in Jennison's depredations happened at Harrisonburg, Missouri. Another outfit had looted the depository of the American Bible Society before Doc's men arrived. They left only a stock of Bibles. So the 7th took the Bibles. Such behavior continued for less than five months. However it left an indelible mark on Missouri.

Missouri was technically in the Union. Many of the citizens despoiled by the Jayhawkers were loyal Unionists. Concerned that the Jayhawkers would create more rebels than they conquered, Federal authorities determined to put them where they could do no further harm. In May 1862 they were sent to Kentucky, then to Tennessee.

Bushwhackers lived in the "bush," or country. Their legs "whacked" the bushes as they rode. They were pretty much a mirror image of the Jayhawkers. They just favored the Confederacy. Some were semi-legitimate soldiers. The Confederate Army, perhaps reluctantly, recognized them. Among them were William Quantrill, "Bloody Bill" Anderson, John Thrailkill, David Pool, Jo Shelby and Jeff Thompson. Other bushwhackers were simply bandits. They used the conflict as an excuse for ambush, robbery, murder, arson and plunder. Their extralegal activities made excellent training for some postwar careers. These careers featured liberating the cash in banks, stagecoaches and railroad trains for their personal use. Frank James and his kid brother Jesse turned their knowledge to good account after 1865. So did their cousins Coleman and Jim Younger.

Jennison's closest Southern counterpart was a sometime schoolteacher, farmer, and gambler. William Clarke Quantrill was a strange young man with blue eyes. Undeniably intelligent, he formed his band of guerrilla troops around Christmas in 1861. Without any ties to the South or to slavery, he chose the Confederacy. This was apparently because in Missouri this allowed him to attack all symbols of authority. He attracted to his gang some of the most psychopathic killers in American history.

His was the largest and best-known band of guerrillas in the state of Missouri. Anyone who wanted to join his band was asked just one question: "Will you follow orders, be true to your comrades, and kill those who serve and support the Union?" At first, most of the Bushwhackers were young farm boys. They were volunteers who wanted to defend their homes and take revenge for things done to them and their families. Later on, a more restless breed flocked to Quantrill's black silk banner. If anything, plundering and murder were more important to them than were states' rights. Attempts have been made to see the Bushwhackers and Jayhawkers as latter-day Robin Hoods. They weren't. Quantrill's force was mustered into Confederate service in 1862, but the groups continued to operate independently. Quantrill was twenty-six years old when he and his followers sacked Lawrence, Kansas, on August 21, 1863. That dramatic attack was deliberate, cold and brutal.

Revenge for Union atrocities, real or imagined, was one stimulus for the Lawrence raid. A three-story brick building in Kansas City was used by the

Federals as a temporary prison for some women alleged to have aided Bushwhackers. On August 14th, the building collapsed. Among the five women who died were the sisters of Bushwhackers "Bloody" Bill Anderson and John McCorkle.

> I was a girl of eleven at the time. I remember that the Union men sent three caskets containing my cousins to Little Blue. With the caskets was the satchel of trinkets and dry goods that my sister and Charity had gone to town to buy. The dead were buried in the old Smith Cemetery near Raytown. We didn't have much time for funerals in those days and the three were buried in one grave.
>
> —Eliza Harris

But revenge was not the only motive for the raid. Loot, of course, was always important. Quantrill needed to invigorate his flagging support. To some extent, there was also the desire to show the Federals that he could operate with impunity within Union territory. And the information that Senator James Lane was in Lawrence whetted Quantrill's appetite. He wanted Lane very badly. Memories were long in the struggle. Confederate forces operating in the two states still hated Lane for his leadership of the free-soil cause.

Quantrill assembled his gang about noon the day before the raid. They started toward Kansas about two o'clock. He led four hundred fifty men (including Frank James) past a Union cavalry camp and on into Lawrence at 7:00 a.m. on August 21st. They used ten farmers as guides. They then killed them. They had with the lists of specific targets for assassination, They also heeded Quantrill's words to "kill every man big enough to carry a gun." The attack was perfectly planned. Every man knew his role. Almost every house was visited and robbed. Many white townspeople stayed and were slain. They had not expected wholesale murder. The black people fared better because they ran out of town at the first alarm.

The cornfield west of town, the river bank, and the ravine which ran through the center of town were filled with refugees. Two hours later, the Bushwhackers rode out. They had cleaned out all the banks. Their saddlebags were laden with booty. Many of them swayed from the effects of whiskey. In one hundred twenty minutes, they had devastated the dusty town of two thousand inhabitants. They had killed one hundred fifty of its male citizens. Many were gunned down before their wives and children. Others died trapped in their flaming homes. The raiders left about eighty widows and two hundred fifty orphans. They torched the entire community. They burned $2-million worth of property before escaping into the Missouri hills.

General Thomas Ewing, the commander of the Union troops along the Kansas-Missouri border felt something drastic had to be done. He issued the famous order known as "Order No. 11." The order was issued on August 25, 1863—four days after the Lawrence raid.

A strip of land along the border, eighty-five miles long and fifty miles wide, was made into a wasteland. Everyone living within those boundaries was given fifteen days to leave the area. Then every home, barn, and outbuilding was burned to the ground. All food was appropriated or destroyed. Twenty thousand families were gone as a result.

> A little after the guard house fell, Order No. 11 was issued. Our house at Little Blue was burned. We went down near Glascow. My sister Nannie walked there after she got away from the Union guard house—almost 100 miles. After the guard house fell, the remaining women were taken to some hotel and kept for a period of time.
>
> —Eliza Harris

Order Number 11 worked. It deprived Bushwhackers of the protection, nurture and victims that fed their attacks.

1. According to the passage, the worst Jayhawker was

   a. David Anthony.
   b. Susan B. Anthony.
   c. James Henry Lane.
   d. Doc Jennison.

2. The most prominent Jayhawker politician was

   a. David Anthony.
   b. Susan B. Anthony.
   c. James Henry Lane.
   d. Doc Jennison.

3. Jennison started his criminal career in

   a. Wisconsin.
   b. Kansas.
   c. Iowa.
   d. Illinois.

4. The 7th Kansas Volunteer Cavalry regiment was never known as

    a. a self-sustaining unit.
    b. Jennison's Jayhawkers.
    c. pro-Confederate.
    d. The Forty Thieves.

5. Of the following, which did the Jayhawkers **not** steal?

    a. slaves
    b. Bibles
    c. silverware
    d. furniture

6. Of the following, which was Jennison most famous for stealing?

    a. food
    b. Bibles
    c. silverware
    d. horses

7. Why did Federal authorities remove the Jayhawkers from Missouri?

    a. They did not like them hanging Missourians.
    b. They did not like them stealing from pro-Unionists.
    c. They did not like them stealing horses.
    d. Stealing Bibles was the last straw.

8. What were the first of Quantrill's volunteers most likely to have been motivated by?

    a. fear
    b. greed
    c. revenge
    d. loyalty to the Confederacy

9. Later, Quantrill's volunteers were motivated mostly by

    a. fear.
    b. love of violence.
    c. revenge.
    d. loyalty to the Confederacy.

10. Do you think that the Lawrence raid was typical of the Jayhawker-Bushwhacker war, or was it worse? Why?

_____

_____

_____

_____

_____

_____

_____

_____

_____

_____

_____

_____

_____

_____

_____

_____

_____

_____

11. Do you think Order Number 11 was the right thing to do? Why or why not?

_____

_____

_____

_____

_____

_____

_____

_____

_____

_____

_____

_____

_____

_____

_____

_____

_____

_____

_____

JOHN FREMONT AND THE BEAR FLAG REVOLT, 1846

by John Bidwell

A little over four weeks after Frémont left I happened to be fishing four or five miles down the river, having then left Sutter's service with the view of trying to put up two or three hundred barrels of salmon, thinking the venture would be profitable. An officer of the United States, Lieutenant A. H. Gillespie, of the marines, bearing messages to the explorer, came up the river in a small boat and at once inquired about Frémont. I told him he had gone to Oregon. Said he: "I want to overhaul him. How far is it to the fort?" And receiving my reply, he pushed rapidly on. He overtook Frémont near the Oregon line. Frémont, still indignant against Castro, who had compelled him to abandon his explorations south, returned at once to California.

Frémont's hasty departure for Oregon and Gillespie's pursuit of him had been the occasion of many surmises. Frémont's sudden return excited increased curiosity. People flocked to his camp. Some were settlers. Some were hunters. Some were good men. Some were about as rough specimens of humanity as it would be possible to find anywhere. Frémont, hearing that one hundred and fifty horses were passing, sent a party of these promiscuous people and captured the horses. This, of course, was done before he had orders or any positive news that war had been declared. When Gillespie left the United States, as the bearer of a despatch to Larkin and Frémont and of letters to the latter, war had not been declared. The letters included one from Senator Benton, who had the confidence and knew the purposes of the Administration. As Gillespie had to make his way through Mexico, he committed the despatch and his orders to memory. He then destroyed them. He rewrote them on the vessel which took him, via the Sandwich Islands, to the coast of California. There had been no later arrival, and therefore no later despatches to Frémont were possible. Though Frémont was reticent, whatever he did was supposed to be done with the sanction of the United States. Thus, without giving the least notice even to Sutter, the great friend of Americans, or to Americans in general, scattered and exposed as they were all over California, he precipitated the war.

Sutter was always outspoken in his wish that some day California should belong to the United States; but when he heard that the horses had been taken from Arce (who made no resistance, but with his men and with insulting messages was permitted to go on his way to Castro at Santa Clara), he expressed surprise that Captain Frémont had committed such an act without his knowledge. What Sutter had said was reported to Frémont, perhaps with some exaggeration.

178

As soon as the horses arrived at Frémont's camp, the same party—about twenty-five in number—were sent to Sonoma. By this party General Vallejo, the most prominent Californian north of the bay, his brother Salvador, his brother-in-law Jacob P. Leese, and Victor Prudon were surprised at night. They were taken prisoners, and conveyed to Frémont's camp. It was over eighty miles distant by the traveled route on the Sacramento River. The prisoners were sent to Sutter's Fort. Frémont arrived at the same time. Then Sutter and Frémont met, face to face, for the first time since Frémont, a month before, had passed on his way towards Oregon. I do not know what words passed between them; I was near, but did not hear. This, however, I know: that Sutter had become elated, as all Americans were, with the idea that what Frémont was doing meant California for the United States. But in a few minutes Sutter came to me greatly excited, with tears in his eyes. He said that Frémont had told him he was a Mexican, and that if he did not like what he (Frémont) was doing he would set him across the San Joaquín River and he could go and join the Mexicans. But, this flurry over, Sutter was soon himself again, and resumed his normal attitude of friendship towards Frémont, because he thought him to be acting in accordance with instructions from Washington.

For want of a suitable prison, the prisoners were placed in Sutter's parlor—a large room in the southwest corner of the second story of the two-story adobe house, which had but one door, and this was now guarded by a sentinel. Frémont gave me special directions about the safety of the prisoners, and I understood him to put them under my special charge. Some of Frémont's men remained at the fort. This adobe house is still standing (1899), within the limits of the city of Sacramento, and is the only relic left of Sutter's Fort. It was built in 1841—the first then, the last now.

Among the men who remained to hold Sonoma was William B. Ide. In some way Ide got the notion that Americans ought to strike for an independent republic. To this end nearly every day he wrote something in the form of a proclamation and posted it on the old Mexican flagstaff. Another man left at Sonoma was William L. Todd. Todd painted, on a piece of brown cotton, a yard and a half or so in length, using old red or brown paint that he happened to find, what he intended to be a representation of a grizzly bear. This was raised to the top of the staff, some seventy feet from the ground. Native Californians looking up at it were heard to say "Coche." That was the common name among them for pig or shoat. More than thirty years afterwards I chanced to meet Todd on the train coming up the Sacramento Valley. He had not greatly changed, but appeared considerably broken in health. He informed me that Mrs. Lincoln was his own aunt. He had been brought up in the family of Abraham Lincoln.

The party at Sonoma now received some accessions from Americans and other foreigners living on the north side of the bay. Rumors began to reach them of an uprising on the part of the native Californians, which indeed began under Joaquín de la Torre. Henry L. Ford and other Americans to the number of thirty met de la Torre—whose force was said to number from forty to eighty— near the Petaluma Ranch. Four or five of the Californians were said to have been killed or wounded. The repulse of the Californians seems to have been complete. A messenger was sent in haste to Sacramento for Frémont. He hurried to Sonoma with nearly all his exploring party. They scoured the country far and near, but found no enemy.

I tried to make the prisoners at Sacramento as comfortable as possible, assisting to see that their meals were regularly and properly brought. Sometimes I would sit by while they were eating. One day E.M. Kern, artist to Frémont's exploring expedition, called me out. He said it was Frémont's orders that no one was to go in or speak to the prisoners. I told him they were in my charge, and that he had nothing to say about them. He asserted that they were in his charge. He finally convinced me that he had been made an equal, if not the principal, custodian. I then told him that, as both of us were not needed, I would go over and join Frémont at Sonoma. Just at this time Lieutenant Washington A. Bartlett of the United States Navy arrived from the bay, inquiring for Frémont. The taking of the horses from Arce, the capture of the prisoners, and the occupation of Sonoma, had been heard of, and he was sent to learn what it meant. So he went over to Sonoma with me.

On our arrival Frémont was still absent trying to find the enemy, but that evening he returned. The Bear Flag was still flying, and had been for a week or more. The American flag was nowhere displayed. There was much doubt about the situation. Frémont gave us to understand that we must organize. Lieutenant Gillespie seemed to be his confidential adviser and spokesman. Gillespie said that a meeting would be held the next day at which Frémont would make an address. He also said that it would be necessary to have some plan of organization ready to report to the meeting. P.B. Reading, W.B. Ide and myself were requested to act as a committee to report such a plan. We could learn nothing from Frémont or Gillespie to the effect that the United States had anything to do with Frémont's present movements.

Hostilities having been begun, bringing danger where none before existed, it now became imperative to organize. It was in everyone's mouth (and I think must have come from Frémont) that the war was begun in defense of American settlers! This was simply a pretense to justify the premature beginning of the war, which henceforth was to be carried on in the name of the United States.

So much has been said and written about the "Bear Flag" that some may conclude it was something of importance. It was not so regarded at the time. It was never adopted at any meeting or by any agreement. It was, I think, never even noticed, perhaps never seen, by Frémont when it was flying. The naked old Mexican flagstaff at Sonoma suggested that something should be put on it. Todd had painted it, and others had helped to put it up, for mere pastime. It had no importance to begin with, none whatever when the Stars and Stripes went up. It never would have been thought of again had not an officer of the navy seen it in Sonoma and written a letter about it.

Under these circumstances on the Fourth of July our committee met. We soon found that we could not agree. Ide wished to paste together his long proclamations on the flagstaff, and make them our report. Reading wrote something much shorter, which I thought still too long. I proposed for our report simply this: "The undersigned hereby agree to organize for the purpose of gaining and maintaining the independence of California." Unable to agree upon a report, we decided to submit what we had written to Lieutenant Gillespie, without our names, and ask him to choose. He chose mine. The meeting took place, but Frémont's remarks gave us no light upon any phase of the situation. He neither averred nor denied that he was acting under orders from the United States Government. Some men had been guilty of misconduct in an Indian village, and he reprimanded them. He wanted nothing to do with the movement unless the men would conduct themselves properly. Gillespie made some remarks, presented the report, and all present signed it.

1. What was John Frémont's first act of war?

    a. returning from Oregon
    b. capturing horses
    c. taking prisoners
    d. meeting with Gillespie

2. With whom was Frémont angry?

    a. Larkin
    b. Sutter
    c. Gillespie
    d. Castro

3. Frémont captured 150 horses with

    a. his scouting party.
    b. the marines.
    c. volunteers.
    d. the Mexican army.

4. Frémont apparently got inside information about the administration's plan to go to war with Mexico in a letter written by

    a. Senator Benton.
    b. President Polk.
    c. Larkin.
    d. Gillespie.

5. General Vallejo and others were arrested by

    a. Jacob B. Leese.
    b. Victor Prudon.
    c. Salvador Vallejo.
    d. the same volunteers who had captured Arce's horses.

6. Frémont may have called Sutter a Mexican because he had heard an exaggerated report of Sutter's

    a. outspoken wish that someday California should belong to the United States.
    b. reaction to using his parlor as a prison.
    c. reaction to the report of Arce's horses being seized.
    d. reaction to the imprisonment of General Vallejo and his friends.

7. Who designed the Bear Flag?

    a. John Bidwell
    b. William B. Ide
    c. William L. Todd
    d. Abraham Lincoln

8. The design on the flag was a

    a. beautiful picture of a grizzly bear.
    b. beautiful picture of a pig.
    c. rough picture of a pig.
    d. rough picture of a grizzly bear.

9. In the battle near Petaluma Ranch,

    a. the Americans had from 40 to 80 soldiers.
    b. Joaquín de la Torre had from 40 to 80 soldiers.
    c. Joaquín de la Torre had 30 soldiers.
    d. the Americans lost 4 or 5 killed or wounded soldiers.

10. Who was really in charge of Frémont's prisoners?

    a. E.M. Kern
    b. John Bidwell
    c. Lieutenant Bartlett
    d. Lieutenant Gillespie

11. Why was Frémont away from Sonoma?

    a. He was at Sutter's fort interviewing the prisoners.
    b. He was at Sacramento.
    c. He was fighting at Petaluma Ranch.
    d. He was searching in vain for an enemy.

12. Who posted proclamations on the flagpole?

    a. William P. Ide
    b. William L. Todd
    c. P.B. Reading
    d. John Bidwell

13. Whose "report" was chosen by Gillespie, read at the meeting, and signed by all present?

    a. William P. Ide's
    b. William L. Todd's
    c. P.B. Reading's
    d. John Bidwell's

14. What do you think of Frémont's behavior?

_____

_____

_____

_____

_____

_____

_____

_____

_____

_____

_____

_____

_____

_____

_____

_____

_____

_____

15. Does Bidwell's assertion that Frémont's excuse for starting a war was a pretense remind you of any other situation when some claimed that a pretense had been used to go to war?

_____

_____

_____

_____

_____

_____

_____

_____

_____

_____

_____

_____

_____

_____

_____

_____

_____

_____

THE TWO LARGEST EARTHQUAKES

A magnitude–7.9 earthquake occurred in the Fort Tejon, California, area on January 9, 1857. It was the largest earthquake ever recorded in California. The earthquake was felt from Marysville south to San Diego. It was felt as far east as Las Vegas, Nevada. Several slight to moderate foreshocks preceded the main shock by one to nine hours. Many aftershocks occurred. Two were large enough to have been widely felt.

The Fort Tejon earthquake occurred on the San Andreas fault. The fault ruptured from near Parkfield (in the Cholame Valley) almost to Wrightwood. The rupture covered a distance of about three hundred kilometers. Horizontal displacement of as much as nine meters was observed on the Carrizo Plain. The earthquake caused one fatality. A comparison of this shock to the San Francisco earthquake—which occurred on the San Andreas fault on April 18, 1906—shows that the fault break in 1906 was longer. The maximum and average displacements in 1857 were larger.

Property loss was heavy at Fort Tejon, an Army post about seven kilometers from the San Andreas fault. Two buildings were declared unsafe. Three others were damaged extensively but were habitable. Still others sustained moderate damage. About twenty kilometers west of Fort Tejon, trees were uprooted. Buildings were destroyed between Fort Tejon and Elizabeth Lake. One person was killed in the collapse of an adobe house at Gorman. Strong shaking lasted from one to three minutes.

Instances of seiches, fissuring, sandblows, and hydrologic changes were reported from Sacramento to the Colorado River delta. Ground fissures were observed in the beds of the Los Angeles, Santa Ana, and Santa Clara Rivers and at Santa Barbara. Sandblows occurred at Santa Barbara and in the flood plain of the Santa Clara River. One report describes sunken trees, possibly associated with liquefaction, in the area between Stockton and Sacramento.

Changes in the flow of streams or springs were observed in the areas of San Diego, Santa Barbara, Isabella, and at the south end of the San Joaquin Valley. The waters of the Kern, Lake, Los Angeles, and Mokulumme Rivers overflowed their banks. Changes in the flow of water in wells were reported from the Santa Clara Valley in northern California.

The famous San Francisco earthquake occurred on April 18, 1906. It was a magnitude-7.8 earthquake. The San Francisco earthquake was one of the most devastating in the history of California. The earthquake and resulting fires caused an estimated three thousand deaths. They caused five hundred and twenty-four million dollars in property loss. Damage in San Francisco resulting only from the earthquake itself was estimated at twenty million dollars. Outside the city, property loss was estimated at four million dollars. The duration of the shaking in San Francisco was about one minute.

The earthquake damaged buildings and structures in all parts of the city and county of San Francisco. Over much of the area, the damage was moderate in amount and character. Most chimneys toppled or were badly broken. In the business district, which was built on ground made by filling in the cove of Yerba Buena, pavement was buckled, arched, and fissured. Brick and frame houses of ordinary construction were damaged extensively or destroyed. Sewers and water mains were broken. Streetcar tracks were bent into wavelike forms.

On or near the San Andreas fault, buildings were destroyed. One was torn apart. Trees were knocked to the ground. The surface of the ground was torn and heaved into furrow-like ridges. Roads crossing the faultline were impassable. Pipelines were broken.

The pipeline that carried water from San Andreas Lake to San Francisco was broken. That shut off the water supply to the city. The fires that ignited soon after the onset of the earthquake quickly raged through the city because of the lack of water to control them. They destroyed a large part of San Francisco. Fires also intensified the losses at Fort Bragg and Santa Rosa.

This earthquake caused the most lengthy rupture of a fault ever observed in the contiguous United States. The displacement of the San Andreas fault was observed over a distance of three hundred kilometers from San Juan Bautista to Point Arena, where is passes out to sea. Additional displacement was observed farther north at Shelter Cove in Humbolt County. Assuming the rupture was continuous, the total length of it would extend four hundred and thirty kilometers. The largest horizontal displacement—6.4 meters— occurred near Point Reyes Station in Marin County.

In areas where dislocation of fences and roads indicated the amount of ground movement, motions of three to four and a half meters were common. Near Point Arena, in Mendocino County, a fence and a row of trees were displaced almost five meters. At Wright's Station, in Santa Clara County, a lateral displacement of 1.4 meters was observed. Vertical displacement of as much as 0.9 meters was observed near Fort Ross in Sonoma County. Vertical displacement was not detected toward the south end of the fault.

Although Santa Rosa lies about thirty kilometers from the San Andreas fault, damage to property was severe. Fifty people were killed. The earthquake also was severe in the Los Banos area of the western San Joaquin Valley, where the intensity more than forty-eight kilometers from the fault zone was IX. Santa Rosa lies directly inland from the region of greatest motion on the San Andreas fault.

Trees swayed violently. Some were broken off above the ground or thrown down. The water in springs and artesian wells either increased or decreased its flow. A few sand craterlets formed in areas where water was ejected through cracks or fissures.

The region of destructive intensity extended over a distance of sixty kilometers. The total affected area included most of California and parts of western Nevada and southern Oregon. The maximum intensity of XI was based on geologic effects, but the highest intensity based on damage was IX. Several foreshocks probably occurred. Many aftershocks were reported. Some of them were severe.

1. The largest earthquake in California's history occurred about _____ years ago.

   a. 50
   b. 100
   c. 150
   d. 250

2. The _____ felt as far east as Las Vegas.

   a. foreshocks were
   b. two aftershocks were
   c. earthquake was
   d. tidal wave was

3. "Horizontal displacement" means

   a. how many people lost their homes.
   b. how far land moved from side to side.
   c. how far land moved up or down.
   d. how far someone lying down was thrown up in the air.

4. The Fort Tejon earthquake was larger than the San Francisco earthquake in all of the following **except**

   a. magnitude.
   b. length of the fault break.
   c. maximum displacement.
   d. average displacement.

5. "Sandblows" are probably

   a. explosions of sand caused by underground pressure or movement.
   b. sandstorms.
   c. windblown sand as if in a hurricane or tornado.
   d. quicksand.

6. "Liquification" probably means _____ turned to liquid.

   a. trees
   b. rivers
   c. ground
   d. houses

7. How much more damage did the resulting fire cause than the San Francisco earthquake itself?

   a. $4 million
   b. $20 million
   c. $500 million
   d. $524 million

8. The rupture in 1906 was _____ kilometers longer than that in 1857.

   a. 100
   b. 130
   c. 300
   d. 430

9. The largest horizontal displacement in 1857 was _____ meters higher than the largest in 1906.

   a. 2.6
   b. 3.4
   c. 6.4
   d. 9

10. Why was the loss of life so much more severe in 1906 than in 1857?

_____

_____

_____

_____

_____

_____

_____

_____

_____

11. How many different kinds of measurement seem to be used to measure earthquakes? Describe them.

_____

_____

_____

_____

_____

_____

_____

BATTLE OF POINT PLEASANT, 1774

In May 1774, Captain James Harrod led about forty men, in boats, down the Ohio River, and camped on the present site of Cincinnati. There they felled the first tree known to have been cut down on that spot by the ax of a white man. Boating on to the mouth of Kentucky River, they turned their little fleet into that stream and ascended to what is now Shaker Landing in Mercer County. Debarking there, they made their way through the forest to a point near Salt Lick. There they built a camp on the present site of Harrodsburg, one hundred yards below Big Spring, beneath the branches of an elm tree.

From this camp the men dispersed, in small squads, to select and survey lands for suitable settlements and to build cabins. These latter were known as "lottery cabins," as they were drawn for among the men by lot. Thus, John Crow, James Brown, and others secured lottery cabins in the vicinity of Danville. James Wiley located three miles east of Harrodsburg. James Harrod went to Boiling Spring, six miles south. The cabins were not built to live in, but were evidence of the first survey made, which gave a first claim on the land. They were but pens of logs, roughly cut, in low cabin form, often without roofs or chimneys.

On June 16th, Harrod and Hite laid off a town site at Big Spring camp, where they had previously erected the first cabin, giving to each man a half-acre lot and a ten-acre outlot. The name given to this place was "Harrodstown," now Harrodsburg. Near the east end of the town, John Harman made a clearing, and there planted and raised the first corn that was known to have grown in Kentucky. On or about the July 20th, four of Harrod's men, out on a survey, were resting at a large spring, some three miles below Harrodstown, when they were ambushed by Native Americans. Cowan was killed. Sandusky and a comrade, believing that the camp had been surprised, made their way to the Falls of Ohio. The fourth man of the party got back to camp with a report of the disaster. Harrod, at the head of a company, went down and buried Cowan, and secured his papers. Douglas, who had returned this year with his party, was engaged in surveying lands on Elkhorn, Hickman, and Jessamine Creeks, on the opposite side of Kentucky River.

John Floyd and Hancock Taylor also led survey parties, locating lands in Woodford and Fayette Counties, and along the Ohio River to the falls, In the latter part of July, Hancock Taylor, while surveying near the mouth of Kentucky River, was shot and seriously wounded by the Native Americans. He died a few days later, while being borne back to Virginia. He was buried two miles south of Richmond. Thus early was offered up to the spirit of border warfare one of the noblest, most gifted, and promising men of the period that gave birth to western civilization.

The colonial government of Virginia was now aroused to a sense of impending danger. Native Americans on the north side of the river watched with jealousy the intrusion by the whites on their favorite hunting grounds. Their tribal dignity had been insulted, and their rights set aside by the Treaty of Stanwix. The whites had failed to comply with promises of rewards for their release of title to Kentucky. Around the Shawnee, and under the lead of the great chief, Cornstalk, a northwestern confederation was formed. Fifteen hundred warriors, painted and armed for war, were in camps at the towns on the Scioto. Governor Dunmore commissioned Daniel Boone to undertake a journey through the wilderness, and to recall all hunters and survey parties, in view of Native American hostilities.

Boone selected Michael Stoner for his companion in this hazardous service. The latter had been trained in backwoods life. Boone and Stoner set out in June. With energy and endurance they pushed on to the Falls of the Ohio. Warning the explorers in turn, they reached Harrodstown at the time the town was being laid out. Boone seems to have taken an interest. A lot was assigned to him, adjoining one of Evan Hinton's. On these two lots a double cabin was built. It was known as "Boone's cabin," or "Hinton's cabin," until it was burned, with others, by the Native Americans, in March 1777. By the closing days of July, Harrod and Hite, with all comrades, were on their return trip to Virginia.

During the latter part of August, Boone and his comrades reached Virginia. He and Stoner had made the trip of eight hundred miles through the wilderness and over mountains and returned in sixty days. Governor Dunmore had called three thousand regulars and volunteers into the field to meet the Native American army threatening to cross the Ohio and invade Virginia. Boone was given charge of three forts on the Kanawha frontier. Dunmore held the main army at Fort Pitt. General Andrew Lewis, skilled in border warfare, led the left wing, of eleven hundred men, made up mainly of the frontiersmen, across the mountains to the mouth of Great Kanawha. Here he met the invading army of the Native Americans, fifteen hundred strong. He defeated them in the battle of Point Pleasant, on October 10, 1774. The vanquished warriors retreated across the Ohio, and to their towns on the Scioto.

The McAfees, Harrods, Hites, Boones, and most of the Kentucky pioneers were volunteers in this short campaign. Their unerring rifles did execution in the historic battle that had such important bearing on the future of the great west. Governor Dunmore, soon after the defeat, crossed his army below Pittsburgh, marched to the Scioto towns, and there compelled the Native Americans to sue for peace. A treaty was signed, in which the Shawnee and their confederates agreed to give up all title to the country south of the Ohio. The results of this short war in several ways pointed most favorably to the future of Kentucky. The men of the hunting and survey parties became, for some months, the army comrades of many citizens. To these they pictured, in radiant colors, the beauty and attractions of the new land of their adoption and adventure.

1. Why did Captain Harrod lead 40 men down the Ohio River?

    a. to establish territory
    b. to trade with Native Americans
    c. to be the first white men to fell trees in Kentucky
    d. to farm the new land

2. Which of the following is **not** true?

    a. Each man built a cabin.
    b. The group dispersed.
    c. The group built a sprawling base camp.
    d. Each man was given twenty acres.

3. The cabins were used

    a. to provide shelter and sleeping accommodations.
    b. to stake claims on the land.
    c. to store harvested corn.
    d. to protect the men from the threat of Native American attacks.

4. Why did the Native Americans kill some of the men?

    a. The Native Americans were fierce and violent.
    b. The two groups were at war.
    c. The Native Americans were angry that the group had intruded on their land.
    d. The men did not take the necessary precautions.

5. Which of the following events occurred **second**?

    a. Boone's cabin burned.
    b. the Battle of Point Pleasant
    c. The peace treaty was signed.
    d. Boone returned to Virginia.

6. What was Boone's important role before the battle began?

    a. to build forts
    b. to make a last-ditch attempt at peace
    c. to recall surveyors
    d. to train colonists in warfare

7. In which state did the Battle of Point Pleasant take place?

    a. Kentucky
    b. Virginia
    c. Ohio
    d. Pennsylvania

8. What was the most important outcome of the Battle of Point Pleasant and the ensuing peace treaty?

_____

_____

_____

_____

_____

_____

_____

_____

_____

9. The ongoing conflict between the Native Americans and the colonists was about land rights. In your opinion, who had actual "rights" to the land? Why? Use evidence from the passage.

_____

_____

_____

_____

_____

_____

_____

_____

_____

_____

_____

_____

_____

_____

_____

_____

_____

_____

TENNESSEE ELK REINTRODUCTION

QUESTIONS & ANSWERS

1. How long has it been since elk roamed wild in the state of Tennessee?

The last elk reported in Tennessee was in 1865. One was reported killed in Obion County during that year.

2. What was the cause of the disappearance of the elk population in Tennessee?

Hunting and habitat destruction are the two biggest reasons for the extinction of elk in Tennessee and elsewhere in the eastern U.S.

3. Where will the elk come from that are to be released in Tennessee?

The subspecies of elk that once roamed in Tennessee (*Cervus elaphus canadensis*) are extinct. A closely related subspecies of elk (*Cervus elaphus manitobensis*) are being released into Tennessee. The initial elk released in Tennessee are from Elk Island National Park in Alberta, Canada. This elk herd is closely monitored for potential health problems. It is considered one of the best sources of wild disease-free elk. Tennessee will also consider obtaining elk from Utah and other western states that have not had disease problems in wild elk. Another source for elk may also be from the Elk and Bison Enclosure at the Land Between the Lakes.

4. How many elk will be reintroduced into Tennessee?

Current plans call for fifty elk to be released into Tennessee for the first year. Four hundred are to be released over the following four years.

5. What will be the sex and age composition of elk released into Tennessee?

For each release approximately seventy-five percent of the elk will be cows. Twenty-five percent will be bulls. For the safety of the animals the bulls will have their antlers removed prior to transporting them to Tennessee. Mature bulls will be transported apart from the rest of the animals. A portion of the elk released will be calves. They will be transported with their mothers. It is also hoped that some of the mature cows will also be pregnant. That will ultimately augment the number of animals released and will cause the Tennessee population to grow faster.

6. How large an area is the Tennessee elk restoration zone?

The elk restoration project calls for elk to be released in a 670,000-acre restoration zone. The zone is located in Scott, Morgan, Campbell, Anderson, and Claiborne Counties. The center of the zone will be the Royal Blue Wildlife Management Area. Elk that wander outside of the restoration zone will be captured and moved back into the restoration zone if possible. They may be destroyed if capture is not possible.

7. Why remove elk that wander out of the restoration zone?

Elk have the potential to cause crop and property damage if they live in areas that have large amounts of row crops and/or have large numbers of people. The restoration zone was selected because it contains few farm crops and few people. It has habitat that is suitable for supporting an elk herd. Areas outside of the zone may be hostile to elk. It is imperative that elk remain in the restoration zone.

8. How far will elk travel?

It is difficult to say how far elk will travel. Their movement patterns are largely determined by habitat. In western areas, elk are very mobile, mostly in response to availability of suitable habitat. This may be influenced by weather conditions. In the eastern states that have elk, elk movements have been a lot less than those seen in western states. Michigan, for example, has an elk herd of 1,300–1,500 elk. It is maintained on 512,000 acres. It is expected that the elk herd in Tennessee will approach this size. The 670,000 acres of the restoration zone should contain suitable habitat to maintain this herd. It is also expected, as has occurred in most eastern elk releases, that a few animals will wander off the restoration area.

9. What will be done if some elk do cause damage in the restoration zone?

The Tennessee Wildlife Resources Agency (TWRA) has hired a full-time elk biologist. Her duties will be primarily to increase the amount of habitat suitable for elk. That will help reduce conflicts with landowner interests. In addition to this duty, the biologist will be responsible for providing assistance to landowners to lessen any damage that elk may be causing to their property. Measures such as fencing and physical harassment will be tried first to solve damage problems. If these techniques fail, then the elk will be moved elsewhere if possible. If it is not possible to move the elk and damage continues, then they may have to be destroyed.

198

10. Will elk be considered for release in other areas of the state?

The present elk restoration zone was chosen since it contains a large amount of public land that has few agricultural crops and is composed of suitable habitat for elk. Also, the area has a great deal of public support for elk. Volunteer groups in the area such as Campbell Outdoor Recreation Association, Tennessee Conservation League, and the Rocky Mountain Elk Foundation provided support for the restoration project. At some future time (and after evaluation of this initial restoration effort), the agency may evaluate the feasibility of restoration in other areas. However, no specific plans exist at this time to restore elk in other areas.

11. How big of a population will be established in the elk release zone?

It is hoped that the population of elk will expand from the four hundred elk scheduled to be released to a population of 1,400 to 2,000. This population level should be obtainable within sixteen years.

12. Will elk ever again be hunted in Tennessee?

For the immediate future, there will be no hunting. However, hunters and non-hunters alike will be able to enjoy viewing the elk and listening to them in the fall.

As the elk population grows in the restoration zone, legal hunting of elk will be a management option. It is speculated that when the elk population exceeds one thousand animals that a hunting program can be implemented. When a hunting program is implemented it is likely that the demand for elk hunting opportunities will greatly exceed that needed to maintain a stable elk population. Most likely hunters will have to submit applications to be selected for an elk hunt. The demand for these hunts may be so high that a hunter is likely to only be drawn once in a lifetime, if at all.

13. Who is paying for reintroducing elk into Tennessee?

The budget for the elk reintroduction project is roughly $300,000 per year. The Rocky Mountain Elk Foundation (RMEF) is providing approximately fifty percent of the funding. The state of Tennessee, the University of Tennessee, and other groups will provide the remainder.

14. Where can people see these newly-released elk in Tennessee?

All elk released will be ear-tagged and fitted with radio collars so that their movements can be tracked. Once the movements of the elk are patterned, plans are to establish viewing areas for the public. The public can assist in helping establish these areas by reporting sightings of elk.

15. Will elk bring diseases to other Tennessee wildlife or to domestic livestock and pets?

All elk brought into Tennessee for release will go through strict disease testing prior to release. This testing will be more thorough than that required for bringing captive elk into Tennessee. Also, the elk brought into Tennessee will come from areas where health surveillance has been ongoing for several years with no history of significant disease. All of these precautions will greatly minimize the risk of any diseases being introduced into the state.

16. What other eastern states have resident wild elk herds?

Michigan, Pennsylvania, Wisconsin, Arkansas, and Kentucky all have resident elk. Several other eastern states are looking into the possibility of also reintroducing elk.

1. Under which question would a reader look to find information about subspecies of elk?

    a. Where can people see these newly-released elk in Tennessee?
    b. How far will elk travel?
    c. Where will the elk come from that are to be released in Tennessee?
    d. Will elk be considered for release in other areas of the state?

2. Why does Tennessee need to reintroduce elk to the state?

    a. They all migrated to Canada.
    b. They are extinct in Tennessee.
    c. They need to be reintroduced to feel comfortable.
    d. They have never been in Tennessee before.

3. Why would the male elks' antlers need to be removed before they are transported?

    a. to keep them from harming each other
    b. to keep people from being scared of them
    c. to fit them into the trucks and train cars
    d. to help them look more like female elk

4. The author was able to make an assumption about how the elk herd would travel and grow in Tennessee by using _____ as an example.

   a. Canada
   b. Michigan
   c. Tennessee
   d. Utah

5. What would be the **last** step taken to prevent elk from damaging people's property?

   a. Destroy the elk.
   b. Fence the property.
   c. Move the elk.
   d. Use physical harrassment techniques.

6. Which of the following would you be **least** likely to see in the selected restoration zone?

   a. elk
   b. wildlife
   c. forests
   d. farmland

7. Why would someone be concerned about elk being hunted again?

   a. Hunting is not an effective way to control animal populations.
   b. An elk cannot be hunted.
   c. Elk will attack hunters if they see them.
   d. Hunting is one cause of elk no longer being in Tennessee.

8. Which of the following people would be **most** interested in reading this passage?

   a. an environmentalist
   b. a chemist
   c. a psychologist
   d. an astronaut

9. What is another way to say "augment," as it is used under the fifth question?

    a. terrorize
    b. introduce
    c. increase
    d. kill off

10. Michael lives far away from the 670,000-acre elk release site. As a zoologist, he wants to be able to observe the elk in their new habitat. He contacts the Tennessee Wildlife Resources Agency (TWRA) to see if they will open a second elk restoration zone closer to where he lives. What would a TWRA representative most likely tell Michael? What could Michael do on his own to learn more about the elk?

GENERAL MARIANO G. VALLEJO
by Guadalupe Vallejo

Mariano Guadalupe Vallejo was born in Monterey July 7, 1808. He died in Sonoma January 18, 1890. He married Francisca Benicia Carrillo in San Diego on March 6, 1832.

The life of young Vallejo at Monterey was not different from other boys of his class. He went to school with soldier schoolmasters. As he grew older he craved other works than the lives of the saints. Governor Sola took much interest in the boys. He helped them to obtain a few books of a more secular nature. As they grew older they procured from visiting shipmasters such books as could be had. They carefully concealed these books from the vigilant eyes of the padres. The padres were ever on guard to confiscate and destroy books of heretical tendency.

In 1830 Vallejo was assigned to the San Francisco company. He was made comandante in 1831. He made several campaigns against the Indians. In 1834 [he] was sent as comisionado to secularize the mission of San Francisco Solano. In 1834 [he] was granted the Petaluma rancho.

In 1835 Vallejo was instructed to lay out a pueblo at the Solano mission. He was made director of colonization at the north. He was authorized to issue grants of land to settlers. The scheme was to prevent, by Spanish colonization, further extension of the Russian establishment of Ross. Vallejo laid out the pueblo. He gave it the Indian name of the valley. He called it Sonoma—Valley of the Moon. He labored very earnestly to establish his pueblo. He succeeded in attracting a number of families to it. He transferred the San Francisco company to Sonoma. He also organized a company of about fifty Indians whom he drilled in the manual of arms.

The neglect of the Mexican government to pay its soldiers had caused the presidial companies to disband. Vallejo supported his military establishment for several years at his own expense. In 1834 he took the preliminary steps for establishing a civil government at San Francisco. On January 1, 1835, he turned over to the ayuntamien control of civil affairs of that pueblo. He was untiring in his efforts to settle and develop the northern frontier. Through his wise management and influence with the Indian chiefs the peace of the frontier was rarely broken.

In the rising of Alvarado and Castro against Gutierrez he took no active part. His sympathies were with his nephew, Alvarado. He accepted office under the government formed by him. He was now (1837) the foremost man in

California and one of the richest. Over the hills of his princely estate of Petaluma roamed ten thousand cattle, four to six thousand horses, and many thousand sheep. He occupied a baronial castle on the plaza at Sonoma. There he entertained all who came with most royal hospitality. Few travelers of note came to California without visiting him. At Petaluma he had a great ranch house called La Hacienda. On his home farm, Lachryma Montis (Tear of the Mountain), he built, about 1849, a modern frame house. He spent the later years of his life there.

Vallejo's attitude towards the Russians at Fort Ross and Bodega was firm and dignified. He maintained that the Russians were on California soil. He notified the Russian manager, Rotchef, that while the use of the port of Bodega by the Russians was tolerated, if he permitted foreigners to land and enter the country in defiance of law he must not be surprised if he found Mexican troops stationed there.

Vallejo also objected to Sutter's establishing an independent principality in the Sacramento valley and his assumption of authority to wage war upon the natives, to grant passports, and to exercise other prerogatives of sovereignty. This made Sutter very angry. He announced that if he were interfered with he would not only defend himself but would declare the independence of California from the Mexican rule.

Vallejo was always friendly to American immigrants. He exceeded his authority in protecting them. He openly advocated the cause of the United States. One can hardly conceive a more ungrateful return for the kindness to immigrants and help to Americans. He was seized and confined in a dismal prison by these same immigrants. He was kept there long after the United States authorities had taken possession and the United States flag was flying over his prison house.

On September 15, 1846, he wrote Larkin:

> I left the [sic] Sacramento half dead and arrived here (Sonoma) almost without life, but am now much better. The political change has cost a great deal to my person and mind and likewise to my property. I have lost more than one thousand live horned cattle, six hundred tame horses, and many other things of value which were taken from my house here and at Petaluma. My wheat crops are entirely lost. The cattle ate them up in the field. I assure you that two hundred fanegas [about 25,000 bushels] of sowing, in good condition. All is lost and the only hope for making it up is to work again.

The town of Vallejo was named for him. A street in San Francisco bears his name. He had sixteen children. Ten lived to maturity. One daughter married

John B. Frisbie, captain of company H, Stevenson's regiment. Another married his brother, Levi. One married Arpad Harasthy. The two younger daughters married Don Ricardo de Empáron and James H. Cutter.

1. Mariano Vallejo lived

    a. in Mexico.
    b. during most of the 19th century.
    c. in a monastery.
    d. on a ship.

2. Vallejo broadened his horizons by reading books obtained from

    a. the padres.
    b. his schoolmasters.
    c. his schoolmates.
    d. passing shipmasters and the governor.

3. When Vallejo was assigned to secularize the mission of San Francisco Solano, he was to

    a. build a presidio or fort for increased security.
    b. develop and populate a settlement or town near the mission.
    c. turn its property over to civilians.
    d. turn its property over to the Russians.

4. When Vallejo was instructed to lay out a pueblo at the Solano mission, his job was to

    a. build a presidio or fort for increased security.
    b. develop and populate a settlement or town near the mission.
    c. turn its property over to civilians.
    d. turn its property over to the Russians.

5. Presidial companies were

    a. businesses located near a presidio.
    b. military units located in a presidio.
    c. civil governments.
    d. ayuntamien.

6. The principal purpose of the settlement in the Sonoma valley was to

    a. stop expansion of the Russian settlement at Ross.
    b. prevent expansion of Sutter's settlement at Ross.
    c. settle and develop the northern frontier.
    d. pacify the Indians in the area.

7. Vallejo's ranch house, La Hacienda, was at

    a. Sonoma.
    b. Petaluma.
    c. Lachryma Montis.
    d. San Diego.

8. Vallejo apparently had the most difficult relationships with

    a. the Mexican authorities.
    b. Governor Alvarado.
    c. Rotchef.
    d. Sutter.

9. Spanish and Mexican land grants gave the right to use the land, but not ownership. Do you think this caused Vallejo trouble eventually? Why?

_____

_____

_____

_____

_____

_____

_____

_____

_____

THE LINCOLNS IN INDIANA

In the fall of 1816, Thomas and Nancy Lincoln packed their belongings. With their two children, nine-year-old Sarah and seven-year-old Abraham, they left their Kentucky home. They were bound for the new frontier of southern Indiana. They arrived in December. Thomas had made an one-hundred-and-sixty-acre claim near the Little Pigeon Creek. Thomas quickly set about building a cabin for his family. In time, he cleared fields. He improved the cabin and outbuildings. He utilized his carpentry skills to establish himself within the community.

His young son assisted Thomas with much of the work. As he grew older, Abraham increased in his skill with the plow and, especially, with the ax. In fact, in later life, he described how he " . . . was almost constantly handling that most useful instrument . . . " to combat the " . . . trees and bogs and grubs . . . " of the "unbroken wilderness" that was Indiana in the early 19th century.

The demands of life on the frontier left little time for young Abraham to attend school. As he later recalled, his education was acquired "by littles" and the total " . . . did not amount to one year." However, despite the limitations he faced, his parents encouraged him in every way possible. Soon, his eyes were opened to the joy of books and the wonders of reading. He became an avid reader. At the age of eleven, he read Parson Weems's *Life of Washington*. He followed it with Benjamin Franklin's *Autobiography*, *Robinson Crusoe*, and *The Arabian Nights*. He could often be seen carrying a book and his ax. For Abraham Lincoln, to get books and read them was "the main thing."

Life was generally good for the Lincolns during their first couple of years in Indiana. Like many pioneer families, though, they could not escape their share of tragedy. In October 1818, when Abraham was nine years old, his mother, Nancy Hanks Lincoln, died of the milk sickness. Milk sickness was scourge of the frontier. It resulted when a person drank contaminated milk. It was contaminated if it came from a cow infected with the toxin from the white snakeroot plant. Nancy had gone to nurse and comfort her ill neighbors. She herself became a victim of the dreaded disease. For young Abraham it was a tragic blow. His mother had been a guiding force in his life. She had encouraged him to read and to explore the world through books. His feelings for her were still strong some forty years later when he said, "All that I am or hope to be, I owe to my angel mother."

The family keenly felt Nancy's absence. Young Sarah and Abraham were now without a mother and Thomas was without a wife. This loneliness led Thomas to return to Kentucky in 1819 in search of a new wife. He soon met Sarah

Bush Johnston. Sarah was a widow with three children. Thomas chose well. The cheerful and orderly Sarah proved to be a kind stepmother. She reared Abraham and Sarah as her own. Under her guidance, the two families became one.

The remainder of his years in Indiana were adventurous ones for Abraham Lincoln. He continued to grow. By the time he was nineteen, he stood at six foot four inches. He could wrestle with the best. Local people remembered that he could lift more weight and drive an ax deeper than any man around.

In 1828, he was hired by James Gentry. Gentry was the richest man in the community. Gentry wanted Abraham to accompany his son, Allen, to New Orleans. They were to travel in a flatboat loaded with produce. While in New Orleans, Lincoln witnessed a slave auction on the docks. It was a sight that greatly disturbed him. The impression it made was a strong and lasting one.

Abraham continued to work for Gentry intermittently at his store. He also began to take an interest in politics. The Gentry store was often a gathering place for local residents. There Abraham listened as a number of political views were aired. At home was more talk of politics. He began to form his own opinions. With a keen mind and a gifted knowledge of words he was able to make his own contributions to the lively discussions.

Another job that Abraham had during his teenage years was operating a ferryboat service across the mouth of the Anderson River. In his spare time, he built a scow to take passengers out to the steamers on the Ohio. One day he rowed out two men and placed them aboard with their trunks. To his surprise each threw him a silver half-dollar. "I could scarcely credit," he said, "that I, a poor boy, had earned a dollar in less than a day."

Although profitable, his business venture also led to one of his first encounters with the legal system. Two brothers, who held the ferry rights across the Ohio between Kentucky and Indiana, charged Lincoln with encroaching on their jurisdiction. Kentucky law, in such cases, said that the violator should be fined. However, because he did not carry his passengers all the way across the river but only to the steamboats, the judge ruled that Lincoln had not violated the law and dismissed the charge.

By all accounts the Lincolns prospered in Indiana, but in 1830, Thomas decided to move to Illinois. Relatives there had described the soil as rich and productive. Milk sickness, which threatened to break out again in the Little Pigeon community, did not exist. With that news, Thomas sold his property and left the state.

Abraham Lincoln lived in Indiana for fourteen years, from the age of seven to the age of twenty-one. During that time he had grown physically and mentally. With his hands and his back, he had helped carve a farm and home out of the wilderness. With his mind, he had begun to explore the world of books and knowledge. He had experienced adventure and he had known deep personal loss. The death of his mother in 1818 and the death of his beloved sister, Sarah, in 1828, left deep emotional scars. However, all those experiences helped make him into the man that he became.

1. As he was growing up, Abraham Lincoln was especially good at

    a. carpentry.
    b. plowing.
    c. cutting down trees.
    d. building cabins.

2. The total number of days Abraham spent in school amounted to

    a. none.
    b. very few.
    c. less than a year's worth.
    d. more than a year's worth.

3. Of the following, which book did Abraham Lincoln read first?

    a. *Arabian Nights*
    b. *Life of Washington*
    c. *Robinson Crusoe*
    d. Benjamin Franklin's *Autobiography*

4. Thomas Lincoln's first wife and Abraham Lincoln's mother was named

    a. Nancy Hanks Lincoln.
    b. Sarah Lincoln.
    c. Sarah Bush Johnston.
    d. Nancy Hanks Johnston.

5. Before she married Thomas Lincoln, Abraham Lincoln's stepmother was named

   a. Nancy Hanks Lincoln.
   b. Sarah Lincoln.
   c. Sarah Bush Johnston.
   d. Nancy Hanks Johnston.

6. Abraham Lincoln helped Allen Gentry

   a. in his father's store.
   b. on a ferryboat from Kentucky to Indiana.
   c. sail from Indiana to steamboats on the Ohio River.
   d. on a trip to New Orleans.

7. Abraham Lincoln was amazed at how much money he earned

   a. in James Gentry's store.
   b. on a ferryboat from Kentucky to Indiana.
   c. on a ferryboat carrying people to steamboats on the Ohio River.
   d. during a trip to New Orleans.

8. Abraham Lincoln saw slavery firsthand

   a. in James Gentry's store.
   b. on a ferryboat from Kentucky to Indiana.
   c. on a ferryboat carrying people to steamboats on the Ohio River.
   d. during a trip to New Orleans.

9. Abraham Lincoln ended up in court because of what he did

   a. in James Gentry's store.
   b. on a ferryboat from Kentucky to Indiana.
   c. on a ferryboat carrying people to steamboats on the Ohio River.
   d. during a trip to New Orleans.

10. What kind of person was 19-year-old Abraham Lincoln? Give reasons for
    your conclusions based on details from the passage.

    _____

    _____

    _____

    _____

    _____

    _____

    _____

    _____

    _____

    _____

    _____

    _____

    _____

    _____

    _____

    _____

    _____

    _____

PINCKNEY'S TREATY GIVES AMERICA ACCESS TO NEW ORLEANS

As a result of Spain's intervention during the French and Indian War she had lost Florida but had been given Louisiana. Then, as a result of Spain's intervention during the American Revolution she had won back the Floridas, which included much of present Alabama and Mississippi. Spain now controlled the entire Gulf Coast, and all of America west of the Mississippi.

Nevertheless, by the 1790s, Spain viewed with alarm the swarms of aggressive Americans who were moving across the Appalachians nearer and nearer to Spanish territory. Two types of countermeasures were tried. Through a system of alliances backed by liberal gifts, the colonial governor at New Orleans endeavored to forge a buffer state of Indian tribes hostile to the Americans. Since the Americans and the Indians of the Southeast were enemies of long standing, this was not too difficult. Forts were built. Commercial treaties were negotiated. Governor Carondelet even dreamed of organizing the thirteen thousand warriors into an army that would drive the Americans back across the mountains.

The other means practiced by the Spanish was to sow dissension among the Americans. Many of the plots to separate the West from the United States were instigated by the Spanish officials. Numerous leading men of the Western settlements had Spanish money in their pockets. It had been paid to them for aiding the Spanish cause and keeping the Spanish informed. It was apparent that Spain realized the danger to Louisiana from the Americans.

In order to appreciate the reasons why Jefferson was concerned over the ownership of Louisiana, we must define U.S. interest in the territory more carefully. By the 1790s, Americans by the thousands were crossing the mountains and building their homes along the Ohio River and its tributaries. For the most part these men were farmers. Since they grew their own food in large measure, they were remarkably self-sufficient. They did not depend on other sections in order to live. On the other hand, their only hope of rising above the subsistence level or of getting ahead in the world was to produce more than they needed at home and to sell the surplus. They could produce salable goods in considerable quantities—flour, meat, tobacco, and cotton, in particular. The great problem was to find a market. The nearest market, of course, was the eastern seaboard. Philadelphia, Baltimore and other centers of population needed agricultural products. Between the Westerners and the cities, however, lay the Appalachian Mountains. The Appalachians are not high, but they are wide and rugged. There was ridge after ridge after ridge. The mountain belt was in places over one hundred miles wide. There were almost no roads and only a few trails wide enough for packhorses. The Westerners could, and did, drive herds of cattle and hogs over the mountains, transporting their surplus meat on the hoof. If their surplus grain was distilled and converted into whiskey, it was possible to carry that over the mountains at a small profit. With these exceptions the mountains were a very effective barrier between the Westerners and their markets. When you pay freight rates of over $100 per ton, there is little to be gained in transporting bulky agricultural produce.

Although the way to the East was barred to commerce, there was a natural outlet for Western crops. They could be floated down the Ohio and Mississippi Rivers to the sea. It was entirely practical for a farmer or small merchant to cut down a few trees, hew and saw out planks, and construct a simple flatboat. The flatboat, which cost little, could be loaded with several hundred barrels of flour, or salt meat, hogsheads of tobacco or bales of cotton. Then the farmer or merchant, with roughly four helpers, would let the flatboat drift with the current down the river. The total cost of the trip was roughly $100 for the boat, $200 for the wages, and $50 for provisions. Upon reaching New Orleans the cargo would be sold to merchants or ship agents who would transfer the goods to sailing ships and carry them to New York, Philadelphia, or Baltimore, or the West Indies, or even to Europe. Since the flatboat was useless for an upstream trip, it was sold for lumber. It was worth about $5. The crew then walked back to Nashville, or Marietta, or whatever had been their starting point by way of the Natchez Trace.

The trip down the river and back overland was cheap, but it was scarcely easy. On the way there was the danger of accident on the uncharted river. The flatboats were of pretty flimsy construction. There were river pirates going down and land pirates coming back. They robbed and murdered without scruple. As you might imagine, it took tough men to carry on this trade. There are many stories of the flatboatmen. One would jump into the air, crack his heels together, flap his arms and crow like a rooster. Then he would proclaim his toughness and challenge any comer to a fight. If his challenge was accepted, the brawl might well end with ears or noses bitten off, an eye gouged out, or similar niceties.

The hope of economic progress in the West thus lay in the navigation of the Mississippi River. There was one grave flaw in the picture. The mouth of the Mississippi did not belong to the United States. From just below Natchez to the sea both banks of the river were Spanish. That meant that the goods of the Westerners had to pass through a foreign port, and import and export duties cut deeply into their prospects of profit. With the population and production of the West growing rapidly, farsighted Americans on both sides of the mountains could say with Thomas Jefferson that the possessor of New Orleans was our "natural and habitual enemy . . ."

The Spanish authorities disliked and feared the Westerners. There were frequent clashes of interest between the two countries over boundaries, the Indians, and particularly over trade on the Mississippi. In 1795, the situation improved greatly when Thomas Pinckney succeeded in negotiating a favorable treaty with Spain. The boundary of Florida was settled to the temporary satisfaction of the United States. Eastern shippers obtained desirable concessions. Of prime interest was the agreement on the Mississippi question. Under the Pinckney Treaty, Spain acknowledged the right of Americans to the free navigation of the river. In other words, American vessels could pass between U.S. territory and the sea without hindrance from Spain.

Spain also granted the right of deposit at New Orleans. The nature of the American export trade made this provision of first importance. Westerners descending the river in their flatboats could enjoy the free use of the river only if an American ship willing to buy their produce happened to be waiting at New Orleans. The boats were too frail to be tied up at the riverbank and to wait until a ship appeared. Frequently they sank under those circumstances. Of course, the goods could be sold to New Orleans merchants, but that was importing, and involved high duties. What Spain granted in the right of deposit was the privilege of landing the flatboat cargoes at New Orleans, storing them in warehouses until a ship arrived and purchased them, and then transferring them to the ship. No duties were charged. The only fee was warehouse rent. The treaty guaranteed the right of deposit at New Orleans for at least three years after which, if it were terminated there, another point would be designated. The Westerners were delighted. Trade down the river swelled in volume. At the end of three years, although the treaty permitted Spain to do so, the right of deposit at New Orleans was not terminated. By 1802, over five hundred flatboats were descending the river annually. They carried over a million dollars worth of produce.

Conditions under Pinckney's Treaty were so favorable that many Americans were willing to let the ownership of New Orleans remain as it was. Spain was no longer a major world power. Jefferson, among others, felt that as long as Spain held the city the United States could bide its time. The West was growing stronger and when the time was ripe, New Orleans could be picked up without difficulty.

1. Spain had to give Florida to the British after Spain

    a. and France won the French and Indian (Seven Years') War.
    b. and France lost the French and Indian (Seven Years') War.
    c. and France helped America win the American Revolution.
    d. sided with Britain against America during the American Revolution.

2. Spain won Florida back after Spain

    a. and France won the French and Indian (Seven Years') War.
    b. and France lost the French and Indian (Seven Years') War.
    c. and France helped America win the American Revolution.
    d. sided with Britain against America during the American Revolution.

3. Of the following, which was **not** part of Spain's efforts to keep Americans away from its territories?

    a. liberal gifts to the Native Americans
    b. building forts
    c. negotiating trade treaties
    d. organizing an army of 13,000 Native-American warriors

4. Of the following, which was **not** part of Spain's efforts to keep Americans away from its territories?

    a. bribing leading Americans
    b. encouraging creating a separate country in the West
    c. attacking American settlements
    d. spying on Americans

5. Western farmers could **not** get their products to the eastern markets because

    a. it cost too much to ship over the Appalachians.
    b. it took too long to ship over the Appalachians and the produce would spoil.
    c. the Appalachians were too high to ship over.
    d. Native-American tribes in the Appalachians were too fierce.

6. For western farmers, the easiest, cheapest way to get products to market was

    a. by way of the Great Lakes.
    b. by way of the Ohio and Mississippi Rivers.
    c. over the Appalachians.
    d. around the Appalachians.

7. Flatboats were mainly propelled by

    a. oars.
    b. sails.
    c. poles.
    d. river currents.

8. Once the crops had reached New Orleans, they were

    a. shipped to Mexico and California.
    b. put on wagon trains for the east coast, West Indies, or Europe.
    c. put on sailing ships.
    d. sold to New Orleans residents for their own use.

9. The biggest problem in shipping Western goods was the

    a. dangers on the river.
    b. long walk back home.
    c. Spanish control of the mouth of the Mississippi.
    d. fact that riverboat men were not nice men.

10. The right of deposit allowed Americans to

    a. sell to New Orleans merchants without paying any duty.
    b. tie up at a riverbank until a ship appeared.
    c. sell produce only if a ship happened to be waiting.
    d. keep produce in New Orleans warehouses without paying duty until it was sold to a ship.

11. Why do you suppose Spain was willing to grant some favorable terms to the United States?

_____

_____

_____

_____

_____

_____

_____

_____

_____

_____

_____

_____

_____

_____

_____

_____

_____

_____

_____

INDEPENDENCE SOUGHT FOR KENTUCKY

The question of government in Kentucky now arose again. Should Kentucky always remain a territory belonging to Virginia? Should Kentucky enter the Union as a separate state? Should Kentucky withdraw from all of it and set up a separate, sovereign government west of the Allegheny Mountains? Should Kentucky accept the overtures of Spain or England to come under the royal protection of one of these? It was a big decision to make.

The war was now over and each colony was free. What would the colonies do about their future government? This question agitated the whole country from Maine to Georgia. For six years the people waited, in doubt as to how the problem of government would be solved. Finally, the federal *Constitution* was adopted on September 17, 1787. Virginia, with its Kentucky territory, was the tenth state to agree to it.

Kentucky hoped for little support from the new government. Because of her distance apart from the rest of the nation, she could not easily transport her products to the eastern seaboard. The Mississippi River afforded the only outlet to foreign markets. The Spanish, who controlled the navigation of the river, offered special privileges of trade to the Kentuckians if they would set up a separate government of their own. The question of Kentucky's future was still pressing. No people loved their country more; none were more patriotic, but the people of Kentucky desired to do what which was best for the themselves.

In the autumn of 1784 information was given out that the Cherokee were preparing to invade the southern frontiers, while Ohio tribes threatened on the northern side. At the call of Colonel Benjamin Logan, a meeting was held to consider the defense. It was the consensus of the meeting that the best policy was to anticipate the enemy, invade his country, and strike a blow from which he could not well recover. Then the questions came up: How should an army be raised, armed, and equipped for such an invasion? Who could call out the men to join an army? There was no law to authorize anyone to act on such a thing. After the treaty of peace with England, the veterans of past conflicts had returned to their land. They were busily at work building their houses and opening their farms.

Kentucky could make no laws and had no authority. She must apply to Virginia and this delay might be fatal. A new sense of the dangers of the situation dawned upon the assembly. It was resolved to hold a convention at Danville on December 27, 1784, to consider the state of the country. There, it was agreed that only a homegrown government could properly provide for

Kentucky. Furthermore, Kentucky was growing so quickly that she would surely qualify for statehood. A resolution was passed in favor of applying to Virginia for an act of separation from the mother state.

On May 23, 1785, the convention reconvened. The following statement to the Virginia Assembly was resolved:

That it is the duty of this convention as they regard the prosperity and happiness of their constituents, to pray the General Assembly at the ensuing session, for an act to separate this district from the present government, on terms honorable to both and injurious to neither, in order that it may enjoy all the advantages and rights of a free sovereign and independent republic.

1. After the Revolutionary War had ended, which of the following was **not** one of Kentucky's options?

   a. Kentucky could become a colony of Spain or England.
   b. Kentucky could establish its own government, separate from its mother colony of Virginia and the rest of the growing nation.
   c. Kentucky could enter the Union as an individual American state.
   d. Kentucky could remain free of all forms of control or government.

2. According to this passage, why did Kentucky feel that it might benefit from becoming a Spanish-controlled colony?

   a. Spain controlled the Mississippi River, which Kentucky had to use for purposes of trade and transportation.
   b. Spain maintained excellent relationships with the Native Americans.
   c. The people of Kentucky felt that Spain would someday gain control of all the colonies.
   d. The people of Kentucky already had a strong trading relationship with Spain.

3. Why were the people of Kentucky unable to authorize a rally call to their men for the defense of their land against any future Native American attacks?

   a. Kentucky was not yet a state and, therefore, could not make such decisions.
   b. Kentucky was land that still officially belonged to Virginia.
   c. All the men in Kentucky had returned to their homes following the war.
   d. Nobody was in charge.

4. What was the result of the reconvention of May 23, 1785?

   a. Kentucky became a state.
   b. Kentucky declared war on the Native Americans.
   c. Kentucky elected its first governor.
   d. Kentucky separated from Virginia.

5. Every colony, and not just Kentucky, struggled with the issue of what to do about its future government. In your own words, describe the issue. What were the pros and cons of each side of the issue?

_____

_____

_____

_____

_____

_____

_____

_____

_____

_____

_____

_____

_____

_____

_____

_____

6. Why was it so important not to delay regarding the decision made
    during the reconvention in May 1785?

_____

_____

_____

_____

_____

_____

_____

_____

_____

_____

_____

_____

from "EARLY HISTORY OF CHEYENNE DOG SOLDIERS"

by W.S. Campbell

Of all the typical Plains tribes, the Cheyennes were most distinguished for warlike qualities. Few in number, they overcame or held in check most of the peoples who opposed them. When the westward movement of European civilization began, they made more trouble than all the rest combined. In short, they were preeminently warriors among peoples whose trade was war.

As in other prairie tribes, the warriors of the Cheyenne were organized into societies or orders. These societies were fraternal, military, and semi-religious organizations with special privileges, duties, and dress. The societies usually tracing [sic] their origin to some mythical culture hero or medicine man. Each society had its own songs and secret ritual, and exacted certain observances and standards of its members.

Of these organizations, none has played such a part in the history of the Plains as the "Dog Soldiers" of the Cheyenne. The story of how it began is told as follows:

> The Dog-Man (Dog Soldier) Society was organized after the organization of the other societies, by a young man without influence, but who was chosen by the great Prophet. One morning the young man went through the entire camp and to the center of the camp circle, announcing that he was about to form a society. No one was anxious to join him, so he was alone all that day. The other medicine-men had had no difficulty in establishing their societies, but this young man, when his turn came to organize, was ridiculed, for he was not a medicine-man, and had no influence to induce others to follow his leadership. At evening he was sad. He sat in the midst of the whole camp. He prayed to the Great Prophet and the Great Medicine Man to assist him.

> At sunset he began to sing a sacred song. While he sang the people noticed that now and then the large and small dogs throughout the camp whined and howled and were restless. The people in their lodges fell asleep. The man sang from sunset to midnight; then he began to wail. The people were all sleeping in their lodges and did not hear him. Again he sang. Then he walked out to the opening of the camp-circle, singing as he went. At the opening of the camp-circle he ceased singing and went out. All the dogs of the whole camp followed him, both male and female, some carrying in their mouths their puppies. Four times he sang before he reached his destination at daybreak.

> As the sun rose he and all the dogs arrived at a river bottom which was partly timbered and level. The man sat down by a tree that leaned toward the north. Immediately the dogs ran from him and arranged themselves in the form of a

222

semi-circle about him, like the shape of the camp-circle they had left. Then they lay down to rest. As the dogs lay down, by some mysterious power, there sprang up over the man in the center of the circle a lodge. The lodge included the leaning tree by which the man sat. There were three other saplings, trimmed at the base with the boughs left at the top. The lodge was formed of the skins of the buffalo.

As soon as the lodge appeared, all the dogs rushed towards it. As they entered the lodge they turned into human beings. They were dressed in a way that members of the Dog-Men Society later followed. The Dog Men began to sing. The man listened very attentively. He learned several songs from them, their ceremony, and their dancing forms. The camp circle and the center lodge had the appearance of a real camp circle for three long days. The Dog Men blessed the man and promised that he should be successful in all of his undertakings and that his people, his society, and his band would become the greatest of all if he carried out their instructions.

Later, the Cheyenne discovered the camp. However,

. . . as they came into view of the wonderful camp the Dog lodge instantly disappeared and the Dog-Men were transformed into dogs. The medicine-men and warriors were by this time very sorry that they had refused to join this man's society—and the next day, according to instructions of the Great Prophet, he again asked the warriors to join his society, and many hundreds of men joined it. He directed the society to imitate the Dog Man in dress, and to sing the way the Dog-Men sang. This is why the other warrior societies call the warriors of this society "Dog-Men Warriors."

The uniform of the society consisted of a bonnet covered with upright feathers of birds of prey, leggings, breechcloth, and moccasins. Each member wore a whistle suspended from a thong round the neck and made of the wing bone of an eagle. The belt was made of four skunk skins. The Dog Soldiers carried a bow and arrows and a rattle shaped like a snake was used to accompany their songs. They had one chief and seven assistants. Four of them were leaders in battle, chosen on account of their extraordinary courage. These four wore, in addition to the usual uniform, a long sash which passed over the right shoulder and hung to the ground under the left arm, decorated with porcupine quills and eagle feathers. Of these four men the two bravest had their leggings fringed with human hair.

The society has a secret ritual that occupies four days. It has a series of four hundred songs used in its ceremonies and dances. It was often called upon to perform police duties in a large camp. It enjoyed certain privileges in the tribe, such as the right to kill any fat dog whenever a feast was in order.

The powers of a warrior society in doing police duty were great. Their punishments were severe against those who violated camp regulations. Not infrequently they whipped delinquents with quirts, beat them with clubs, or killed their ponies. For small offenses they might cut up a man's robe, break his lodge poles, or slash his tipi cover. They had charge of the tribal buffalo hunt, and saw to it that the rules governing the hunt were observed and that all men had an equal chance to kill meat. They prevented any individual hunting until after the needs of the camp had been supplied.

About 1830 all the men of a certain Cheyenne band joined the Dog Soldiers in a body. Since that time the society has comprised about half the men in the tribe. It has been the most distinct, important, and aggressive of all the warrior societies of the Cheyenne. In fact, the name of the tribe, Cheyenne, has by some been derived from the French *chien*, (dog) in direct allusion to the organization, through this derivation is now discredited by the best authorities.

The Cheyenne had engaged in a very disastrous drawn battle with the Kiowas, Comanches, and Apaches in 1838. By 1840 the Dog Soldiers were so influential that the Cheyenne chiefs left it to them to decide whether or not peace should be made with these tribes. The peace then made by the Dog Soldiers has never been broken.

A disastrous fight with the Pawnees in 1852 was also a great misfortune to the Cheyennes. In the following year those who had lost relatives brought presents to the Dog Soldiers, urging them to avenge the dead. Accordingly, the Dog Soldiers led a campaign against the Pawnees. Finding them reenforced by a number of Pottawatomies, equipped with firearms, the Dog Soldiers were forced to withdraw.

1. Why was the young man sad?

   a. He had been ridiculed.
   b. He was not a medicine man.
   c. He had no influence.
   d. No one from the camp would join his society.

2. When did all the dogs follow the young man?

   a. at sunset, when he began to sing a sacred song
   b. at midnight, when he began to wail
   c. as he fell silent and left the camp
   d. at daybreak

224

3. From whom did the Dog-Men Society learn how to dress and sing?

    a. dogs from the camp that became human
    b. men from the camp dressed like dogs
    c. the Great Prophet
    d. the Great Medicine Man

4. Why did the Cheyenne warriors and medicine men change their minds about joining the society?

    a. They saw the dogs turned into men.
    b. They were sorry they had not done it before.
    c. The Great Prophet instructed them to.
    d. They saw the Dog lodge.

5. Who always wore a whistle and carried a rattle shaped like a snake?

    a. the two bravest men only
    b. the four leaders in battle only
    c. one chief and seven assistants only
    d. all the Dog Soldiers

6. Who dressed with a long sash over the right shoulder?

    a. the two bravest men only
    b. the four leaders in battle only
    c. one chief and seven assistants only
    d. all the Dog Soldiers

7. The most important function of the Dog Soldiers in the Cheyenne tribe was

    a. performing the secret fair day ritual with 400 songs.
    b. deciding when a fight was to be held.
    c. acting as tribal policemen.
    d. organizing the buffalo hunt.

8. The Dog Soldiers' most important leadership role was

    a. entering into the 1838 battle with three other tribes.
    b. making peace with three other tribes.
    c. entering into the 1852 battle with the Pawnee.
    d. deciding not to attack the Pawnee and their allies in 1853.

9. Write a story about a young Cheyenne warrior trying to decide whether or not to join the Dog-Men Society. Use details from the passage to make your writing more interesting.

_____

_____

_____

_____

_____

_____

_____

_____

_____

_____

_____

_____

_____

_____

_____

_____

_____

_____

THE SPANISH CLOSE
THE PORT OF NEW ORLEANS

On October 18, 1802, the Spanish intendant at New Orleans issued a proclamation canceling the American right of deposit at that city. He pointed out that the original 1795 treaty called for the right of deposit to last three years. The proclamation was a bombshell. Western trade was based on the free deposit at New Orleans. The economic well-being of hundreds of thousands of people depended on it. On the afternoon of October 18th, two American flatboats reached the city. They tied up, as usual, at the muddy batture just above the town. Imagine the surprise and anger when they were forbidden to land. Recalling the proverbial toughness of the men who handled the flatboats, you can guess that the official who forbade their landing did not go unguarded. The news of the closure swept back up the river and created a storm of controversy. Demands for action were made, of which this letter published in the *Kentucky Gazette* is a good example:

> The reptile Spaniards act in a most hostile manner towards our citizens and commerce. With degrading remarks that the people of the United States have no national character—that they are divided, weak, quarrelsome people, without energy—and that they have nothing to fear from them. Such language is too insulting.

> To give you a further view of our aggrieved situation, I will only state that a few days since a parcel of cotton arrived at New Orleans, the bales being so damaged that it was necessary to have them repacked before shipped. They were landed by paying 6 per cent duty, and cannot be re-shipped on board an American vessel, but must on re-shipment pay 6 per cent more as Spanish produce on board a Spanish bottom. This rule will hold good in all instances where a landing is made in any case. I trust 700,000 persons will not wait for Mr. Jefferson to go through all the forms, ceremonies and etiquette of the courts of Spain and Bonaparte, before they determine whether it will be best to drive the miscreants from their waters or not. I say start and drive them with the spring flood and then negotiate. We can now get the whole province without the loss of one drop of blood, and let the French get there 'twill be otherwise.

> P.S. I have it in my power to state that the fortifications at New Orleans are in no sort of repair, and that there are no effective troops in the province. The town duty is now done by the militia, and that from one end of the province to the other they are almost in a state of revolt. In my humble opinion three thousand Kentucky militia could put the U.S. in possession of the fairest country in the universe, without the shedding of one man's blood. Good God! can all western America be dead to the their true interests, and will they pass over the present favorable moment to possess themselves of advantages that

will never have an end, or will they blindly allow themselves to come under the French yoke of tyranny? How is it that the pens of thousands lie dormant on this most alarming occasion? That which is and will be death to western America if allowed, and life if speedily stopped. Let me beseech all those who subsist on the branches of the Mississippi to arm and defend their dearest rights and national privileges.

The Westerners were angry. They demanded action from the government or they would take matters in their own hands. Jefferson's political enemies jumped in to egg on the warmongers. Thus the intendant's proclamation caused grave concern in Washington. The people of New Orleans also were surprised and dismayed by the order. The American trade was a large part of the city's business. Much of the food supply came down in the American flatboats. They, too, demanded the reopening of the river.

Not only were the Westerners, the United States government and the people of New Orleans amazed at the sudden proclamation; other Spanish officials in America were shocked and horrified. The governor of Louisiana, who shared the administration of the colony with the intendant and had political authority over treaty matters, was strongly opposed to the measure, but he was too old and vacillating to dare to cross the intendant. The Spanish minister to the United States ordered him in the king's name to restore the deposit—and received the reply that he had no more right than the intendant to speak in the king's name. Even the captain-general in Havana, who was a direct supervisor of the intendant, failed to swerve him. Here was a mystery. The intendant was a relatively meek man who had never distinguished himself for boldness. He was a civilian official of rather limited authority, yet he calmly defied every effort to countermand the proclamation. He claimed no authority higher than his own interpretation of his duty, but he refused to budge. Everyone thought they knew why, but no one was sure. They thought he had secret orders and that the orders were from Napoleon.

Historians have searched the archives of Louisiana, Spain and France and have solved the mystery in part. The intendant did have orders from Madrid. They were marked "Very Secret." They told him to terminate the right of deposit and do it without revealing his instructions to do so. The mystery which remains is why the order was issued. What was the closure to accomplish?

At any rate, the closure at New Orleans affected the Westerners and, through their indignation, the administration in Washington. With the West aroused and the French interest in Louisiana becoming more and more apparent, action was necessary. Jefferson's foes introduced a war measure in Congress. Thomas Jefferson did not want war. The country was still small and was unprepared. He was struggling to maintain an economical administration. An attack on New Orleans, he knew, would not stop there. It meant war with France and Spain. American maritime commerce, which then was second only to England's, would be swept from the seas. It would be long, costly, and the result was not certain. While Jefferson did not want war, he saw clearly that U.S. national interests demanded possession of the Isle of Orleans.

1. Who ordered the right of deposit to be terminated?

   a. the governor of Louisiana
   b. the intendant of Louisiana
   c. the captain-general in Havana
   d. the Spanish minister to the United States

2. Why did so meek a man ignore even his direct superior?

   a. No one knows.
   b. He had secret orders from Napoleon.
   c. He had secret orders from the United States government.
   d. He had secret orders from Madrid.

3. What did the *Kentucky Gazette* letter writer want his readers to do?

   a. join the Kentucky militia and attack New Orleans
   b. write letters supporting an attack on New Orleans
   c. write letters asking the Spanish to reconsider
   d. write letters asking the French to reconsider

4. How much was the total duty that caused such indignation and calls for war?

   a. 12%
   b. 16%
   c. 20%
   d. 50%

5. What do you think was really behind the calls for war?

_____

_____

_____

_____

_____

_____

_____

_____

6. Is the title of this passage an accurate one? Why or why not?

_____

_____

_____

_____

_____

_____

_____

_____

_____

LIFE IN EARLY 19TH-CENTURY KENTUCKY

Travelers found the log cabin to be the most common settler dwelling of the Appalachian West. Cabins were crude buildings. They were sixteen to twenty feet in length and no more than twelve or sixteen feet wide. The interior typically held a single room centering on a fireplace along one wall with an unfinished loft above. Furniture was simple. There were table, a few stools or chairs, and mattresses stuffed with corn shucks. Windows were rare and frequently without glass. During the winter months, they were covered with wooden shutters and animal skins.

More financially stable families lived in frame, brick, or stone houses that grew larger with expanding wealth. Many of these houses were two stories tall with two or four rooms on each floor. Some had separate kitchen wings.

Furnishings varied greatly with the financial circumstances of the family. They typically included a table and chairs, a chest, or a bedstead. Wealthy homeowners were able to import higher quality finished goods and luxury products from the eastern seaboard and Europe. Also present, for owners of sufficient wealth, were one or more slaves, usually housed in separate cabins or outbuildings on the property.

Families could be both large and extended. Particularly in the early years of settlement, houses were often shared by grandparents, in-laws, and cousins. Deaths from war or disease left widows, widowers, or orphans who needed the support of family or friends. Women played key roles in the development of the Appalachian West. They shared the dangers of migration and the hard labor of clearing fields and raising crops. Wives and daughters bore responsibility for managing households and caring for children and the elderly.

Kentucky's climate, while temperate, was not warm enough to support large plantings of crops such as cotton or rice. The soil of the bluegrass was rich, but a wooden plow could not cut through its dense roots. Clearing dense forests thus became the preferred method for creating farmland. Small trees and bushes were chopped down and burned. The rough ground with stumps still in place was broken with a light plow or hoe. Then the first seeds were planted. It was said that the average adult male could clear five or six acres of wooded land a year in this fashion.

Farms varied greatly in size and organization. The wealthiest farmers could own as much as one thousand two hundred acres or more. Part was used for planted fields, another for free-range livestock. Less wealthy farmers with smaller parcels of land, under thirty acres, worked hard to raise enough crops to feed their families with perhaps small surpluses to sell or barter. The smallest farms were those of the squatters. They cleared only a few acres and stayed on the land until they had enough money to buy a farm elsewhere.

Education was an early interest for western settlers. However, the rigors of frontier life and lack of trained teachers made schooling a rare experience for most children. Simple lessons taught by rote, supported by a few elementary textbooks, were the norm. For young girls from wealthier families, female academies offered more genteel training in literature, languages, and the arts.

In an age when herbal remedies were common, illness often carried the danger of death. Whooping cough, scarlet fever, and measles killed or disabled many. The "ague," a kind of malarial fever, was associated with swamps and standing water. "Milk sick" brought death to those who drank milk produced by cows that had eaten poisonous plants. Most serious of all were the epidemics of smallpox and cholera that swept through whole communities. However, as threatening as these diseases were for the white settlers, they were often even more devastating for Native Americans who lacked any immunity at all to them.

In a region where hard work and danger was a daily commonplace, recreation was therefore treasured and quite varied. In remote settlements, activities necessary to rural life such as hunting, shucking corn, or quilting could be made into pleasant shared events for the scattered communities. Dances and church socials offered other opportunities for friends and relatives to gather. Public speeches offered by politicians provided other occasions.

In villages and towns, more resources were available. Larger populations could support newspapers and libraries. Touring companies of players presented theater productions. Lecturers entertained in courthouse squares and lodge halls. Musical groups performed in parlors. Private tutoring on musical instruments was available for the well-to-do.

Public taverns were also centers of lively entertainment. In the large public rooms of these establishments, locals and travelers mingled and exchanged gossip. In one corner of the main room or in a separate room, a bar offered refreshment. Guests who made their way upstairs at the end of the evening rarely went to private rooms. More frequently they went to a common dormitory room to share beds with strangers.

1. By the early nineteenth century, the population of Kentucky was mainly comprised of

    a. wealthy families.
    b. primitive pioneer families.
    c. slaves.
    d. all of the above.

2. Which of the following is **not** true of Kentucky life in the early nineteenth century?

    a. Log cabins were the characteristic homes of pioneers.
    b. Economically successful families resided in elaborate mansions.
    c. Families residing together were often large and extended.
    d. Slaves were often housed in separate cabins.

3. The wealthy could import high quality goods from

    a. Mexico.
    b. California.
    c. Europe.
    d. Canada.

4. Which of the following do we know **not** to be true about the role of women in the early nineteenth century?

    a. Women were just as important to western development as men.
    b. Women labored to clear fields and raise crops with men.
    c. Women managed entire households.
    d. Women managed the family finances.

5. Most Kentucky children in the early nineteenth century

    a. attended frontier schools.
    b. memorized lessons out of textbooks at home.
    c. never had any schooling.
    d. were well-trained in literature, languages, and the arts.

6. Why did many people succumb to illness in the early nineteenth century?

    a. People could not afford health care.
    b. Disease were much worse back then.
    c. Doctors were not trained well.
    d. Health care was still quite primitive.

7. Why were recreational activities particularly cherished?

   a. Laughter was known to be the best medicine.
   b. Leisure time was rare.
   c. Everyone needed to relax after a long day of work.
   d. Kentuckians loved their recreational activites.

8. Which of the following were **not** popular diversions around the 1800s?

   a. taverns and music
   b. newspapers and libraries
   c. stickball and footraces
   d. church socials and political speeches

9. The passage says that day-to-day activities such as hunting, shucking corn, or quilting could be made into pleasant shared events. How might the early Kentuckians have made such tasks more exciting?

_____

_____

_____

_____

_____

_____

_____

_____

_____

_____

10. Why were diseases such as smallpox and cholera even more devastating to Native Americans than to the settlers?

_____

_____

_____

_____

_____

_____

_____

_____

_____

_____

_____

_____

_____

_____

_____

_____

RACCOONS AND RABIES

Physical Characteristics

Raccoons are medium-sized mammals. They have distinctive black face masks outlined in white. Each raccoon has also have four to seven dark rings on its thickly furred tail. The pelt of the raccoon is generally gray and sprinkled with black buff, which gives the coat a grizzled appearance. The average size of a raccoon is between twelve and thirty pounds.

General Biology

Found throughout Tennessee, the raccoon is the official state mammal. Raccoons are omnivores. They eat fruit, nuts, frogs, insects, grains, crawfish, bird eggs, mice, and anything else they can get their hands on. Generally nocturnal animals, raccoons den in hollow trees or hollow logs and spend most of the daylight hours there. Strong climbers and swimmers, raccoons are generally found in habitats associated with water such as hardwood swamps, marshes, and bottomland forests. Raccoons do most of their foraging near or in waterways. All too often, however, raccoons make their homes in urban and residential areas where there is plenty of cover and an abundance of food to scavenged at night.

The raccoon's mating season begins in February. Typically, two or three cubs per litter are born in April or May. Raccoons are born with their eyes and ears closed. They are covered in dark fur and have no rings on their tails. The mother cares for the young on her own. The youngsters leave their mother when they are weaned.

Raccoons have few natural predators. Therefore, hunters and trappers, who kill thousands of raccoons annually, are the primary means of population control. Many raccoons are also struck and killed by vehicles on the roadways. This is particularly true in the spring, when the young are dispersing and the males are searching for mates.

Disease

Raccoons are capable of transmitting rabies, canine distemper and parvovirus to domestic dogs. They can transmit rabies and roundworms to humans. Disease may become a significant problem when raccoon populations reach levels that cannot be supported by their available food and habitat.

Rabies

Rabies, also known as "hydrophobia," is a fatal disease that can affect all mammals, including human beings. Triggered by a virus that attacks the central nervous system, rabies causes inflammation of the brain. The rabies virus lives in the saliva of infected animals and is most often transmitted through their bites. It can also be transmitted through licks. Inhalation of the rabies virus has been known to occur, but only in very special circumstances (such as inhalation in confined areas).

The incubation period, the time between exposure to the disease and the onset of symptoms, varies from a few days to several months. A rabid animal may even appear healthy while the virus is incubating. However, once symptoms appear, there is no treatment and it is almost always fatal. An animal that has contracted rabies will have flu-like symptoms, severe headache, and fever. As the disease progresses, the animal will become confused. It will begin to hallucinate as the brain ceases to function properly. The animal's jaw will often drop, causing it to drool or foam at the mouth. Rabid foxes and raccoons may not behave normally, appearing during daylight hours.

There are two types of rabies in animals. One is called "furious form rabies." Animals with this type of rabies may exhibit early symptoms such as restlessness, agitation, and increased aggressiveness. This is followed by depression, paralysis and eventually death. The other form of rabies is called "dumb form rabies." These animals are lethargic, depressed, and partially paralyzed. They may appear unusually tame. They will also eventually die. You cannot diagnose an animal with rabies by simply observing the animal. There is currently no test that can be performed on a live animal to detect the presence of the rabies virus. In order to test for the presence of rabies, brain tissue must be sampled.

The disease can be effectively prevented in humans and domestic animals through the administration of rabies vaccines. Prevention and control among wild animals, however, is much more complicated. Rabies can be abundant and wildly distributed in wild animals and there are many different variants of the virus (skunk-strain, fox-strain, raccoon-strain, bat-strain etc.). Each strain may infect any species of mammal. Therefore, it is extremely important for people to stay away from wild or domestic animals, especially bats, foxes, raccoons and skunks. Also, any animal acting in a strange or unusual manner should be treated with caution and avoided.

BAT-STRAIN RABIES

Since the late 1970s, seventy-five percent of human rabies cases in the United States have been caused by the bat strain of rabies. Bats have very small teeth so a bite from a bat may not be detectable.

RACCOON-STRAIN RABIES

Raccoon-strain rabies is a strain of rabies carried mainly by raccoons. This strain was virtually unknown prior to the 1950s. Florida experienced the first case of raccoon rabies. During the next three decades, the disease then spread slowly into Georgia, Alabama, and South Carolina. In 1978 Virginia experienced an outbreak of raccoon strain rabies due to the translocation of raccoons from Georgia and Florida. The first cases in West Virginia and Virginia appeared in the late 1970s. Since then, raccoon rabies in the area has expanded to form the most common form of rabies found in the United States. The strain now occurs in all the eastern coastal states, as well as in Alabama, Pennsylvania, Vermont, West Virginia, Ohio, and even in southern Ontario in Canada.

The United States Department of Agriculture, Animal and Plant Health Service, Wildlife Services launched an oral rabies vaccination program in 2002. The goal of the program is to stop the westward spread of raccoon strain rabies. Aircraft in East Tennessee distributed an oral rabies vaccine. Following distribution of the oral vaccine, active rabies surveillance has been conducted in the baiting zone.

In Tennessee, raccoon-strain rabies was first documented in June 2003, when four raccoons tested positive in Carter County and a feral cat tested positive in Johnson County. A second occurrence of raccoon strain rabies was discovered in January 2004, when seven raccoons tested positive for raccoon strain rabies in Hamilton County.

Raccoons and skunks may incubate rabies for long periods (many months) without becoming ill. They may shed the virus in saliva two weeks prior to showing symptoms. Within the baiting/surveillance zone, capturing an animal appearing normal and releasing it in another area later can be extremely hazardous. An animal that appears healthy may later develop the symptoms of clinical rabies. In order to protect the public and monitor the spread of rabies in wild populations, the translocation of all rabies vector species inside the oral vaccination baiting/surveillance zone has been terminated.

State law currently prevents the Tennessee Wildlife Resources Agency from undertaking any direct rabies control. The Tennessee Department of Health is responsible for the investigation of any potential human rabies exposure. If a person is bitten by a wild or domestic animal, he or she should wash with soap and water immediately and then go to the doctor, where a rabies shot can be administered as soon as possible.

RABIES PREVENTION INFORMATION

- Respect and observe wild animals from a distance.
- Do not feed wild animals.
- Do not approach or handle wild animals.
- Secure food and garbage; do not allow wild animals access to them.
- Place trash out for pickup on the same day it will be picked up.
- Seal openings in attics, basements, porches, sheds, and barns.
- Cap chimneys with screens.
- Vaccinate all pets.

1. This passage was written to
   a. inform readers about keeping raccoons for pets.
   b. persuade readers to read more about rabies.
   c. educate readers about the importance of rabies prevention.
   d. compare and contrast various wild animals.

2. Which of the following statements is **true** about raccoons?
   a. Raccoons are nocturnal animals.
   b. Raccoons do not eat meat.
   c. Raccoons spend their days climbing and swimming.
   d. Raccoons only live near waterways.

3. Why might the hunting of raccoons be encouraged?
   a. Raccoon meat is a staple food in many states.
   b. Humans are frequently attacked by raccoons.
   c. Raccoon fur is worth a lot of money.
   d. The raccoon population needs to be controlled.

4. The author says that rabies is most often transmitted through

   a. inhalation.
   b. the bite of a rabid animal.
   c. contact with a wild or domestic animal.
   d. contact with a vaccinated animal.

5. According to the article, rabies is

   a. caused by a virus that attacks the nervous system.
   b. caused by inflammation of the brain.
   c. caused by paralysis.
   d. also known as hypochondria.

6. What does "cease," as used in the seventh paragraph, mean?

   a. starts
   b. continues
   c. tries
   d. stops

7. Once an animal begins to show symptoms of rabies,

   a. the incubation period will begin.
   b. it may appear healthy.
   c. it will almost always die.
   d. the rabies test can be administered.

8. Which of the following is **least** likely to acquire rabies?

   a. unvaccinated domestic pets
   b. vaccinated domestic pets
   c. wild animals
   d. unvaccinated humans

9. If a human is bitten by an animal, he or she should

   a. wait a few days to see what happens.
   b. call the Department of Health.
   c. wash the affected area and go to the doctor immediately.
   d. schedule an appointment with a doctor for the following week.

10. While you are walking down the street on a warm spring afternoon, a raccoon comes out of the woods. It seems to want to come closer to you. What should you do?

   a. Give it food and water.
   b. Call it to you and look at it closely.
   c. Follow it.
   d. Call the Tennessee Department of Health.

11. Why do raccoons often leave the wilderness to wander into urban and residential areas?

_____

_____

_____

_____

_____

_____

_____

_____

_____

_____

_____

_____

_____

_____

_____

242

12. Why is rabies typically more difficult to prevent among wild animals than it is humans and domestic animals? What are Tennessee wildlife groups doing to try to remedy this problem?

_____

_____

_____

_____

_____

_____

_____

_____

_____

_____

_____

_____

_____

_____

_____

_____

_____

_____

FIRST SETTLERS

Judge Richard Henderson was born in Virginia, but moved with his parents to North Carolina. Raised in poverty, his education was limited. Yet by studious diligence and energy, he attained a high rank in the legal profession and became chief justice of the colonial court.

Judge Henderson opened an office for the sale of lands in Transylvania soon after his arrival in the spring of 1775. The price of lands was fixed, for one year, at 13 1/3¢ per acre. Buyers also had to pay half a cent per acre annual rent, to begin in 1780. Any settler might enter six hundred forty acres for himself at these rates. The effect of this apparent possession and steady settlement of the country attracted many. By December 1775, five hundred and sixty thousand acres had been sold.

The Transylvania parties were not the first to arrive in Kentucky in 1775. Captain James Harrod had returned with his party of the year before to their cabin settlements at Harrodstown and its vicinity. Other parties followed. Harrodstown was soon fortified. The stockade fort, much like that at Boonesborough, was located south of the old spring and on the brow of the adjacent hill. It became a central rallying point for all nearby settlements.

Meanwhile, Benjamin Logan had gathered a company who desired to better their fortunes. The expedition was well prepared and well provided with implements for building a strong station, and for clearing and tilling lands. To assist in these labors, some slaves had been brought along. Cabins and defenses were built so well that no future attacks were ever successful upon them. Clearings were made. The settlement had a homelike appearance before the completion of the first year. It was soon ready to receive the female members of the families, who were much missed. This year was the first that white women came to settle in Kentucky. Their coming was at Boone's suggestion. Determined to raise his family in Kentucky, he set out with a small party to collect his wife and children from North Carolina. The trip resulted in the arrival of the wives and families of many of the male pioneers. The colonies now seemed more homelike and with a new spirit of content.

1. What was Judge Henderson's most important contribution to the new country?

    a. saving the lives of Harrod's group
    b. achieving a high rank in the legal profession
    c. being a diligent student and a hard worker
    d. overseeing the sale of land to settlers

2. Which of the following can be said about Logan's cabin forts?

   a. They were homey and comfortable.
   b. They proved to be resilient to attack.
   c. They were frequently destroyed.
   d. They were impenetrable.

3. What became of Harrodstown?

   a. It became a centralized fort.
   b. It was overtaken by Native Americans.
   c. It was destroyed.
   d. It became the first permanent settlement.

4. Why did the pioneers build fortified cabins?

   a. to keep out the wild animals
   b. to be prepared in case the Revolution came to Kentucky
   c. to provide shelter for weary pioneers
   d. to ward off the threat of Native American attack

5. Which of the following **best** describes how Daniel Boone felt about Kentucky?

   a. He felt it was a beautiful but dangerous country.
   b. He thought it had a good future.
   c. He loved it and wanted his family to settle there as soon as possible.
   d. He loved it but knew that it was not a place to settle permanently.

6. Which event occurred to make the Kentucky settlements feel more homelike?

   a. The Americans beat the British in the Revolution.
   b. The first group of women and children arrived.
   c. Boone returned to North Carolina.
   d. The cabins were furnished.

7. How do you think Judge Richard Henderson's background affected his dealings in colonial Kentucky?

_____

_____

_____

_____

_____

_____

_____

_____

_____

_____

_____

_____

_____

_____

_____

_____

PONTIAC'S CONSPIRACY

A deep-rooted dislike on the part of the Indians for the English grew after 1760 with great rapidity. They sorely missed the gifts and supplies lavishly provided by the French. They warmly resented the rapacity and arrogance of the British traders. The open contempt of the soldiery at the posts galled the Indians. The confiscation of their lands drove them to desperation. In their hearts hope never died that the French would regain their lost dominion. Again and again rumors were set afloat that this was about to happen. The belief in such a reconquest was adroitly encouraged, too, by the surviving French settlers and traders. In 1761, the tension among the Indians was increased by the appearance of a "prophet" among the Delawares. He called on all his race to purge itself of foreign influences and to unite to drive the white man from the land.

Protests against English encroachments were frequent and, though respectful, none the less emphatic. At a conference in Philadelphia in 1761, an Iroquois sachem declared, "We, your Brethren, of the several Nations, are penned up like Hoggs. There are Forts all around us, and therefore we are apprehensive that Death is coming upon us." A petition of some Christian Oneida addressed to Sir William Johnson ran as follows:

> We are now left in Peace and have nothing to do but to plant our Corn, Hunt the wild Beasts, smoke our Pipes, and mind Religion. But as these Forts, which are built among us, disturb our Peace, and are a great hurt to Religion, because some of our Warriors are foolish, and some of our Brother Soldiers don't fear God, we therefore desire that these Forts may be pull'd down, and kick'd out of the way.

The leadership of the great revolt that was impending fell naturally upon Pontiac. Since the coming of the English, he had established himself with his squaws and children on a wooded island in Lake St. Clair. He was barely out of view of the fortifications of Detroit. In all Indian annals no name is more illustrious than Pontiac's. No figure more forcefully displays the good qualities of his race. He was principal chief of the Ottawa tribe. By 1763, he was also the head of a powerful confederation of Ottawa, Ojibwa, and Potawatomi. He was a leader known and respected among Algonquin peoples from the sources of the Ohio to the Mississippi. While capable of acts of magnanimity, he had an ambition of Napoleonic proportions.

More clearly than most of his forest contemporaries, Pontiac perceived that in the life of the Indian people a crisis had come. He saw that, unless the tide of English invasion was rolled back at once, all would be lost. The colonial farmers would push in after the soldiers. The forests would be cut away. The hunting grounds would be destroyed. The native population would be driven away or enslaved. In the silence of his wigwam he thought out a plan of action. By the closing weeks of 1762, he was ready. Never was a plot more shrewdly devised and more artfully carried out.

During the winter of 1762–1763, his messengers passed stealthily from nation to nation throughout the whole western country. They carried the pictured wampum belts and the reddened tomahawks that symbolized war. In April 1763, the lake tribes were summoned to a great council on the banks of the Ecorces, below Detroit. There Pontiac in person proclaimed the will of the Master of Life as revealed to the Delaware prophet. He then announced the details of his plan. Everywhere the appeal met with approval. Not only the scores of Algonquin peoples, but also the Seneca branch of the Iroquois confederacy and a number of tribes on the lower Mississippi, pledged themselves with all solemnity to fulfill their prophet's injunction "to drive the dogs which wear red clothing into the sea." While keen-eyed warriors sought to keep up appearances by lounging about the forts and begging in their customary manner for tobacco, whiskey, and gunpowder, every wigwam and forest hamlet from Niagara to the Mississippi was astir. Indian women chanted the tribal war songs. In the blaze of a hundred campfires chiefs and warriors performed the savage pantomime of battle.

A simultaneous attack, timed by a change of the moon, was to be made on the English forts and settlements throughout all the western country. Every tribe was to fall upon the settlement nearest at hand. Afterwards all were to combine—with French aid, it was confidently believed—in an assault on the seats of English power farther east. The honor of destroying the most important of the English strongholds, Detroit, was reserved for Pontiac himself.

1. Of the following, which did the French do for the Native Americans that the British did **not** do?
   a. lavish gifts and supplies on them
   b. display greed and arrogance
   c. display contempt
   d. confiscate their lands

2. Who or what did the Indians apparently resent the most after 1760?

   a. French fur traders
   b. French forts
   c. British forts
   d. British fur traders

3. Pontiac was chief of the

   a. Delaware.
   b. Ottawa.
   c. Ojibwa.
   d. Potawatomi.

4. A prophet had arisen among the

   a. Delaware.
   b. Ottawa.
   c. Ojibwa.
   d. Potawatomi.

5. All of the following were members of Pontiac's confederation **except** the

   a. Delaware.
   b. Ottawa.
   c. Ojibwa.
   d. Potawatomi.

6. Pontiac's plans met with the approval of all of the following **except**

   a. most of the Algonquin people.
   b. most of the Iroquois people.
   c. the Seneca.
   d. some lower Mississippi tribes.

7. How did the Native Americans pretend to be friendly?

   a. chanting tribal war songs
   b. performing pantomimes of battle
   c. begging for tobacco, whiskey, and gunpowder
   d. spying on forts

8. The most important English stronghold in Indian territory was

    a. Detroit.
    b. on the banks of the Ecorces below Detroit.
    c. Chicago.
    d. Vincennes.

9. Do you think Pontiac's plans succeeded? Why or why not?

_____

_____

_____

_____

_____

_____

_____

_____

_____

_____

_____

_____

_____

_____

_____

PONTIAC ATTACKS

The date fixed for the rising was the 7th of May, 1763. Six days in advance Pontiac with forty of his warriors appeared at the fort at Detroit. He protested undying friendship for the Great Father across the water. He insisted on performing the calumet dance before the new commandant, Major Gladwyn. This aroused no suspicion. However, four days later a French settler reported that his wife had visited the Ottawa village to buy venison. She had observed the men busily filing off the ends of their gunbarrels. The blacksmith at the post recalled the fact that the Indians had lately sought to borrow files and saws without being able to give a plausible explanation of the use they intended to make of the implements.

The English traveler Jonathan Carver visited the post five years afterwards. He relates that an Ottawa girl with whom Major Gladwyn had formed an attachment betrayed the plot. Though this story is of doubtful authenticity, there is no doubt that, in one way or another, the commandant was amply warned that treachery was in the air. The sounds of revelry from the Indian camps, the furtive glances of the Indians lounging about the settlement, and the very tension of the atmosphere would have been enough to put an experienced Indian fighter on his guard.

Accordingly when, on the fated morning, Pontiac and sixty Indians, carrying their shortened muskets under long blankets, appeared before the fort and asked admission, they were taken aback to find the whole garrison under arms. On their way from the gate to the council house they were obliged to literally march between rows of glittering steel. With uneasy glances, the party crowded into the council room, where Gladwyn and his officers sat waiting.

"Why," asked the chieftain stolidly, "do I see so many of my father's young men standing in the street with their guns?"

"To keep them in training," was the laconic reply.

The scene that was planned was then carried out, except in one vital particular. In the course of his speech professing strong attachment to the English, Pontiac came to the point where he was to give the signal for slaughter by holding forth the wampum belt of peace inverted. Instead he presented the emblem—to the accompaniment of a significant clash of arms and roll of drums from the mustered garrison outside—in the normal manner. After a solemn warning from the commandant that vengeance would follow any act of aggression, the council broke up. To the forest leader's equivocal announcement that he would bring all of his wives and children in a few days to shake hands with their English fathers, Gladwyn deigned no reply.

Balked in his plans, the chief retired, but only to meditate fresh treachery. A few days later, with a multitude of followers, he sought admission to the fort to assure "his fathers" that "evil birds had sung lies in their ears." He was refused. He called all his forces to arms, threw off his disguises, and began hostilities. For six months the settlement was besieged with a persistence rarely displayed in Indian warfare. At first the French inhabitants encouraged the besiegers, but, after it became known that a final peace between England and France had been concluded, they withheld further aid. Throughout the whole period, the English obtained supplies with no great difficulty from the neighboring farms. There was little actual fighting. The loss of life was insignificant.

For three years the movements of this disappointed Indian leader are uncertain. Most of the time, apparently, he dwelt in the Maumee country, leading the existence of an ordinary warrior. Then, in the spring of 1769, he appeared at the settlements on the middle Mississippi. At the newly-founded French town of St. Louis, on the Spanish side of the river, he visited an old friend, the commandant Saint Ange de Bellerive. Thence he crossed the Mississippi to Cahokia, Illinois. There Indian and creole alike welcomed him. They made him the central figure in a series of boisterous festivities.

An English trader in the village jealously observed the honors that were paid the visitor. He resolved that an old score should forthwith be evened up. A Kaskaskian Indian was bribed, with a barrel of liquor and with promises of further reward. The bargain was hardly sealed before the deed was done. Stealing upon his victim as he walked in the neighboring forest, the Indian assassin buried a tomahawk in his brain. "Thus basely," in the words of Parkman, "perished the champion of a ruined race." Claimed by Saint-Ange, the body was borne across the river and buried with military honors near the new Fort St. Louis. The site of Pontiac's grave was soon forgotten. Today the people of a great city trample over and about it without heed.

1. The Great Father across the water was

    a. the king of England.
    b. the king of France.
    c. the king of Spain.
    d. George Washington.

2. The Native Americans filed the ends of their gunbarrels to make them

   a. more attractive.
   b. more accurate.
   c. look like Native American weapons.
   d. easier to hide.

3. According to the author, which of the following probably did **not** help alert Major Gladwyn to the Native Americans' plans?

   a. revelry at the Native American camp
   b. his Native American girlfriend
   c. furtive glances by Native Americans
   d. a tense atmosphere

4. By "taken aback," as used in paragraph 3, the author means that the Native Americans

   a. stepped backwards.
   b. were carried or pushed backwards.
   c. were taken back in time, or remembered a previous, similar occurrence.
   d. were surprised.

5. "Laconic," as used in the third paragraph, means

   a. humorous, joking.
   b. brief, short.
   c. arrogant, boastful.
   d. angry, hostile.

6. Pontiac's signal to attack was planned to be

   a. professing strong attachment to the English.
   b. presenting the wampum belt of peace in the normal manner.
   c. presenting the wampum belt of peace inverted.
   d. bringing his wives and children to shake hands.

7. Pontiac attacked the fort at Detroit for

   a. a few days.
   b. six months.
   c. three years.
   d. an unknown amount of time.

8. After failing to conquer Detroit, Pontiac

    a. went straight to St. Louis.
    b. went straight to Cahokia.
    c. attacked other English forts.
    d. went to live among the Maumee.

9. Pontiac was killed by

    a. an English trader.
    b. a Kaskaskian Native American.
    c. Saint Ange de Bellerive.
    d. a French settler (a creole).

10. Do you think Pontiac deserved a more noble end? Why or why not?

_____

_____

_____

_____

_____

_____

_____

_____

_____

_____

_____

_____

AN INDIAN RESERVE

The ink with which the Treaty of Paris was signed was hardly dry. The king of England and his ministers were confronted with the task of providing a government for the new possessions. They also had to solve the problems of land tenure and trade. Still more imperative were measures to conciliate the Indians. Pontiac's rebellion had been in progress for four months. The entire backcountry was aflame.

The easiest solution of the difficulty was to let things take their course and let seaboard populations spread at will over the new lands. Maybe they should allow these people to carry on trade in their own way and make whatever arrangements with the native tribes that they desired. Colonies such as Virginia and New York had extensive western claims. They would have been glad to see this plan adopted. Strong objections, however, were raised. Colonies that had no western claims feared the effects of the advantages that their more fortunate neighbors would enjoy. Men who had invested heavily in lands lying west of the mountains felt that their returns would be diminished and delayed if the backcountry were thrown open to settlers. Some people thought that the Indians had a moral right to protection against wholesale white invasion of their hunting grounds.

It was the king and his ministers who had it in their power to settle the question. From their point of view it was desirable to keep the western territories as much apart from the older colonies as possible. It was in their interest to regulate their settlement and trade. Eventually, it was believed, the territories would be cut into new colonies. The experience with the seaboard dependencies was already such as to suggest the desirability of having the future settlements more completely under government control from the beginning.

After due consideration, King George and his ministers made known their policy on October 7, 1763, in a comprehensive proclamation. The disposition made of the great rectangular area bounded by the Alleghenies, the Mississippi, the Great Lakes, and the Gulf of Mexico was fairly startling. With fine disregard of the chartered claims of the seaboard colonies and of the rights of pioneers already settled on frontier farms, the whole was erected into an Indian reserve. No "loving subject" could purchase land or settle in the territory without special license. Present residents had to "forthwith remove themselves." Trade would be carried on only by permit and under close surveillance. Officers were stationed among the tribes to preserve friendly relations and to apprehend fugitives from colonial justice.

The objects of this drastic scheme were never clearly stated. Benjamin Franklin believed that the main purpose was to conciliate the Indians. George Washington agreed with him. Later historians have generally thought that what the English government had chiefly in mind was to limit the bounds of the seaboard colonies. They felt that this would help to preserve imperial control over colonial affairs.

Very likely both of these motives weighed heavily in the decision. Lord Hillsborough presided over the meetings of the Lords of Trade when the proclamation was discussed. He subsequently wrote that the "capital object" of the government's policy was to confine the colonies so that they should be kept within easy reach of British trade and of the authority necessary to keep them in due subordination to the mother country. He added that the extension of the fur trade depended "entirely upon the Indians being undisturbed in the possession of their hunting-grounds."

It does not follow that the king and his advisers intended that the territory should be kept forever intact as a forest preserve. They seem to have contemplated that, from time to time, cessions would be secured from the Indians. Tracts would then be opened for settlement. Nevertheless, every move was to be made in accordance with plans formulated or authorized in England. The restrictive policy did not win universal assent in the mother country. The Whigs generally opposed it. Burke thundered against it as "an attempt to keep as a lair of wild beasts that earth which God, by an express charter, has given to the children of men."

In America, there was a disposition to take the proclamation lightly, as being a mere sop to the Indians, but wherever it was regarded seriously, it was hotly resented. After passing through an arduous war, the colonists were ready to enter upon a new expansive era. The western territories were theirs by charter, by settlement, and by conquest. The Indian population, they believed, belonged to the unprogressive and unproductive peoples of the earth. Every acre of fertile soil in America called to the thrifty agriculturist. Every westward-flowing river invited to trade and settlement as well. Therefore, to seek to keep back the ocean with a broom would be like trying to stop by mere decree the tide of homeseekers. Some of the colonies made honest attempts to compel the removal of settlers from the reserved lands beyond their borders. Pennsylvania went so far as to decree the death penalty for all who should refuse to remove. However, the law was never enforced.

1. The Treaty of Paris gave Illinois and the rest of the old northwest to

   a. France.
   b. Spain.
   c. the United States.
   d. England.

2. After the Treaty of Paris, the king had to solve all of the following problems **except**

   a. land tenure.
   b. trade.
   c. war with France.
   d. war with the Native Americans.

3. Who objected to a policy of colonies settling their own problems?

   a. Virginia
   b. New York
   c. people who had no interest in lands lying west of the mountains
   d. people who had invested heavily in lands lying west of the mountains

4. Who thought the king should restrict access to the west?

   a. people who thought the Native Americans had a moral right to their lands
   b. Virginia
   c. New York
   d. people who wanted to settle out west

5. The British government decided to

   a. throw open the west to settlement.
   b. restrict all access to the west to the Indians only.
   c. let the colonies as a whole decide what to do.
   d. let Virginia and New York decide what to do.

6. Why were officers going to be stationed among the tribes?

   a. to grant licenses to purchase land
   b. to grant licenses to settle
   c. to grant licenses to trade
   d. to apprehend fugitives and preserve friendly relations

7. Why did the British government pursue the policy they did?

    a. to conciliate the Indians
    b. to preserve imperial control over colonial affairs
    c. both of the above
    d. neither of the above

8. One reason the British government decided to restrict access to the west was that they

    a. felt bad about what they had done to the Native Americans.
    b. wanted to expand the fur trade with the Native Americans.
    c. wanted to make peace with the Spanish.
    d. wanted to make peace with the French.

9. Why did so many Americans oppose the law?

_____

_____

_____

_____

_____

_____

_____

_____

_____

_____

_____

_____

_____

10. What would America be like if the law was still in effect?

_____

_____

_____

_____

_____

_____

_____

_____

_____

_____

_____

_____

_____

_____

_____

_____

_____

_____

WILLIAM MACCATE BINESSI

When my brother, William, was about twelve or thirteen years of age, the Protestant Mission School started at Mackinac Island. My father thought best to put him to that school. After being there less than a year, he was going around with his teachers, acting as interpreter among the Indian camps at the Island of Mackinac. I was perfectly astonished to see how quick he had acquired the English language. After the mission broke up at the island, William came home and stayed with us for about two years. Then he was again taken by Bishop Reese of the Catholic mission at Little Traverse. Our little sister, a very lovely girl, also went. They were taken down to Cincinnati, Ohio, where they were put into higher schools. There my brother attained the highest degree of education, or graduation as it is called.

From thence he was taken across the ocean to the city of Rome, Italy, to study for the priesthood, leaving his little sister in Cincinnati. It is related that he was a very eloquent and powerful orator. He was considered a very promising man by the people of the city of Rome. He received great attention from the noble families, on account of his wisdom and talent and his being a native American; and yet he had a much lighter complexion than his cousin, Aug Hamlin, who was also taken over there and represented as half French.

Here is a letter he sent from Rome:

ROME, April 17, 1833 MY DEAR SISTER:

It is the custom of the College of the Propaganda, on the feast of Epiphany each year, that the students should deliver a discourse in their own respective languages. This year there were thirty-one different languages delivered by the students, so you may judge what kind of a college this is. At present it is quite full; there are ninety-three, of which thirteen are from the United States.

On Easter Sunday the Holy Father celebrated mass in the church of St. Peter. It is very seldom that his holiness is seen personally celebrating mass in public except on great festivals. The church was crowded with spectators, both citizens of Rome and foreigners. On the front part of the church there was an elevated place beautifully ornamented. After the solemn ceremonies the Holy Father went up and gave his paternal benediction to the people. There is a large square before St. Peter's, and it was crowded so that it was impossible to kneel down to receive the benediction.

This week we are quite merry; we seem to employ our minds on the merriment which is always displayed amongst us on such occasions. Our secretary is now

Cardinal, and to-morrow he will be crowned with the dignity of the Cardinal. Our college has been illuminated these two evenings. The congregational halls of the Propaganda were opened on this occasion. The new Cardinal then received all the compliments of the Cardinals, Bishops, Prelates, Ambassadors, Princes, and other distinguished dignities. There are two large beautiful rooms, in one of which the new Cardinal was seated and received all those who came to pay him compliments. The visitors all came through the same passage, and there was a man posted in each room who received them and cried out to others that such man was coming, and so on through all those that were placed for the purpose, and one called the Cardinal gentleman introduced them to the new Cardinal. If there were such a thing in America it would be quite a novelty.

I remain your most affectionate brother,

William Maccate Binessi

William died almost the very day when he was to be ordained a priest. He received a long visit from his cousin Hamlin that evening. They sat late in the night, talking on various subjects, and particularly on American matters and his ordination. My brother was perfectly well and robust at that time, and full of lively spirits. He told his cousin that night, that if he ever set his foot again on American soil, his people, the Ottawa and Chippewa of Michigan, should always remain where they were. The United States would never be able to compel them to go west of the Mississippi, for he knew the way to prevent them from being driven off from their native land. He also told his cousin that as soon as he was ordained and relieved from Rome, he would at once start for America, and go right straight to Washington to see the President of the United States, in order to hold conference with him on the subject of his people and their lands.

There was a great preparation for the occasion of his ordination. A great ceremony was to be in St. Peter's Church. A Native American, son of the chief of the Ottawa tribe of Indians, a prince of the forests of Michigan, was to be ordained a priest, which had never before happened since the discovery of the Aborigines in America.

In the morning, at the breakfast table, my brother William did not appear. Every one was surprised not to see him at the table. After breakfast, a messenger was sent to his room. He soon returned with the shocking news that he was dead. Then the authorities of the college arose and rushed to the scene. There they found him on the floor, lying in his own blood. When Hamlin, his cousin heard of it, he too rushed to the room. After his cousin's body was taken out, wrapped up in a cloth, he went in. He saw at once enough to tell him that it was the work of the assassin.

When the news reached to Little Traverse, now Harbor Springs, all the country of Arbor Croche was enveloped in deep mourning. A great lamentation took place among the Ottawa and Chippewa in this country with the expression, "All our hope is gone." Many people came to our dwelling to learn full particulars of my brother's death, and to console and mourn with his father in his great bereavement.

No motive for the assassination has ever been developed. It remains to this day a mystery. It was related that there was no known enemy in the institution previous to his death; but he was much thought of and beloved by every one in the college. It was an honor to be with him and to converse with him, as it is related that his conversation was always most noble and instructive. It was even considered a great honor to sit by him at the tables; as it is related that the students of the college used to have a strife amongst themselves who should be the first to sit by him.

There were several American students at Rome at that time. It was claimed by the Italians that my brother's death came through some of the American students from a secret plot originating in this country to remove this Indian youth who had attained the highest pinnacle of science and who had become their equal in wisdom, and in all the important questions of the day, both in temporal and spiritual matters. He was slain, it has been said, because it was found out that he was counseling his people on the subject of their lands and their treaties with the government of the United States. His death deprived the Ottawa and Chippewa Indians of a wise counselor and adviser, one of their own native countrymen; but it seems that it would be impossible for the American people in this Christian land to make such a wicked conspiracy against this poor son of the forest who had become as wise as any of them and a great statesman for his country. Yet it might be possible, for we have learned that we cannot always trust the American people as to their integrity and stability in well doing with us.

William died almost the very day when he was to be ordained a priest. He was assassinated in Rome. Soon after the death of my brother, William, my sister, Margaret, left Cincinnati, Ohio. She came to Detroit, Michigan. She was employed as teacher of the orphan children at a Catholic institution. She left Detroit about 1835. She came to Little Traverse. She at once began to teach the Indian children for the Catholic mission. She has ever since been very useful to her people. Now she is a decrepit old lady. She sometimes goes by the name of Aunty Margaret, or Queen of the Ottawas. She is constantly employed in making Indian curiosities. She is wearing out her fingers and eyes to make her living and keep her home.

Like many others of her race, she has been made the victim of fraud and extortion. Some years ago a white man came to the Indian country. He committed many crimes, for some of which he is now in prison. Soon after he came here, this wicked man pretended he was gored by an ox—although there were no marks of violence. He claimed the ox belonged to Mr. Boyd, Aunty Margaret's husband. He therefore sued Mr. Boyd for damages for several hundred dollars. The ox which he claimed had injured him did not belong to Mr. Boyd. There was no eyewitness in the case. Nevertheless, he obtained judgment for damages against him. A mortgage had to be given on the land which the Government had given her. The Indian's oath and evidence are not regarded in this country, and he stands a very poor chance before the law. Although they are citizens of the State, they are continually being taken advantage of by the attorneys of the land. They are continually being robbed and cheated out of their property. They can obtain no protection nor redress whatever.

Before Mr. Hamlin, my cousin, left Italy, he was asked by the authorities if William had any younger brother in America of a fit age to attend school. He told the authorities that the deceased had one brother just the right age to begin school. That was myself. Then there was an order for me to be sent to Rome to take the place of my brother. When my father heard of it, he said, "No; they have killed one of my sons after they have educated him, and they will kill another."

Hamlin came home soon after my brother's death. Sometime after the Treaty of 1836 he was appointed U.S. Interpreter. He continued to hold this office until 1861. I succeeded him.

1. About how old was William when he became an interpreter?

    a. 11 or 12
    b. 13 or 14
    c. 15 or 16
    d. 17 or 18

2. Margaret and William attended school

    a. at the Protestant Mission School at Mackinac Island.
    b. at the Catholic mission at Little Traverse.
    c. in Cincinnati.
    d. in Rome.

3. In Rome, William studied for the priesthood at the

    a. College of the Propaganda.
    b. feast of the Epiphany.
    c. church of St. Peter.
    d. large square before St. Peter's.

4. What did William plan to do as soon as he was ordained?

    a. stay in Rome
    b. go home to Michigan
    c. visit his sister in Cincinnati
    d. meet with the president of the United States

5. What did William hope to achieve once he was ordained?

    a. convert as many of his people as possible
    b. rise to bishop
    c. preserve his people's lands
    d. open a school

6. Why was there great excitement in Rome on the day William was to be ordained?

    a. It was the feast of the Epiphany.
    b. The Holy Father was celebrating Mass in public.
    c. The secretary of William's college was to be crowned Cardinal.
    d. The first Native American was to be ordained a priest.

7. How did Aug Hamlin determine that his cousin had been assassinated?

    a. He saw his cousin's body.
    b. He saw the signs of violence in his cousin's room.
    c. He saw the assassin.
    d. He spoke to eyewitnesses.

8. In Cincinnati, Aunty Margaret

    a. taught Native American children at a Catholic mission.
    b. taught at an orphanage.
    c. made Native American curiosities.
    d. sued Mr. Boyd.

9. As soon as she came to Little Traverse, Aunty Margaret

    a. taught Native American children at a Catholic mission.
    b. taught at an orphanage.
    c. made Native American curiosities.
    d. sued Mr. Boyd.

10. Of the following, which is **true**?

    a. The man who sued was gored by an ox.
    b. The ox belonged to Aunty Margaret's husband.
    c. There were eyewitnesses.
    d. The man was a liar and a criminal.

11. Who won the lawsuit?

    a. Aunty Margaret
    b. Mr. Boyd
    c. the man in prison
    d. the eyewitness

12. Why were Native Americans cheated in court so often?

    a. They were not allowed to testify in court.
    b. They were not allowed to hire lawyers.
    c. No lawyers would work for them.
    d. The lawyers were all dishonest.

13. When did the author become an interpreter for the United States?

    a. 1835
    b. 1836
    c. the late 1840s
    d. 1861

14. Why didn't the author go to school in Rome?

_____

_____

_____

_____

_____

_____

_____

_____

_____

_____

_____

_____

_____

_____

_____

_____

_____

THE CONQUEST OF CALIFORNIA
by John Bidwell

As yet Frémont had received advice from Washington no later than those brought by Gillespie. His object in going to Monterey must have been to confer with Commodore Sloat and get positive information about the war with Mexico, which proved to be a reality, as we learned even before our arrival there. There was now no longer uncertainty; all were glad. It was a glorious sight to see the Stars and Stripes as we marched into Monterey. Here we found Commodore Sloat. The same evening, or the next, Commodore Stockton, a chivalrous and dashing officer, arrived around Cape Horn to supersede him. Plans were immediately laid to conquer California.

A California Battalion was to be organized. Frémont was to be lieutenant colonel in command. Stockton asked Frémont to nominate his own officers. P.B. Reading was chosen paymaster, Ezekiel Merritt quartermaster, and, I think, King commissary. The captains and lieutenants chosen at Sonoma were also commissioned. Though I did not aspire to office, I received a commission as second lieutenant.

Merritt, the quartermaster, could neither read nor write. He was an old mountaineer and trapper. He lived with an Indian squaw. He went clad in buckskin fringed after the style of the Rocky Mountain Indians. He chewed tobacco to a disgusting excess, and stammered badly. He had a reputation for bravery because of his continual boasting of his prowess in killing Indians. The handle of the tomahawk he carried had nearly a hundred notches to record the number of his Indian scalps. He drank deeply whenever he could get liquor. Stockton said to him: "Major Merritt" (for he was now major), "make out a requisition for some money, say two thousand dollars. You will need about that amount at the start. Bring your requisition on board, and I will approve, and direct the purser to honor it." Major Reading wrote the requisition. Merritt got the money, two thousand Mexican silver dollars. That afternoon I met him in Monterey, nearly as drunk as he could be. He said: "Bidwell, I am rich; I have lots of money"; and putting both hands into the deep pockets of his buckskin breeches he brought out two handfuls of Mexican dollars, saying, "Here, take this, and if you can find anything to buy, buy it, and when you want more money come to me, for I have got lots of it."

Merritt was never removed from his office or rank, but simply fell into disuse. He was detailed, like subordinate officers or men, to perform other duties, generally at the head of small scouting parties. Merritt's friends—for he must have had friends to recommend him for quartermaster—in some way managed to fix up the accounts relating to the early administration of his office. In fact, I tried to help them myself, but I believe that all of us together were never able to find, within a thousand dollars, what Merritt had done with the money. How he ever came to be recommended for quartermaster was to every one a mystery. Perhaps some of the current theories that subsequently prevailed might have had in them just a shade of truth, namely, that somebody entertained the idea that quartermaster meant the ability and duty to quarter the beef!

The first conquest of California, in 1846, by the Americans, with the exception of the skirmish at Petaluma and another towards Monterey, was achieved without a battle. We simply marched all over California, from Sonoma to San Diego, and raised the American flag without opposition or protest. We tried to find an enemy, but could not. So Kit Carson and Ned Beale were sent East, bearing despatches [sic] from Commodore Stockton announcing the entire conquest of California by the United States.

Frémont was made Governor by Stockton at Los Angeles, but could not enter upon the full discharge of the duties of his office till he had visited the upper part of California and returned. He sent me to take charge of the Mission of San Luis Rey, with a commission as magistrate over the larger portion of the country between Los Angeles and San Diego. Stockton and all his forces retired on board their vessels. Frémont went north, leaving part of his men at Los Angeles under Gillespie, part at Santa Barbara under Lieutenant Talbot, and some at other points. Pio Pico and José Castro, respectively the last Mexican governor and commander-in-chief, remained concealed a while and then withdrew into Mexico.

Suddenly, in about a month, Frémont being in the north and his troops scattered, the whole country south of Monterey was in a state of revolt.

Then for the first time there was something like war. As there were rumors of Mexican troops coming from Sonora, Merritt was sent by Gillespie to reconnoiter towards the Colorado River. Gillespie was surrounded at Los Angeles, and made to capitulate. I fled from San Luis Rey to San Diego. Merritt and his party, hearing of the outbreak, also escaped to San Diego. Meanwhile, Frémont enlisted a considerable force (about four hundred), principally from the large Hastings immigration at Sacramento, and marched south. Commodore Stockton had landed and marched to retake Los Angeles, and failed.

All the men-of-war, and all the scattered forces, except Frémont's new force, were then concentrated at San Diego, where Commodore Stockton collected and reorganized the forces. They were composed of sailors, marines, men of

Frémont's battalion under Gillespie and Merritt, volunteers at San Diego, including some native Californians and that portion of the regular troops under General S.W. Kearny that had escaped from the field of San Pascual—in all between seven hundred and eight hundred men. Of these forces I was commissioned and served as quartermaster. This work of preparation took several months. Finally, on December 29, 1846, the army set out to retake Los Angeles. It fought the battles of San Gabriel and the Mesa, which ended the insurrection. The enemy fled, met Frémont at San Fernando, and surrendered to him the next day. The terms of surrender were so lenient that the native Californians from that time forth became the fast friends of Frémont.

Time does not permit me to do more than allude to the arrival at San Diego of General Kearny with one hundred soldiers, and with Kit Carson and Beale, from New Mexico; or to his repulse at San Pascual.

Unfortunate differences regarding rank had arisen between Stockton and Kearny. Frémont was afterwards arrested in California by Kearny for refusing to obey his orders, and was taken to Washington and court-martialed. Stockton, however, was largely to blame. He would not submit to General Kearny, his superior in command on land. That led Frémont to refuse to obey Kearny, his superior officer. Frémont's disobedience was no doubt owing to the advice of Stockton who had appointed him governor of California.

1. Before reaching Monterey, Frémont discovered that

    a. the U.S. had declared war on Mexico.
    b. Commodore Sloat had arrived.
    c. Commodore Stockton had arrived.
    d. no more news was available.

2. Who was named quartermaster?

    a. John Frémont
    b. P.B. Reading
    c. Ezekiel Merritt
    d. John Bidwell

3. Who was named a second lieutenant?

    a. John Frémont
    b. P.B. Reading
    c. Ezekiel Merritt
    d. John Bidwell

4. Who told the quartermaster to requisition $2,000?

    a. John Frémont
    b. P.B. Reading
    c. Commodore Stockton
    d. Commodore Sloat

5. Who actually wrote the requisition?

    a. John Frémont
    b. P.B. Reading
    c. Ezekiel Merritt
    d. Commodore Stockton

6. A paymaster's duty is probably to

    a. quarter beef.
    b. buy liquor.
    c. pay the troops.
    d. purchase food and equipment for the troops.

7. A quartermaster's duty is probably to

    a. quarter beef.
    b. buy liquor.
    c. pay the troops.
    d. purchase food and equipment for the troops.

8. When the passage says that Stockton retired on board his vessel, it means that he

    a. no longer felt it necessary to command on ship.
    b. was through with government service and on his way home.
    c. was through with government service and planned to live on board his ship.
    d. went to sleep.

9. The last Mexican governor of California was

    a. General Vallejo.
    b. Pio Pico.
    c. Jose Castro.
    d. Joaquín de la Torre.

10. Who was **not** part of Commodore Stockton's force at San Diego?

    a. Frémont and his Hastings contingent
    b. Frémont's battalion under Gillespie and Merritt
    c. sailors and marines
    d. native California volunteers

11. General Kearny lost a battle at

    a. Los Angeles.
    b. San Pascual.
    c. San Gabriel.
    d. Mesa.

12. The battles which ended the insurrection were fought at

    a. San Pascual and San Diego.
    b. Los Angeles and San Fernando.
    c. Monterey and Sacramento.
    d. San Gabriel and Mesa.

13. Do you think Frémont or Stockton should have been court-martialed? Both? Neither? Or which one? Why?

_____

_____

_____

_____

_____

_____

_____

_____

_____

ULYSSES S. GRANT IN MISSOURI

My family, all this while, was at the East. It consisted now of a wife and two children. I saw no chance of supporting them on the Pacific coast out of my pay as an army officer. I concluded, therefore, to resign, and in March applied for a leave of absence until the end of the July following, tendering my resignation to take effect at the end of that time. I left the Pacific coast very much attached to it, and with the full expectation of making it my future home. That expectation and that hope remained uppermost in my mind until the Lieutenant–Generalcy bill was introduced into Congress in the winter of 1863–1864. The passage of that bill, and my promotion, blasted my last hope of ever becoming a citizen of the further West.

In the late summer of 1854, I rejoined my family, to find in it a son whom I had never seen, born while I was on the Isthmus of Panama. I was now to commence, at the age of thirty-two, a new struggle for our support. My wife had a farm near St. Louis, to which we went, but I had no means to stock it. A house had to be built also. I worked very hard, never losing a day because of bad weather, and accomplished the object in a moderate way. If nothing else could be done I would load a cord of wood on a wagon and take it to the city for sale. I managed to keep along very well until 1858, when I was attacked by fever and ague. I had suffered very severely and for a long time from this disease, while a boy in Ohio. It lasted now over a year and, while it did not keep me in the house, it did interfere greatly with the amount of work I was able to perform. In the fall of 1858 I sold out my stock, crops and farming utensils at auction, and gave up farming.

In the winter I established a partnership with Harry Boggs, a cousin of Mrs. Grant, in the real estate agency business. I spent that winter at St. Louis myself, but did not take my family into town until the spring. Our business might have become prosperous if I had been able to wait for it to grow. As it was, there was no more than one person could attend to, and not enough to support two families. While a citizen of St. Louis and engaged in the real estate agency business, I was a candidate for the office of county engineer, an office of respectability and emolument which would have been very acceptable to me at that time. The incumbent was appointed by the county court, which consisted of five members. My opponent had the advantage of birth over me (he was a citizen by adoption) and carried off the prize. I now withdrew from the co-partnership with Boggs. In May 1860, I removed to Galena, Illinois, and took a clerkship in my father's store.

While a citizen of Missouri, my first opportunity for casting a vote at a Presidential election occurred. I had been in the army from before attaining my majority and had thought but little about politics, although I was a Whig by education and a great admirer of Mr. Clay. But the Whig party had ceased to exist before I had an opportunity of exercising the privilege of casting a ballot; the Know-Nothing party had taken its place, but was on the wane; and the Republican party was in a chaotic state and had not yet received a name. It had no existence in the Slave States except at points on the borders next to Free States. In St. Louis City and County, what afterwards became the Republican party was known as the Free–Soil Democracy, led by the Honorable Frank P. Blair. Most of my neighbors had known me as an officer of the army with Whig proclivities. They had been on the same side, and, on the death of their party, many had become Know-Nothings, or members of the American party. There was a lodge near my new home, and I was invited to join it. I accepted the invitation; was initiated; attended a meeting just one week later, and never went to another afterwards.

I have no apologies to make for having been one week a member of the American party; for I still think native-born citizens of the United States should have as much protection, as many privileges in their native country, as those who voluntarily select it for a home. But all secret, oath-bound political parties are dangerous to any nation, no matter how pure or how patriotic the motives and principles which first bring them together. No political party can or ought to exist when one of its corner-stones is opposition to freedom of thought and to the right to worship God "according to the dictate of one's own conscience," or according to the creed of any religious denomination whatever. Nevertheless, if a sect sets up its laws as binding above the state laws, wherever the two come in conflict this claim must be resisted and suppressed at whatever cost.

1. Of the following roles in Ulysses S. Grant's history, which came **first**?

    a. real estate agent in St. Louis
    b. farmer near St. Louis
    c. soldier in Panama
    d. resignation from the army in California

2. Which came **last**?

    a. real estate agent in St. Louis
    b. farmer near St. Louis
    c. over a year of illness
    d. resignation from the army in California

3. What did Ulysses S. Grant do when farming did not go well in 1854–1855?

   a. He sold his stock.
   b. He sold his crops.
   c. He sold his farming utensils.
   d. He chopped and sold firewood.

4. How old was Grant when he entered the real estate business?

   a. 32
   b. 34
   c. 36
   d. 38

5. While in St. Louis, Ulysses S. Grant briefly joined the _____ party.

   a. Republican
   b. American, or Know-Nothing,
   c. Democratic
   d. Free-Soil Democratic

6. What party do you think Grant voted for in his first presidential election? Why?

   _____

   _____

   _____

   _____

   _____

   _____

   _____

   _____

7. What do you think of Grant's explanation and defense of his party membership? Explain your opinions.

_____

_____

_____

_____

_____

_____

_____

_____

_____

_____

_____

_____

_____

_____

_____

_____

_____

_____

NEW ENGLAND'S INFLUENCE ON MICHIGAN

New England had an important influence on the development of Michigan, especially in the areas of religion, government, education, and architecture. Immigrants brought their New England ideals of hard work, responsibility, home, church, and education. "Nowhere in the West did Yankee stock predominate as much as in Michigan."

Many people had moved into western New York from New England in the hope of improving their lives. However, by 1825 many had perceived that things were not improving. A number of farmers had purchased land on easy terms from a large land company, but had not been able to make the payments. The abundance of cheap land further west with easy access via the Erie Canal attracted many of these New York/New England farmers to migrate to Michigan in the hope of starting over on more productive land.

One method used to encourage interest in immigration was the distribution of maps and gazetteers in the eastern states. To entice people who were reluctant to leave family and friends, one gazetteer suggested forming "colonies for immigration" in which a number of families would agree to emigrate together. It painted a very optimistic financial picture:

> A father may sell his small farm in the East for a sum that will purchase a dozen large ones in the West, of the best quality of the land. He may thus better his own condition, and settle a handsome property upon each of his family, who, in a few years, may become wealthy and independent, without the least difficulty.

These were brave words, considering that the East was in the midst of a depression following the panic of 1837.

Some New England influences on the development of Michigan were:

Township Government

The township form of government was taken from the New England model. In the territories, the "township" replaced the "town" as the unit of local government. The town meeting was the governing body. Every adult male had the right to take part. The township was not unique to Michigan. It followed the pattern set by Ohio and Indiana of establishing township government. In 1825, Congress authorized Michigan voters to select all township officials except judges.

Religion

Many of the pioneers' ancestors had crossed the ocean in search of religious freedom. The earliest settlements in New England were centered on the church. Its teachings dictated the way people conducted their everyday lives. The early settlers to Michigan brought their religious convictions with them. Soon after settlement, they began to gather for services.

A Methodist minister traveled a "circuit" of local communities. The Methodist circuit rider was a welcome sight to lonely settlers in the wilderness. The minister did not merely offer spiritual guidance. He baptized the young, performed marriages, and buried the dead. He also brought news of the outside world and from other communities in the area. Circuit riding was a grueling and demanding occupation that took the rider away from home and family for long periods of time. Consequently, the circuit rider would often serve for a period of time and then look for a more settled way to minister.

Schools

Just as firmly held as their religious beliefs by the new settlers was the value of education as a means of improving their lives. In 1826, a territorial law reserved the sixteenth section of every township for the state of Michigan. Proceeds from the sale or lease of the lands were designated for a perpetual fund, the interest of which was to be used for primary education. An 1827 law specified that every township composed of fifty households should provide itself with a schoolteacher of "good moral character." The people of the school districts were responsible for financing, building, operating, and maintaining the schools.

Housing

The first task of the pioneer was to build a shelter, usually of logs. The first house would have been a log cabin, usually one room about fourteen by sixteen feet. Notching the logs together at the corners held them in place. The floor was made of logs cut in half, laid with the flat side facing up. The chimney was made of sticks, covered with mud plaster an inch or two thick to prevent fire. The fireplace was very large and constructed of stone. The roof consisted of wood shakes or shingles about three feet long. Once the pioneer had the logs ready, he would call for a house "raising," since the logs were too much for one or two people to handle. All the neighbors from miles around would come for a "raising bee." A log cabin was usually one room, while a log house consisted of two rooms or more, one and a half to two stories high.

In time, the log cabin or house would be replaced with a more refined house, when the settler might either add on to his present house or build an entirely new one. If a farmer was prosperous enough, he might build his home in the Greek Revival style that was predominant between 1830 and 1850. After the Revolutionary War, the old colonial styles were abandoned because they reflected the influence of England. People wanted a style that reflected their newly-won independence. The Greek Revival style developed from the great interest in the Greek War for Independence and the recent archeological discoveries of the classical world. This style came with the pioneers from New York and New England in the 1830s. They adapted it to suit their agricultural and frontier way of life.

1. Many Michigan settlers came from _____ with a stopover in _____.

   a. New England . . . New York
   b. New York . . . New England
   c. Pennsylvania . . . New England
   d. New England . . . Pennsylvania

2. The allure of Michigan was

   a. easy access to the Erie Canal.
   b. abundant land.
   c. cheap, more productive land.
   d. escape from creditors.

3. Who probably promoted immigration to Michigan?

   a. map and gazetteer publishers
   b. colonies for immigration
   c. land companies with land for sale in Michigan
   d. the state of Michigan

4. Of the following, where was the town meeting **not** the local form of government?

   a. Ohio
   b. Indiana
   c. New England
   d. Virginia

5. The sale of land in Michigan was used to finance

    a. local government.
    b. local education.
    c. building churches.
    d. paying for a minister.

6. Michigan law required that the _____ be of "good moral character."

    a. pioneer
    b. farmer
    c. settler
    d. schoolteacher

7. The _____ of a log house was made of logs cut in half.

    a. wall
    b. floor
    c. chimney
    d. fireplace

8. The Greek Revival style did **not**

    a. reflect the influence of England.
    b. come from New York and New England.
    c. reflect an interest in the Greek War of Independence of ancient Greece.
    d. appeal to more prosperous farmers.

9. How do you think pioneer life in Tennessee or Kentucky differed from life in Michigan described in the passage above? How was it similar?

_____

_____

_____

_____

_____

_____

LANSING, MICHIGAN, 1837–1890

The city of Lansing was founded as Michigan's capital city. Its establishment was the result of a provision of the 1837 Michigan constitution. The constitution established Detroit as the state's temporary capital, but required the legislature to select a permanent site in ten years. Thus, in 1847, the legislature was faced with making a choice. At one time or another, virtually every town of any size in the state was given consideration. In the end, however, all were rejected.

At this juncture, the name of Lansing Township was proposed as a compromise. James Seymour of Rochester, New York, owner of lands in the area, made the suggestion. The township was located nearly midway across the state. It lay north of the part of the state that was already thickly settled. Thus, its selection was seen as a means of promoting the growth of the more northerly parts of the state. Accordingly, Lansing Township was adopted as the site.

Commissioners were appointed by the 1847 legislature to select the location for the "Village of Michigan." The settlement's name was changed to Lansing in 1849. The commissioners chose section 16. It was bounded by Saginaw Street on the north, Logan on the west, St. Joseph Street on the south, and the railroad tracks east of Larch Street on the east. This area is now the heart of the city. In the spring of 1847, they platted the section into streets and lots. They designated a large square as the site for the capitol building. Another block, located to the southeast of the capitol square (bounded by Allegan and Kalamazoo Streets and Capitol and Washington Avenues) was reserved for temporary state buildings. On this latter block, a temporary capitol and a house for the governor were soon constructed. They were unpretentious Greek Revival structures.

The legislature recognized Lansing's isolation. In 1848, the legislature financed the opening of roads from the town to other important points. The legislature authorized the completion of the important Grand River Road. It was to run from Detroit through Howell and what is now North Lansing to Grand Rapids and the mouth of the Grand River. The section from Howell to North Lansing (present-day Grand River Avenue) was finally opened in 1849. Several of the new roads, including the Grand River Road and the road to Mason, were turned over to turnpike companies in the 1850s. They were rebuilt as plank roads.

The state government's move to Lansing, and the relatively convenient communication with the rest of the state, led to the rapid development of the sections of Lansing Township near the capitol. As early as 1847, three villages existed in close proximity along the Grand River. The north village was known as the lower village because of its location downstream from the others. It grew up around a dam and sawmill just south of the Grand River Avenue crossing of the Grand River. The dam had been built in 1843 by John W. Burchard. He was the area's first settler. Workmen on the payroll of James Seymour built the mill the following year.

In 1847, following the selection of Lansing as the capital, a bridge was built across the river. Stores and hotels began to appear along what is now Grand River Avenue between North Washington Avenue and Center Street and north on Turner Street. Largely rebuilt in the 1875–1920 period, the North Lansing commercial district now contains Lansing's largest assemblage of Late Victorian business blocks. The district is listed in the National Register of Historic Places.

The south, or upper, village began to develop in 1847 along Main Street and South Washington Avenue. In 1847, a Main Street bridge was constructed over the Grand River. The village's central element was the Benton House. It was a four-story, brick, Greek Revival–style hotel. Because of its distance from the capitol site, the upper village remained relatively undeveloped. The Main Street bridge was not even replaced when it washed out in 1860.

The middle village, centered on Washington and Michigan Avenues near the capitol, quickly became Lansing's focal point. The first Michigan Avenue Grand River bridge was built in 1848.

In 1859, the Village of Lansing was incorporated as a city. It consisted of three settlements. It had about three thousand residents. Its population swelled to 5,241 in 1870 and to 8,326 in 1880. The 1874 Beers' atlas shows that the built-up area then extended from Cedar and Larch Streets on the east to Sycamore on the west, and from Willow and North Street on the north to Main Street on the south.

The routing of railroads through the city was a major reason for this growth. Lansing's first rail link connected the city with Owosso and other towns to the northeast. It was opened as far as North Lansing in 1861 and into the center of the city two years later. Lines were opened to Jackson in 1866, to Battle Creek and Ionia in 1869, to Detroit in 1871, and to Eaton Rapids–Albion–Jonesville in 1873.

Good rail service fostered industrial development. In the 1860s and 1870s, the area along both sides of the river from Grand River Avenue southward to below Michigan Avenue and along the Northern Michigan Central tracks to the east of the river became the site of sawmills, chair factories, and other light industries using the area's rich timber supply until it was depleted in the 1880s. The area also contained a number of steam- and water-powered flour and gristmills. Several mills produced flour exclusively for the New England market.

As the native timber disappeared, Lansing began to switch to heavy industry. In 1869–1870, Edwin Bement and his son, Arthur, moved their foundry and machine shop from Fostoria, Ohio, to Lansing. They wanted to take advantage of the growing demand for farm implements. By the 1880s, the firm of E. Bement & Sons was one of the city's largest employers. They manufactured stoves and farm equipment such as harrows and plows. They were more widely known for their sleds. Another prominent manufacturing firm was the Lansing Wheelbarrow Company. It was later known simply as "The Lansing Company." Founded in 1881, it became one of the largest wheelbarrow-manufacturing firms in the country.

1. The 1837 Michigan constitution provided that Detroit would be the capital

    a. unless the legislature decided otherwise.
    b. permanently.
    c. only until the legislature would choose another site in 1847.
    d. until moved to Kalamazoo in 1847.

2. The original name for Michigan's new capital was

    a. Kalamazoo.
    b. Saginaw.
    c. Village of Michigan.
    d. Lansing Township.

3. The area chosen for the capital was _____ of the railroad tracks.

    a. east
    b. south
    c. north
    d. west

4. The temporary capitol was constructed _____ of the permanent site.

    a. southeast
    b. southwest
    c. northeast
    d. northwest

5. Turnpike companies improved

    a. plank roads.
    b. toll roads.
    c. the Grand River Road and the road to Mason.
    d. concrete roads.

6. The north village commercial district began

    a. around a dam and sawmill just north of the Grand River Avenue crossing of the Grand River.
    b. around a dam and sawmill just south of the Grand River Avenue crossing of the Grand River.
    c. from 1875–1920.
    d. upstream from the other two villages.

7. The sawmill was built

    a. in 1843 by John W. Burchard.
    b. in 1843 by workers for James Seymour.
    c. in 1844 by workers for James Seymour.
    d. in 1844 by John W. Burchard.

8. Of the following, which is **not** true of the upper village?

    a. It was the furthest north.
    b. It was along Main Street and South Washington Avenue.
    c. In 1847, Main Street bridge was built over the Grand River.
    d. The principal building was a hotel.

9. Of the following, which is **not** true of the upper village?

    a. The village did not grow rapidly.
    b. The village was quite a distance away from the capitol.
    c. The Benton House was the focal point of the village.
    d. The bridge was replaced when it was washed out in 1860.

10. Between 1859 and 1880, the Village of Lansing added about _____ residents.

    a. 2,240
    b. 3,000
    c. 5,326
    d. 8,326

11. In 1874, the built-up area of Lansing extended from Main Street

    a. south.
    b. north.
    c. east.
    d. west.

12. The key to the development of Lansing in the 1860s and 1870s was

    a. steam power.
    b. water power.
    c. bridges over the Grand River.
    d. good rail service.

13. The earliest industries established in Lansing were those producing

    a. wood products and flour mills.
    b. stoves and farm equipment.
    c. sleds and wood products.
    d. wheelbarrows and flour mills.

14. Had it not been the state capital, do you think Lansing would have been created at all or would it have prospered? Why or why not?

_____

_____

_____

_____

_____

_____

_____

_____

_____

_____

_____

_____

_____

_____

_____

_____

_____

_____

_____

286

FOLK TACKLES ST. LOUIS CORRUPTION

In 1900, Missouri was home to one of the most important of the nation's new metropolises. St. Louis, with more than 575,000 people, was larger than it would be at the twentieth century's end. At the time it was America's fourth largest city (behind New York, Chicago, and Philadelphia). Like the other big cities it was justly famous for its filth and overcrowded ethnic tenement slums. The Irish lived in "Kerry Patch." African Americans lived in "Clabber Alley." Italian immigrants on "Dago Hill." A bewildering Babel of voices could be heard from southern and eastern Europe. Some public schools were conducted in German. Public health was an ever-present concern. Garbage was strewn everywhere. When it rained the mud in St. Louis' poorly paved streets and even its sidewalks was virtually inescapable. At night one might find prostitutes but, notoriously, not street lights. In addition to these, St. Louis was "celebrated" for polluted air and water. Filthy smoke created by the cheap soft coal brought from the nearby Illinois coal fields darkened the day and filled the lungs. The nation's most infamous water supply—filthy dark brown water from the Mississippi River, rich with sand and Chicago sewage—poured from the city's water taps.

City government was not doing its job. To the extent that needs were met, it was through political corruption. In St. Louis corruption was symbolized by the powerful Irish political boss "Colonel" Edward Butler. He was a former blacksmith. His rise to power began with his monopoly on the horseshoeing of St. Louis' streetcar lines. Butler did not have complete political control of the city. He hardly had a monopoly on corruption. (Although Butler was a Democrat by profession, St. Louis enjoyed a competitive two-party system. Butler was quite willing to work with Republicans as necessity dictated.) However, he was the worst case.

His minions engaged in conventional electoral bad behavior. They beat up politically incorrect voters. They intimidated election judges. They stuffed ballot boxes. They repeatedly voted. They even moved election polls to confuse the supporters of rival political opponents. Butler controlled the city's elective government through lucrative bribes as needed. Those upon whose loyalty he could always count were termed "the Combine." His urban base was such that he was regarded, appropriately, as something of a power in state politics.

As big city bosses of the period run, Butler is of about average interest. He had neither the power nor the inventiveness of Kansas City's Thomas Pendergast. While Butler's gang may have done this or that, of far greater importance is the crusade they set off that made an obscure Tennessee migrant to St. Louis nationally famous, then governor, and finally a contender for the presidency.

Joseph Folk came to St. Louis in 1893 to join his judge uncle in a law partnership. He was a minor player in local Democratic politics. He gained a measure of good publicity for his work in negotiating an end to a particularly vicious streetcar strike. When approached to run for circuit attorney in 1900 he received the blessing of all factions of the Democratic Party, including Ed Butler. During his campaign Folk said that he would come down hard on wrongdoing wherever he found it. The Democratic bosses paid little attention. They had heard it all before. To their shock, however, that is exactly what Folk did. Upon taking office he first went against those who corrupted the electoral process—men who had, in fact, just used those very methods to help get Folk elected. Intense pressure quickly fell on Folk from people who told him to go after the Republican crooks but to leave the Democratic crooks alone. A year later, he went after Boss Butler himself. Butler was found guilty of attempting to bribe two members of St. Louis' Board of Health to steer garbage removal contracts to him.

Eventually Butler received more sympathy from Missouri's Supreme Court who, despising Folk, overturned Butler's conviction, but the Boss's power was permanently broken. Folk was, in fact, a sloppy prosecutor. He often achieved his convictions with the aid of sympathetic lower court judges. His convictions of the politically corrupt were overturned upon appeal with remarkable regularity. Folk's crusade won him fame nonetheless. Folk was actually not principally concerned with sending people to jail. He was much more interested in changing Missouri's political culture.

In the process of prosecuting corrupt politicians, however, Folk made an important discovery. They all had ties to businessmen—rich ones. Many of the city's social elite lived in nice mansions in the city's Central West End. They became collectively known as the "Big Cinch." They owned banks, speculated in real estate, ran corporations, and were powerful lawyers. However, here matters got more complicated. Their work gave them extensive business dealings with government. Many of these businessmen were shamelessly greedy, looking for the special privileges that only government could bestow. Nevertheless, the problem was larger than mere knavery. Even respectable businessmen were deeply implicated in political corruption. Work and jobs had to be given and payoffs had to be made in order to get their goals achieved. Bribes were common, ordinary. Corruption was regarded as perhaps unfortunate, but that was the price of doing business. Everybody understood it, everybody did it, and nobody wasted much time agonizing over it. They may have been caught in a system, but

288

they didn't complain much. For those in a position to afford such things, the system worked reasonably well.

Joseph Folk's greatest accomplishment was his challenge to this culture. Corruption had become so established that his wholesale rejection of it was as shocking as a slap in the face. In 1902 Folk brought charges against wealthy Kansas Citian Robert Synder for his bribery of St. Louis Municipal Assembly members to create a streetcar monopoly. Synder's attorney, Henry S. Priest, stated a bit more openly than was prudent the conventional belief that "there are worse things than bribery; bribery is, after all, not such a serious crime. It is a conventional offense…a trifling offense, a mere perversion of justice." Folk electrified Missouri and then the nation with his repudiation of this kind of thinking, famously declaring that "bribery is treason, and the givers and takers of bribes are…traitors." Folk's point, which he tirelessly made, was that "boodle," as political corruption for monetary advantage came to be known, undermined representative government and placed all government power and preferment in the service of a wealthy oligarchy. What kind of a democracy did you have when corrupt elections made voting meaningless, and government became the servant solely of those who could afford to purchase its favors? It was not the people's will being served.

As long as Folk went after notorious figures like Butler and the lesser political thugs who corrupted the political process, he enjoyed widespread support. When he started going after businessmen, he lost it. Much of the local press and the city elite rallied against him. He was accused of ruining St. Louis' business climate. Some visited him privately, others publicly, and they threatened him with ruin or physical violence. He was beseeched for mercy. He was called a traitor to his party.

Folk's hour, however, had arrived. There was no stopping him. His moment came in no little measure because it was also the moment of Lincoln Steffens, who was poised to become one of America's foremost muckraking journalists. Working with St. Louis journalist Claude Wetmore, Steffens wrote his famous 1903 essay, "Tweed Days in St. Louis," for the popular magazine, *McClure's*. The essay, which made Folk nationally famous, became the opening story for Steffen's classic book, *The Shame of the Cities*. (When it appeared in 1904, it would also include a second unflattering essay on the city entitled, "The Shamelessness of St. Louis.")

It did not take long for his rising fame to lead Folk to think about running for higher office. Indeed the presidency was soon on his mind, but he settled for Missouri's governorship as a necessary stepping-stone. He was helped in this ambition when it became all too spectacularly apparent that the state legislature was as corrupt as St. Louis's municipal government. For years, a loose group in and around state government known as the "Lobby" had worked on behalf of special interests for a price.

In late 1902, a scandal erupted. It was revealed that commercial competitors had purchased legislation banning alum's use. A Cole County grand jury probing state government corruption in the wake of the scandal concluded that:

> The extent of the venality existing among the makers of our State laws is alarming to those who believe in free government . . . the evidence before us shows that corruption has been the usual and accepted thing in State legislation. . . . Laws have been sold to the highest bidder in numerous instances.

Working with Attorney General Edward Crow, Folk, still prosecuting attorney, managed to carve out a role for himself in the alum investigation. It eventually lead to the indictment and resignation of the lieutenant governor and several legislators.

By the alum scandal's conclusion Folk's gubernatorial candidacy and subsequent election were almost a certainty. His run for office was, in fact, more moral crusade than campaign. On the stump Folk not only offered the state, but the nation, "the Missouri Idea," that a reawakened civic morality would drive commercialism and grafters out of government, that laws were for enforcing, and that politicians were public servants of a democracy, not the private servants of an oligarchy.

Folk did win a smashing victory, but it was a personal one. The Republicans took control of the legislature. The rest of the Democratic ticket went down to defeat. While Folk was exhilarated, he became a man without a party. During the campaign Folk had engaged in a lot of pious anti-party rhetoric: "if a party cannot get along without rascals, the people should get along without the party." Many Democratic party activists came to hate Folk or "Holy Joe," as they scornfully called him, a man who would ruin his own party for personal advantage. When Folk in his inaugural address declared that there were those who were lying in wait to resume power believing that the 'Missouri Idea' was "only a passing virtuous spasm," he was not far from the mark.

Folk's administration proved troubled. Democrats as well as Republicans were ready to resist his leadership. He tried to pass a law to virtually eject lobbyists from Jefferson City. He attempted to clamp down on the popular gift of railroad passes given to legislators. He pushed for a public service commission to control utilities, commercial travel, and communication. He worked for the passage of a law implementing initiative petition, referendum, and recall. He sought the adoption of primaries. He urged that voting be made compulsory. He tried to enforce all laws to their full rigor. In a few areas he was successful, but in most he was not. His inflexible and literal-minded application of the law made him many new enemies. The most famous incident was when he closed down Sunday openings of St. Louis' beer gardens, which traditionally spilled over with respectable ethnic German families on that day. The scandalized Germans felt themselves under cultural assault with the criminalization of their traditional recreation.

By the conclusion of his administration, Folk's political aspirations were not at an end, but his electoral career was. In 1908, he made a primary run for a Senate seat against incumbent Senator Joel Stone. Stone was a slick popular former governor. He had been embarrassingly implicated as an influence peddler during the alum scandal. Nevertheless, Folk lost badly. The traditional Democrats had impatiently laid in wait. Folk had no organization. The parties, for all their faults, were still full in the saddle.

1. What was the fourth largest city in the U.S. in 1900?

   a. New York
   b. Chicago
   c. Philadelphia
   d. St. Louis

2. Which immigrant group had the greatest influence on public education in St. Louis in 1900?

   a. Italians
   b. Irish
   c. Germans
   d. Poles

3. Edward Butler's rise to power began when he obtained the right to

   a. horseshoe all the horses pulling streetcars in St. Louis.
   b. elect judges.
   c. decide where polling would take place.
   d. work with Republicans as well as Democrats.

4. St. Louis' elite lived in

    a. Kerry Patch.
    b. the Central West End.
    c. Clabber Alley.
    d. Dago Hill.

5. The rich businessmen of St. Louis were known as the

    a. "St. Louis Board of Health."
    b. "Big Cinch."
    c. "Combine."
    d. "Supreme Court."

6. Joseph Folk first came to prominence by

    a. attacking Ed Butler.
    b. practicing law with his uncle.
    c. helping to settle a strike.
    d. saying he would come down hard on corruption.

7. Butler was found guilty of trying to bribe

    a. election officials.
    b. health officials.
    c. streetcar officials.
    d. judges.

8. Of the following, who was involved in Kansas City, not in St. Louis?

    a. Robert Synder
    b. Thomas Pendergast
    c. Edward Butler
    d. Joseph Folk

9. Who declared that bribery is not a serious crime?

    a. Henry Priest
    b. the Missouri Supreme Court
    c. Edward Butler
    d. Joseph Folk

10. Who declared that bribery is treason?

    a. Henry Priest
    b. the Missouri Supreme Court
    c. Edward Butler
    d. Joseph Folk

11. What did Folk lose when he started prosecuting corrupt businessmen?

    a. public support
    b. his mind
    c. his attention to detail
    d. support of the Missouri Supreme Court

12. Folk became nationally famous due to a journalist named

    a. Tweed.
    b. Wetmore.
    c. Steffens.
    d. Crow.

13. State government was corrupted by a group known as the

    a. "Big Cinch."
    b. "Lobby."
    c. "Combine."
    d. "Muckrackers."

14. The alum scandal suggested that the _____ had been bribed by _____.

    a. lieutenant governor . . . the alum industry
    b. lieutenant governor . . . competitors of the alum industry
    c. attorney general . . . competitors of the alum industry
    d. attorney general . . . the alum industry

15. Why did Folk lose in 1908?

_____

_____

_____

_____

_____

_____

_____

_____

_____

_____

_____

_____

_____

_____

_____

_____

_____

_____

_____

_____

16. What do you think would happen to a politician like Folk in Missouri today? Explain your reasoning.

_____

_____

_____

_____

_____

_____

_____

_____

_____

_____

_____

_____

_____

_____

_____

_____

_____

_____

Made in the USA
Coppell, TX
24 August 2022

81953553R00168